RESEARCHES

OF THE

REV E SMITH AND REV H G O DWIGHT

IN

ARMENIA

INCLUDING A JOURNEY

THROUGH ASIA MINOR AND INTO GEORGIA AND PERSIA

WITH A VISIT TO THE

NESTORIAN AND CHALDEAN CHRISTIANS

OF OORMIAH AND SALMAS

IN TWO VOLUMES—VOL I

BY ELI SMITH

Missionary of the American Board of Commissioners for
Foreign Mission

BOSTON
PUBLISHED BY CROCKER AND BREWSTER
47 Washington Street
NEW YORK   JONATHAN LEAVITT
182 Broadway

1833

GRIFFIN & CO PRINTERS.

ADVERTISEMENT

A LARGE extent of territory in the countries lying around the Mediterranean had been surveyed by the missionaries of the American Board of Commissioners for Foreign Missions before Messrs Smith and Dwight entered upon the tour described in these volumes Messrs Fisk and Parsons, in the year 1820 had traversed the country embracing the Seven Churches of Asia Messrs Fisk and King had as cended the Nile as far as Thebes in Upper Egypt in 1823 Messrs Parsons Fisk King Bird Goodell and Smith had at different times explored the whole of Palestine and the greater part of Syria within the years 1821—1827 In 1827 Mr Gridley travelled from Smyrna into Cappadocia, and in that year and the two following Messrs Brewer, King Smith and Anderson visited the Peloponnesus and the more important of the Ionian and Ægean islands Tri poli and Tunis on the northern coast of Africa were vis-ited by Mr Bird in 1829

These investigations together with those of missionaries employed by other societies had laid open the religious and moral condition of the Coptic Maronite and Greek churches to the minute observation of their brethren in this western world

Some sects there were however having their principal residence farther east of which, though enough was known to excite interest there was not enough to determine defi nitely what should be attempted for their spiritual improve-ment Such among others were the Armenians, Geor gians Nestorians and Chaldeans

To ascertain what it was practicable for the churches of America to do for these sects, and also for the Turks, Turk mans, Kurds and Persians among whom they reside, the Prudential Committee of the Board resolved to send two missionaries into Armenia on a tour of investigation   The Rev Eli Smith was selected for one on account of his experience as a traveller and his acquaintance with the Arabic language with which he had made himself familiar in Syria, and also with Turkish which a little practice would enable him to employ in conversation   The Rev H G O Dwight although but just come into the Mediterranean was associated with him in full confidence that he would render important aid in the service

It is due to these brethren to say that they executed their commission to the entire satisfaction of the Committee   The result has been the collection of a mass of interesting and valuable facts the relation of which in the independent journals of the two travellers deposited at the Missionary Rooms occupies more than a thousand pages of manuscript   The use which Mr Smith has made of the journal of his companion is explained in the Preface

It may be proper to add that the Committee have taken measures, since receiving these reports to commence a mission among the Nestorians of Oormiah in Persia   and they hope soon with the leave of Providence to occupy a number of new stations in that part of the world

We regard the statements contained in these volumes as possessing an accuracy and value far beyond what is common in books of travels   and as being worthy of the attentive perusal of the geographer and historian as well as of missionaries and directors of missionary societies   and indeed of all who are interested in the publication of the gospel in the east and in the intellectual and moral improvement of man

Missionary Rooms, Boston
    Jan 17 1833

B B WISNER
R ANDERSON } *Secretaries*
DAVID GREENE

PREFACE

―――――

An important fact brought to light by the experience of pro-
estant missions in Western Asia has for some time interested
the benevolent in the relics of the *Oriental Churches*. While pa
pists are hedged around by inveterate prejudice and moslems by
their intolerant law against apostasy, *those churches are accessible*.
The importance of evangelical labors among them therefore has
been naturally regarded as enhanced, not only by the prospect of
effecting their own improvement but by the very inaccessibleness
in other ways of the regions they inhabit. One of the largest of
the oriental churches is the ARMENIAN. From what missionaries
had seen of its scattered members along the coast of the Levant the
American Board of Missions had been led to hope that *in Armenia
itself* might be found some promising fields for missionary culture.
To investigate this point their Prudential Committee directed the
journey narrated in the following pages to be undertaken. Their
Instructions bearing date the 19th of January 1830 may be found
published in part in the Missionary Herald vol xxvi p 75. They
were received at Malta on the 27th of February, and the journey
was accomplished during the remainder of that and the first six
months of the following year

1*

The manner of the journey will be sufficiently declared by the narrative itself One point only need be alluded to here The reader will find occasional descriptions perhaps sometimes disgusting ones, of circumstances of inconvenience which were often encountered In a country where no accommodations for comfortable travelling exist there can be only the alternative of furnishing one s self or of dispensing with them entirely Two English friends, who will be alluded to in the course of the narrative adopting the former course took in their train from Persia to Trebizond, fifteen or sixteen animals bearing tents beds chairs, tables and other articles of convenience with servants in proportion and another, for a small family and a brother is known to have hired no less than thirty Had such arrangements been adopted for this journey the reader would have been rarely told of the uncomfortable circumstances now alluded to What was deemed a desirable regard for missionary economy with other considerations prevented and the other part of the alternative was adopted Innumerable annoyances, some expense of health and risk of life even were among the consequences but there was the serious advantage also, of a more thorough introduction to the domestic condition of the people than would otherwise have been had This advantage it has been found convenient in the course of a faithful narrative to impart also to the reader While enjoying it he will have no disposition, it is hoped to interpret any description as a gratuitous appeal to his sympathies in personal sufferings and if in any case his taste is annoyed by a picture drawn offensively naked it is presumed he will not complain when he reflects what the experience of the reality must have been

The advantages enjoyed for conducting investigations to a true result will also appear in part from the narrative It may be proper to state here, that the disposition universally prevalent to give information with little regard to truth has been it is believed, fully appreciated Besides re questioning and cross questioning the same informant several persons when opportunity has offered, have often been interrogated respecting the same fact, before the truth of it was regarded as ascertained. At Shoosha a large part of the general ground touching the Armenians was brought under the review of the Rev Mr Dittrich whose studies and experience had qualified him to be an excellent informant. And in the end, at Malta notes were very faithfully compared with bishop Dionysius, one of the best informed ecclesiastics of the Armenian nation, now attached to the American mission press in that island. He furnished in fact much additional information. Through him were obtained all the extracts from works in the Armenian language. For, during the journey, only the Turkish language had been made familiar, that being understood everywhere and a dragoman being always at hand to interpret when it was found convenient to resort to the Armenian. A missionary might perhaps in some cases have made a better *selection* of extracts than the bishop on the topics of inquiry proposed to him but full reliance may be placed upon the faithfulness of his *translation* of them into Turkish. In converting them from that language into English no pains have been spared in the use of the best helps to attain perfect accuracy —After all it would be vain to hope that false information has not perhaps in many cases been credited. Should the effect of such errors be to lead others to ascertain the truth their occurrence will be less regretted. The reader is specially warned to regard nearly all the statistical estimates of population as liable to great uncertainty they being in hardly one case founded upon a regular census

The course taken to secure a correct record of observations it may be well briefly to explain. It was often found impossible when thrown at night exhausted from fatigue and hunger into a dirty stable or a noisy family room to record more than brief memoranda of the observations of the day. With these to aid the memory fuller journals were drawn up at the next convenient stopping place, generally after a very few days. At the direction of the Committee, each kept his own memoranda of facts and opinions and wrote out his journal independently of the other to serve as a mutual check

against errors and omissions.   With hardly more than one exception
(where an important conversation happened to be carried on in a
language understood by but one) neither knew what was in the
records of the other until the final reports to the society were drawn
up at Malta   Then also each made out a separate report from the
data in his own possession   Upon the comparison at the end it was
a source of gratification to find, that though one had preserved many
things which the other had not very rarely did any serious dis
crepancy exist   In this state the two reports were submitted to the
Committee   From them the following work was ordered by the
Committee to be prepared and published   In executing their order
Mr Dwight's report has been constantly at hand and has been
freely drawn from whenever it was found to contain the fullest ex
hibition of facts and opinions   and the reader is requested to under
stand that Mr Dwight has shared equally in the labor of collecting
the materials for the whole   It is a matter of sincere regret, that af
ter contributing so much enterprise, firmness and uniform Chris
tian affection toward the successful and happy prosecution of the
journey his absence from his native land has forbidden the possibil
ity of his sharing, likewise the responsibilities of authorship in the
publication of the results to which it has led

The form of letters was adopted in both of the reports submitted to
the Committee for their many obvious advantages   A mere contin
uous journal throwing into each day only its own events would ne
cessarily have occasioned much diffusiveness and repetition and sep
arated far from each other scraps of information needing to be joined
in order to a complete view of any given subject   Letters written
at the end of the journey while they have still allowed the preser
vation of regular dates for such events as demanded a chronological
order have given liberty whenever occasion introduced any topic,
to complete the discussion of that topic by throwing into one suc
cinct view all the information that was obtained respecting it in any
part of the journey   Some advantage has been reaped at the same
time, from the informality of the epistolary style of writing   In de

ciding to whom his letters should be directed, neither writer felt at
any loss   They were addressed to the REV RUFUS ANDERSON
one of the Secretaries of the Board   He had drawn up the Instruc
tions which had guided the investigations of the journey and was
already personally acquainted with the affairs of the Mediterranean
both looked to him as a proper organ of communication with the
Committee, and one had already shared with him the labors and
pleasures of a similar journey of missionary investigation in Greece
The reader is requested to bear in mind, that the letters were origin
ally composed not for popular nor for devotional purposes but for
an official report to the executive officers of a missionary society
with special reference to their business arrangements and if, in
preparing them for the public it has not been found easy to divest
them entirely of their original character, he will, it is hoped need no
apology

The *map* which accompanies the work has been compiled for the
purpose   no single one being found already in existence that could
be advantageously used   The greater part of Armenia is still *terra
incognita* to the topographer and, being divided between three
great empires and in their remotest corners it has received less at
tention than some others equally little known   In laying out this
map a recent Russian map of the countries between the Black and
Caspian seas has been followed in the northern part a map in Mo
rier s Journeys to Persia has helped to settle the localities of Ader
baiján Kinneir s journey in Armenia and Kurdistán has thrown
light upon some very unfrequented parts Niebuhr has been relied
upon for some localities in Mesopotamia and an Armenian map in
Mukhtar s Armenian Dictionary has been frequently consulted, be
sides other more common authorities which need not be named
After all it is to be regarded as only an approximation to an accurate
delineation of the country

Travellers from *other nations* have repeatedly visited the regions
here described   The most important publications they have given
to the world, viz those of Chardin Tournefort, Kinneir, Morier

Porter and Le Gamba have been consulted in these researches
Where their authority has been relied upon for any fact, credit has
been scrupulously given with one exception to be mentioned in its
place The attention of *Americans* has been very little directed to
Armenia perhaps hardly enough to create a desire for further in
formation respecting it For an evil sometimes incident to a new
thing is that it is too far from the common range of knowledge for
its bearings to be fully appreciated It is hoped that the fact that
the reader is now presented with the observations of the first Americans who have trod the soil of Armenia, will not be one that shall
detract from his interest in their perusal The work is submitted
to the religious public, with the earnest prayer that it may contrib
ute to forward the great work of benevolence, to which the author
and his coadjutor have devoted their lives

ELI SMITH

Boston January 1833

CONTENTS

INTRODUCTION

LETTER I

LETTER II

LETTER VI

LETTER VII

LETTER VIII

LETTER IX

LETTER X

LETTER XI

DIRECTIONS

FOR THE PRONUNCIATION OF FOREIGN WORDS

THE author bespeaks the reader's patience with the *hard names* which he will encounter in perusing this work. To give an account of any country without mentioning the names of persons and places which are found in it is evidently impossible. Such exotic names must in *most* cases contain some sounds or combinations of sounds not familiar to an English ear. *Armenia* unfortunately *abounds* in such as are uncouth. The difficulty therefore, was not to be avoided. The author has met it in the best way he was able, but he can truly say that hardly any thing in the preparation of the work has given him more trouble. Had he in order to divest names of their barbarous aspect brought them within the scope of ordinary English spelling to the entire neglect of foreign sounds no scholar would have forgiven him. He has therefore had recourse to the *native orthography* and has been so successful as to collect a list of most of the names which occur as they are written by Armenian Turkish Arabic Persian or other authors to whose languages respectively they belong. It was for a time in contemplation to publish such a list in an appendix. But the number of readers who are acquainted with the Arabic and Armenian characters is so small that the project was abandoned.

In fixing upon the letters by which to represent particular sounds little difficulty has been experienced in regard to *consonants* the use of our consonant letters being sufficiently uniform to express with little ambiguity any sounds that are common to our language and certain combinations having been pretty unanimously agreed upon to represent the more common ones which are foreign. But in regard to *vowels* if one would adhere closely to the *English* use of them the difficulty is insurmountable. To comprehend its nature let any one attempt to write a foreign word in which the two sounds of *a* in *fate* and in *father* occur so that a stranger will pronounce it correctly.

The system adopted in this work both for vowels and consonants (except in some words where a vulgar spelling has gone into too general use to be corrected) is explained so far as explanation is needed by the following *illustrations*. In comparing it with the native orthography the scholar will need to be reminded that the sounds of Turkish and Persian words, especially unaccented *vowels* are but very imperfectly represented by the Arabic characters in which those languages are written and as much regard has been had therefore to the manner in which they are pronounced as to that in which they are written   The same Arabic and Armenian *consonants* have been pretty uniformly expressed by the same consonants in English —In writing *ee* and *oo* instead of *i* and *u* the author has made a compromise with the taste of the common reader at the expense of a loss of the uniformity which would please the scholar

ILLUSTRATIONS

a	has uniformly the sound	of	*a*	in	*father*
ai	"	of	*i*	in	*pine*
ch	"	of	*ch*	in	*church*
e	"	{ of	*a*	in	*fate*
		{ or of	*e*	in	*met*
ee	"	of	*ee*	in	*feet*
g	"	of hard *g*		in	*get*
gh	"	of the Arabic *Ghain*			
	[The common d ay p onou c t l k n pl l d g]				
i		of	*i*	in	*pin*
j		of	*j*	in	*jar*
kh		of the Arabic *Kha*			
	[The co n on ead m y pro ou c] k mpl *k*]				
o		of	*o*	in	*note*
ö		{ of the German *o* in			*horen*
		{ or of the French *eu* in			*beurre*
oo	"	of	*oo*	in	*cool*
s		of	*s*	in	*son*
	[N to l p ono in ʃ l k]				
u		{ of	*u*	in	*gulf*
		{ or a Turkish and Armenian sound resembling it			
ü		{ of the German *u* in			*uber*
		{ or of the French *u* in			*vue*
v		{ of the German *w*			
		{ between the English *v* and *w*			
y final		of	*y*	in	*folly*

An *accent* over a vowel indicates the *syllable* which is to be accented without deciding whether the *vowel* itself is long or short

———

For the value of foreign *coins* and measures of *distance* see NOTE at the end of the second volume   Some of the *foreign words* also which most frequently occur are explained in the INDEX

INTRODUCTION

HISTORICAL SKETCH OF ARMENIA

To give a just and intelligible view of the present state of Armenia frequent references to its ancient history will be necessary   A concise historical sketch of that country, therefore which may serve to explain such references, can not be considered an irrelevant introduction to the following work   It will add to the interest of the subject by showing in how many of the greatest revolutions of mankind, Armenia has been concerned   And should any of the pictures of semi barbarism and demoralization which will occasionally be given tend to excite disgust, such a feeling will be turned into the most charitable compassion, by a view of the wars, persecutions, lawless cruelty, and systematic oppression, which have rolled over or rested upon Armenia, and crushed its inhabitants to the dust   Indeed, if the reader s reflections take the same course as the au thor's he will wonder not so much that the Armenians have merely the name of Christianity as that they have even that, and will discover, in so providential a preservation of the forms of religion, an indication of God's intention, ere long to restore its spirit

2

In the great scarcity of materials elsewhere to be found, Armenian authors have been principally relied upon for this sketch of Armenian history Nor has their testimony to early events confessedly traditionary been rejected, unless contradicted by more credible foreign historians For, whether their own accounts of their early fortunes are more or less rational than the Grecian fables related of them by Strabo and others they are fully believed by the Armenians themselves and a knowledge of them is necessary to a perfect acquaintance with the character of the nation

Armenia is an inland country at the eastern extremity of Asia Minor lying at short distances from the Mediterranean on the southwest the Black sea on the northwest the Caspian on the northeast and at a much greater distance from the Persian gulf on the southeast Its western boundary is not far from six hundred miles east of Constantinople On the north are the ancient Albania Iberia and Colchis, or the modern Georgia and the adjacent provinces , on the west Pontus and Cappadocia on the south Mesopotamia and Assyria and on the east the ancient Media Atropatene or modern Aderbaijan It extends about four hundred and thirty miles in longitude, and about three hundred in latitude

Being an elevated and mountainous region watered with abundant rains and covered for some months in the year, with deep snows, it gives rise to several large and celebrated rivers The noble Euphrates begins here, in two distinct branches themselves not small rivers, its long and solitary course towards the Persian Gulf The Tigris also springs from numerous sources within the Armenian boundary and soon after crossing it washes the soil of ancient Nineveh The Jorokh (Akampsis) carries a part of the waters of Armenia into the Black sea In a mass of mountains between the two branches of the Euphrates rises the rapid and furious Aras (Araxes)   while the still larger Koor (Cyrus) finds its origin not far to the north, and both at length discharge their united waters into the Caspian sea   Armenia, in the most flourishing period of its history, was divided into fifteen provinces which again were subdivided into almost as many cantons as there are valleys in that mountainous region   In the centre of them all was the province of Ararad (Ararat) distinguished for its extent and fertility and which, from its having been almost invariably the residence of the Armenian court is uniformly mentioned in the Bible instead of Armenia itself * On the mountains of this province Scripture tells us the ark rested after the flood   Here was the second cradle of the human race, and from hence were scattered over the face of the earth, the first progenitors of every nation †

* See Gen 8 4 Jer 51 27 (and 2 Kings 19 37 Is 37 38 in Heb)

† The following are the fifteen provinces into which Armenia was divided viz Oodi and Kookáik on the north   Daik on the northwest High Armenia on the west   Fourth Armenia on the southwest   Aghdznik Mogk and Gorjaik on the south   Persarmenia on the southeast   Vasbooragan on the east   Sunik Artsákh and Paidagaran on the northeast and Doorooperán and Ararád in the interior

For a more extended geographical account of Armenia the reader is referred to the first volume of the very learned *Mémoires Historiques et Géographiques sur l Arménie* of M J Saint-Martin   It was our travelling companion and guide and though composed principally from Armenian authors without the aid of personal observation it constantly surprised us by its extreme accuracy

Saint Martin s work also has been constantly referred to in composing this historical sketch and besides contributing many important new facts it has aided much in digesting and correcting information obtained elsewhere   The work to which most frequent reference has been had however is a history of Armenia by the Vartabed Michael Chamchean of Venice   Three editions of this history have been published by its author   The principal is in three large octavo volumes in the Armenian language and the other two are abridgments of this one in Armenian and the other in Armeno-Turkish   The Armenian abridgment has been translated into English and published by Johannes Avdall an Armenian of Calcutta   The other called *Gulzári Tevarikh* the Rose Garden of History was published in 1812 and is the one referred to

Armenian tradition has availed itself of this interesting locality of the nation to trace its history up to the remotest and even to a sacred antiquity It tells us that *Haig* a son of Togarmah the grandson of Japhet was the father of the Armenian race.   Hence to this day they invariably call themselves in their own tongue *Haik* their country also they name *Haik* or *Hayasdan* Haig they believe accompanied his kindred the other descendants of Noah, from the region of Ararad to the land of Shinar   where he assisted at the building of Babel and was affected by the confusion of tongues   Subsequently disgusted with the tyranny of Nimrod he retired with his numerous family towards his native country and established himself in the plain of Moosh to the west of the lake of Van   Finding many there, who, not having followed the tide of emigration to Shinar had remained unaffected by the curse of God at Babel he and his family learned again from them their mother tongue *
Hence have the Armenians a favorite notion that they still speak the language of Noah †

The immediate successors of Haig upon the throne of Armenia removed northward to the banks of the Aras where the third of the dynasty built the city of Armavir (Armavria) which for about eighteen centuries was the residence of the Armenian monarchs ‡   Here reigned *Aram* the seventh of the dynasty of Haig who by his heroic exploits first extended abroad the fame of his coun

in this sketch   though the references will generally answer also for Avdall s translation   The History of Armenia by Moses of Khoren commonly called Moses Chorenensis is Chamcheán s principal authority in the early part of his work and frequent references have been made to it for confirmation

* Mosis Chorenensis Hist Armen. Lib 1 cap 4 9 Chamcheán s Gulzári Tevaríkh Part 1 chap 1

† The arguments in support of this idea are drawn out at length in the preface of Mesrób's Armenian Grammar printed at Constantinople 1826

‡ Chamcheán Part 1 chap 2 Moses Choren L 1 c 11 St Martin Mém sur l Armén vol 1 p 123

trymen, and thus caused them among foreigners, to be named after himself *Armenians* a name almost universally given to them except by themselves, to this day His country also which he freed from invaders received from him, among other nations the name of *Armenia* *

The same distinguished monarch extended his victorious arms into Cappadocia, and gave laws and his name successively to the regions called first second, and third Armenia which united under the general name of Armenia Minor extended from the Euphrates to Cesarea and from the mountains of Pontus to those of Cilicia. Their oldest and principal city was Cesarea it having been founded under the name of Majak (Mazaca) by Mushag their first Armenian governor †

Armenia Minor passed early from Armenian into Roman hands but deserves even at this day on account of the number of Armenians who inhabit it to retain its ancient name

The principal foreign relations of Armenia whether hostile or friendly, during this early and traditionary part of its history were with the neighboring kingdoms of Assyria Media and Babylon It was subjected to Assyria by Shamiram (Semiramis) who built a city for her own residence on the lake of Aghtamar which was originally named after her Shamiramagérd but now bears the name of Van ‡ Subsequently it aided Arbaces the Mede in his rebellion against her successor Sardanapalus and the consequent establishment of the Median kingdom § But the monarchy which it had thus contributed to establish Dikran (Tigranes) the first king of Armenia whose name occurs in Grecian history || lent his aid to destroy For he assisted

---

* Chamcheán P 1 c 8 Moses Choren L 1 c 11 12

† Chamcheán P 1 c 8 St Mart vol 1 p 17 180 Moses Choren L 1 13

‡ Moses Choren L 1 c 14, 15 St Mart vol 1 p 187 Chamcheán, P 1 c 8 § Chamcheán P 1 c 5 Moses Choren L 1 c 2 0.

|| Xen Cyr L III

2 *

Cyrus, the Persian, at the destruction of the Median monarchy, and, transporting the family of Ajtahag (Astyages), its
last king into Armenia, established them in the canton of
Nakhchevân, where originated from them a distinct clan
He aided also, according to Armenian report, in the accom-
plishment of prophecy by assisting Cyrus at the taking of
Babylon * A little more than two centuries after his distinguished reign, Alexander, whose empire absorbed so many
oriental monarchies extended his conquering arm over Armenia, and 328 A C extinguished the dynasty of Haig,
which until then had held uninterrupted possession of the
throne †

The family of Ajtahag is not the only foreign branch, that,
according to the same tradition, was engrafted into the Ar
menian stock during the period we have now reviewed
Scripture informs us that Adrammelech and Sharezer after assassinating their father Sennacherib king of Assyria,
fled into the land of Armenia ‡ Armenian tradition adds,
that the king of that country assigned to the latter the region of mount Sim near the eastern sources of the Tigris §
where his descendants formed the clan of Sanasoons or Sa
soons , and that a little to the southeast of him, was establish
ed the former from whom sprang the Ardzroonies and Knoo-
nies || One branch of this race was, in the course of time
crowned kings of Vasbooragán and a member of the other
after expelling the invading Huns was appointed by a
Persian king, governor of Armenia ¶ We are told also
that an Armenian king being an ally of Nebuchadnezzar

* Chamcheán P 1 c 6 Moses Choren L 1 c 23—30 and L 2 c
46 Compare Jer 51 27

† Chamcheán P 1 c 12 Moses Choren L 1 c 30

‡ 2 Kings 19 37 Is 37 38   § St Mart vol 1 p 54.

|| Chamcheán P 1 c 5 Moses Choren L 1 c 22 St Mart vol 1
p 163.   ¶ Chamcheán P 4 c 13

at the taking of Jerusalem brought away with him a Jewish noble named Shampád from whom sprang the clan of
Pakradians, so called from Pakarad one of his descend
ants,* different branches of which afterwards ascended the
thrones of Armenia and Georgia —These with numerous
other clans more or less powerful, many of whom traced their
origin directly to some son or grandson of Haig anciently
composed the Armenian nation, and the names of their nobles often occur in its history

After Armenia had yielded to the arms of Alexander, it
was ruled by governors sometimes of Greek and sometimes of native origin who derived a delegated authority
alternately from Seleucia and from Macedonia or laid
claim to entire independence as for the time suited their
wishes or ability   In the days of Ardashas (Artaxias)
one of these governors, the celebrated Hannibal found in
Armenia a temporary refuge from the vengeance of Rome
and caused to be built on the banks of the Aras a city,
which named after his protector Ardashad (Artaxata) be
came for a time the capital of the kingdom †

The power that overturned the empire of the Seleuci
dæ in the East, and formed an impassable barrier to the
ambition of Rome numbered Armenia among its early
conquests, but, instead of retaining it as a province bestowed upon it a race of independent and powerful kings
In the year 149 A C Aishag the Great (Arsaces called
also Mithridates I), grandson of the founder of the Parthian empire placed his brother Vagharshág (Valarsaces)
upon the throne of Armenia   Under this branch of the
Arsacidæ, which reigned 577 years, the Armenians boast
of greater prosperity and a higher grade in the scale of
nations, than they have at any other period enjoyed   To

---

* Chamcheán P 1 c 10 Moses Choren L 1 c 21

† Chamcheán P ii   St Mart vol 1 p 117

Vagharshag, they believe themselves to be indebted for a true history of their nation up to its very origin in Haig For that prince, desirous himself of information on this point, obtained the consent of his royal brother of Persia to search the ancient records of Nineveh and there found a manuscript, professing to have been translated from the Chaldee into Greek by command of Alexander, which contained in due order the annals of the Armenian nation Upon such a foundation would the tradition we have been following base itself *

Vagharshag and his son Arshág are reported to have conquered the regions on the southeastern shores of the Black sea, and at the foot of mount Caucasus And the Armenians would have us believe that Ardashes the third of the dynasty on the one side overran Asia Minor subdued Thrace and defeated the Lacedæmoni ans in the Peloponnesus and on the other reduced to a secondary rank the monarchy of Persia † Dikrán his successor was an ally of Mihrtad (Mithridates) the great king of Pontus in his renowned wars with Sylla and Lucullus ‡ and was also crowned king of Seleucia § Such relations soon involved him in a direct war with Rome which Pompey after destroying Mihrtád ended by imposing upon him humiliating conditions of peace ‖ Discontented with these he soon formed an alliance with Arshez, of Persia and their united army under the com mand of Pagoor (Pacorus) son of the Persian king and Pazaprán (Barzapharnes), an Armenian prince entered Palestine, and placed a new soverergn upon the rego-pon

* Chamcheán P 3 c. 1 Moses Choren L 1 c 7 8, and L 2 c 3 St Martin vol 1 p 259

† Moses Choren L 2 c 4 8 11 12 Chamcheán P 3 c 2

‡ Chamcheán P 3 c 3 § Justin Hist L 40 c 1

‖ Chamcheán P 3 c 4

tifical throne of Jerusalem * In the sequel of these hos-
tilities thus induced between the Armenians and Romans,
the whole country was overrun by Antony in his Parthian
wars 34 A C The part north of the Aras was given to
his son who however was soon expelled, and the remain
der became permanently tributary to Augustus † With
this division of territory the reigning family after the lead
ing members had died in captivity was also divided The
northern branch, alternately upheld and dethroned by the
Romans and Persians, was at length supplanted by Georgian princes who again yielded to a brother of the king
of Persia, and finally after a separation of eighty five
years, the whole country was reunited under the southern
branch ‡

Important events had in the meantime occurred in the
dominions of the latter The Armenian Arsacidæ at the
commencement of their reign fixed their royal residence
at Medzpin (Nisibis) For from a remote antiquity, the
northwest part of Mesopotamia embracing Nisibis Mar-
din and Orfah (Edessa) was inhabited by a race of people
resembling the Armenians in manners, language and
form and, at the commencement of the Christian era,
constituted, according to Armenian report, under the name
of Mesopotamia of the Armenians an integral part of
Armenia and was the residence of the court for 228
years § Abgar, one of their sovereigns they say transferred the seat of government to Orfah, and was there con
verted to Christianity In their account of this event they

---

* Chamcheán P 3 c 5 Jos Ant L 24 c 24 25. Moses Cho
ren L 2 c 18 † Chamcheán P 3 c 6

‡ St Mart vol 1 p 293 Chamcheán P 3 c 9 Comp Taciti
Ann L 2 c 1—4 56

§ St Mart vol 1 p 157

have taken care to diminish naught from the circumstances so credulously reported by Eusebius They say that Abgár, having believed in Christ from mere report corresponded with him received from him his portrait miraculously impressed by himself upon a handkerchief and was instructed more perfectly and baptized, together with many of the inhabitants of Orfah, by Thaddeus whom the apostle Thomas in obedience to the command of Christ, sent on this mission Others of the Armenians in the interior were subsequently converted by Thaddeus * But the immediate successors of Abgár apostatized from the faith, martyred besides many common Christians, several of the apostles and disciples of our Lord, and nearly exterminated Christianity in the country † We learn of its continuing to exist by being told about two centuries after that a certain king martyred some of the Christians in his dominions and reduced others to slavery ‡

The third in succession from Abgar having obtained from Vespasian A D 75 the dominion of the whole of Armenia proper, by ceding to the Romans his possessions in Mesopotamia, removed his court to the province of Ararad § The subsequent history of Armenia is varied by little except occasional attempts to throw off the *surveillance* of Rome in the struggles of the Romans with

---

* Chamcheán P 3 c 7 Moses Choren L 2 c 26—30 Compare Euseb L 1 c 12 —Asseman in his abstract of the *Chronicon Edessenum* contends that Abgár was not king of Armenia and never governed any part of that country The chronicle represents him to have been the fifteenth in a series of princes who reigned at Edessa (Bib Orient vol 1 p 420)—Tacitus calls Abgar (or as he writes his name Acbarus,) king of the Arabs (Ann L 12 c 12) and in speaking of Armenia during this period he evidently has in mind only the country whose capital was Artaxata Ann L 2 p 56

† Chamcheán P 3 c 8 Moses Choren L 2 c. 31

‡ Chamcheán P 3 c 14

§ Chamcheán P 3 c 10 Moses Choren L 2 c 35

the Parthians of Persia, until the Sassanidæ ascended the throne of Persia A D 226 * It was not to be expected that the Armenian Arsacidæ who had always considered their own interests more or less connected with the for tunes of their kindred of the Persian branch would be unmoved spectators of this revolution Khosrov who then sat upon the throne, first succeeded in expelling Ardasheer (Artaxerxes) the first Sassanian from Persia , † but was himself finally murdered by a hired assassin of the Persian His kingdom was consequently overrun, and his family almost annihilated ‡

Christianity was now revived in Armenia The instru ment employed by Providence to bring about this great event was Gregory styled by the Armenians *Loosavorich*, the Illuminator than whom no saint ranks higher in the Armenian calendar His father a Persian Pehlevi, of the royal family of the Arsacidæ was the very assassinator of Khosrov Gregory being then in his infancy was carried for safety to Cesarea where he was educated in the Christian faith § Durtad (Tiridates) a surviving son of Khosrov at length marched from Rome by order of Diocletian, to take possession of his rightful throne and Gregory attached him self to his suite But having refused to join the king in his idolatry and his relationship to the murderer of his father becoming known he was subjected to tortures and impris oned for fourteen years Delivered at length by the inter position of God he effected, by preaching and miracles, the conversion of the king and court Then, having been

* Chamcheán P 3 c 11—14. Moses Choren L 2 c 40—66.

† The Armenian testimony to this fact is not credited by Gibbon

‡ Chamcheán P 3 c 14 Moses Choren L 2 c 68—71

§ Chamcheán P 3 c 7 14 Moses Choren Lib 2 c 77

consecrated bishop by Leontios of Cesarea, A D 302 he baptized the king and the whole nation *

The Sassanians of Persia, who were ever ready to do an injury to a race of kings, so nearly related to the dynasty they had overturned and who had acted so hostile a part at the commencement of their own reign became still more inimical when those kings professed Christianity in consequence of their well known desire forcibly to restore and establish the religion of Zoroaster, wherever their power extended The Armenians unable to maintain their independence between two such rival powers as Persia and Rome were inclined by religious sympathy to lean upon the latter but gradually came completely into the power of the former as it gained the ascendency in the East Often was their country unceremoniously trampled upon and crushed in the repeated shocks of their warring neighbors † Nor did the church escape without oppression Two of their most powerful chiefs A D 377 renounced the Christian religion for that of Persia and finding Shabooh Second (Shahpoor) moved by true Sassanian intolerance and left by his victory over Julian to deal with Armenia as he pleased were aided by him in repeatedly devastating the country and one of them named Meroojan was promised the sovereignty of it if he would convert the nation to the religion of Zoroaster The bishops and priests were in consequence carried in chains to Persia where many perished

---

* Chamchean P 3 c 15 Moses Choren L 2 c 88 89 —The ancient Greek ecclesiastical historians from Eusebius to Evagrius maintain a remarkable silence respecting this distinguished character and the whole subject of Christianity in Armenia Sozomen (L 2 c 7) reports a tradition that Tiridates king of Armenia was converted by a vision became a very zealous Christian and ordered all his subjects to believe in Christ But he says nothing of Gregory Even the Armenian Moses Chorenensis gives but a very brief account of him Hist Armen L 2 c 61 77 88

† Chamchean P 3 c 16—20 Moses Choren L 3 c 1—24

by torture and in prison, and Magi, accompanied by executioners, were stationed in the towns and villages to convert the people to the worship of fire * Moved by the entreaties of the Armenian Catholicos, as the head of the Armenian church is called, the emperor Theodosius the Great interfered A D 381, and placed upon the throne a king of his own choice. But the interference resulted only in a formal division of Armenia, A D 381 between the king of Persia and the emperor of Constantinople, which divided also the reigning family, and filled the land with civil broils and bloodshed †

Hitherto we have had little occasion to notice the cause of learning in Armenia for we only learn that king Ardashes A D 87 promoted the study of history, astronomy, geometry &c by the establishment of schools, in which the pupils were taught from books written in Armenian with the Persian or Syriac character, ‡ and that Meroojan in his unhallowed enterprise, destroyed all books in the Greek character, which had been used to some extent in writing Armenian and ordered only the Persian i e Syriac character to be used § But the invention of the Armenian alphabet, A D 406 was a new era in Armenian literature Its inventor, a learned monk named Mesrob, having found human ingenuity insufficient betook himself to prayer, and the result was an immediate formation of thirty six of the Armenian characters in perfection || He then instituted schools in which this alphabet was taught and learned men were sent by him and Isaac the Catholicos to Edessa and Constantinople to translate into Armenian the learned works of other nations The most

* Chamcheán P 3 c 21 Moses Choren L 3 c 26.

† Chamcheán P 3 c 22 23. Moses Choren L 3 c 36—47

‡ Chamcheán P 3 c 11

§ Chamcheán P 3 c 21 Moses Choren L 3 c 36

|| Two others were added in the twelfth century

important result of this literary effort was the translation of the Bible into Armenian, A D 411, by Isaac and Mesrob. They first attempted it from the Syriac but the learned men just mentioned having brought from Constantinople a correct copy of the Septuagint, they translated the whole from that version * This is the translation that is still in use, and it is the oldest Armenian book extant The next is Moses of Khoren's History of Armenia, which was composed about half a century later †

After a series of oppressive and persecuting measures on the part of Persia, and of disunion and disloyalty on the part of the Armenian nobles, Vram Fifth (Bahrám) destroyed A D 428, the dynasty of the Arsacidæ of Armenia and degraded that country to the rank of a dependent province ‡ The division of the country between the Greeks and Persians still continued but the share of the former embraced only two or three of the western provinces The remainder was ruled by governors of Persian appointment, though sometimes of native origin till the Sassanian dynasty crumbled under the growing power of the kalifs. Armenia now experienced the most relentless and bloody religious persecution which her annals or those of almost any other nation, have recorded Hazgerd Second (Yezdigérd) the Persian sovereign began A D 449, by using his personal influence to induce the Armenian chiefs to embrace the worship of fire while absent from their country aiding him in his wars with the Huns Mild measures failing of success, he tortured a number of them to death, martyred multitudes of the common people, and harassed the country with insupportable taxes Twice were the principal nobles drawn away from their country, and plunged in the dungeons of Persia The Catholicos and

---

* Chamcheán P 3 c 24 Moses Choren L 3 c 47 49 53, 54

† Chamcheán P 4 c 4

‡ Chamcheán P 3 c 25, 26. Moses Choren L 3 c 64

his leading clergy were carried off in chains, and, after an imprisonment of two or three years, suffered martyrdom Desolating armies ravaged the country, and Magi in their train, by the force of such arguments, sought to make converts to their faith   Some chiefs of the distinguished Mamigonian clan, in this extremity rallied the sinking spirits of their countrymen, collected around their standard other nobles of kindred feelings and bravely defended their religion and their country   Armenian history tells us that their ancestor Mamkon was a nephew of the king of China who, upon the occasion of some revolution in that distant country, sought an asylum in Persia and finally settled in Armenia about the middle of the third century *   The Mamigonians took a high rank among the nobles of their adopted country, and more than one was honored with the office of commander in-chief   They now performed prodigies of valor and, facing with equal firmness the force of superior numbers and the influence of secret treachery not only prevented during two per secuting reigns the Armenian church from becoming en tirely extinct but finally brought the Persian king A D 484 to make peace upon terms of the most complete tol eration of Christianity and the renunciation of every effort to make converts to the faith of the Magi   In fact a Mamigonian was shortly after appointed governor of Ar menia, and under him the country enjoyed a season of quiet and prosperity.†

During this season, the Armenians, by rejecting the council of Chalcedon, subjected themselves to the charge of heresy which is still brought against them by the churches of Greece and Rome   Although neither the

* Moses Choren L 2 c 8. St Mart. vol 2 p 23 —Gibbon at tributes to Mamkón a somewhat different origin (Hist L xiii) But his authority is Moses of Khoren who narrates distinctly the facts as given above.   † Chamchean P 4 c 1—11

civil nor spiritual head of the nation had been present at
the council of Nice, its decrees when brought into the
country, had received the subscription of Gregory, who
was then still living and Armenia seems never to have
been troubled by the Arian heresy * When the canons of the
council of Ephesus also were sent to Armenia, at the
close of its sessions, the nation formally assented to them at
a special synod And an additional barrier was raised to
the introduction of Nestorianism by a speedy condemnation
of the books of Theodorus of Mopsuestia and Diodorus of
Tarsus ,† and by a successful opposition to the proselyting
attempt of Barsumas of Nisibis about forty years afterwards.‡
When the council of Chalcedon assembled, the Armenian
church was too deeply involved in its desperate struggle for
existence with the fire worshipers of Persia to take a part
in its deliberations and Barsumas the Syrian monk of
Samosata, subsequently found means from his retreat in
Mesopotamia, of prejudicing the Armenian clergy against it
through his disciple Samuel § Previous intimacy between
the two nations,‖ facilitated his access to the Armenians
and it was no difficult matter to convince them, that a
council which had treated the works of Theodorus with
indulgence was itself infected with Nestorianism Being
confirmed in this prejudice by the condemnation it received
in the *Henoticon* of Zeno ¶ the Armenian bishops met,
A D 491, and formally rejected it. But at the same time
they most inconsistently anathematized Eutyches **

The fires of persecution continued to be repeatedly kin-

* Chamcheán P 3 c 15. Moses Choren L 2 c 87

† Chamcheán P 3 c 25 Summa Concihorum p 368 Moses Choren L 3 c 51   ‡ Chamcheán, P 4 c 4

§ Asseman Bib Orient. vol 2 p 296

‖ Two native Syrians had already been Catholicoses of Armenia.
Chamcheán P 3 c 17 and P 4 c 1. Compare St Mart vol 1 p 306

¶ Evag Hist L 3 c 4

** Chamcheán P 4 c 12. Compare P 4 c 17

dled by the bigotry of Magism, without excepting even the reign of Nooshirwán the Just, until the Magi themselves were swept away by the besom of Saracen destruction, and Persia became a province in the empire of the kalifs of Mohammed * Armenia, at an early period, felt the rapacious grasp of the Arabian monarchs. Their first incursion was in A D 637,† and ten years after, the nation submitted to pay the *kharaj*, or capitation tax, imposed by Mohammedans upon all tolerated sects.‡ The jealousy of the emperors of Constantinople, who in the last years of the Sassanian dynasty had again extended their dominion over the whole of Armenia, was consequently provoked, and for seventy years that miserable country was a bone of contention between the rival powers of Constantinople and Damascus Being claimed by both and defended by neither, as often as it yielded to the arms of one, it was punished for disobedience by the other and was almost equally devastated by the orthodox Greeks, and the infidel Arabs. From the time that the Greeks again retired within their own division the remainder of the country was governed by representatives of the kalifs, of whom the Armenians have recorded but few complaints except for their extortion until the last who had orders to carry on a war of religious persecution and extermination The city of Tovin was their usual residence §

By a singular change of measures, the court from which these cruel orders emanated soon afterwards established a dynasty of native sovereigns that for 160 years occupied the throne of Armenia The noble family of Pakradians, which at the destruction of Jerusalem had been transported to Armenia has been already noticed They were known as Jews in the reign of Dikran, the fourth of the Ar

---

* Chamchean P 4 c 1—16   † Ibid P 4 c 17

‡ Chamchean P 4 c 18.   § Ibid P 4 c 18—22.

sacian dynasty, and under that dynasty generally enjoyed
the hereditary right of crowning the sovereign and filled
many important offices.* They were distinguished, and
raised to offices of trust and power, by the Mohammedan
governors, and at last Ashod the Pakradian, having already for many years held the office of govenor, was presented, A D 885, with a tributary crown by the kalif of
Bagdad † But the throne of the Pakradians, built upon the
already declining power of the kalifs was a tottering one
from the beginning At this period of the Saracen empire,
the governors of the provinces receiving but little assist
ance from the capital, and acknowledging as little allegiance hardly consulted aught but their own inclinations and
power, in the treatment of their subjects and their neighbors Thus left to themselves the Armenian kings were
neither strong enough to put down internal rebellion nor
to repel foreign aggression Many of the southern nobles
became Mohammedans and we soon cease to hear of the
southeastern provinces as a part of Armenia Kookark and
Oodi the northern provinces owned but a reluctant allegiance and were the scene of protracted and bloody wars
In fact a branch of the Pakradians assumed in Kookárk
the title of king A D 982 and we hear of their descendants occasionally as late as A D 1260 ‡ The Ardzroonies,
whose Assyrian origin has been already mentioned yielded to
the Pakradians, from the beginning but a turbulent obedience, and A D 908, Kakig their head received from a
neighboring vizeer the crown of Vasbooragan thus completing their independence and severing from Armenia
one of its largest provinces This petty Armenian kingdom
whose capital was the city of Van struggled for an unen
vied existence till A D 1021, when Senekerim its king
alarmed at the first invasion of the Seljookians transferred

* Moses Choren L 2 c 3, 13 Chamcheán P 3 c 2
† Chamcheán P 5 c 1   ‡ St Mart vol I p. 365 422

his kingdom, by a regular exchange of deeds, to the emperor Basilius and received in return the province of Sebastia, whither he migrated with his army and about one third of his subjects. In A D 961 a branch separated from the original stock of the Pakradians and peaceably established the kingdom of Kars, which continued to exist even after the parent throne was overturned

The worst foreign enemy of the Pakradians was the vizeer of Aderbaiján He repeatedly ravaged the country drove the king from his throne to retired mountain fastnesses, and subjected the people to the horrors of war and of religious persecution The Abkház (Abasgi) too made frequent incursions upon the northern frontier But all the neighboring enemies of Armenia were at length crushed by another power which trampled alike upon it and upon them Central Asia that ocean of nomadic hordes whose waves had often from the remotest antiquity burst acrost the Jihon (Oxus) to deluge the plains of Persia, and in the sixth century had even extended in the persons of the Huns its desolating influences to Armenia now sent forth a vast inundation which undermined successively the walls of Bagdád and of Constantinople and spread over Armenia the foreign race that occupies and oppresses it at the present day We have just seen one of the petty Armenian kingdoms take to flight at the approach of Toghrul beg at the head of his Turks * The very next year the representative of the main branch of the Pakradians affrighted by the same enemy bequeathed to the Greek emperor his capital and his kingdom upon condition of being defended during life from foreign invasion The Greeks succeeded by sword and by treachery in executing this testament A D 1046,

* Tóghrul's nation were Turks his family Seljookians Seljook the grandfather of Tóghrul having by his greatness provoked the jealousy of his sovereign the king of the Turks fled to save his life and drew after him a large portion of his nation who thence forward followed the fortunes of his family Sar Hist of Georg Almac p 267

and the family, who pretended to a direct descent from King David of Jerusalem, saw themselves transferred from the throne of Armenia, where they had enjoyed the pompous title of *Shahanshah* (king of kings), to the proprietorship of a few obscure towns in Cappadocia.*

We hear much of the church during the dark ages which we have just reviewed, but little that is grateful to the evangelical Christian. As evidence of her prosperity, we are told of numerous churches and convents built, of new ceremonies and precious relics introduced, of multitudes of legendary and scholastic books composed, and of incredible miracles performed † while disputes about the council of Chalcedon the ambition and rivalries of Catholicoses and the introduction of demoralizing heresy, give proof of the low state of religion We hear nothing of eloquent preachers going through the nation and stirring it up to salutary reform , or of the establishment of schools for the education of the common people in religious knowledge and useful science The best fruit of religion that is presented to us is the unyielding steadfastness with which Magian and Mahommedan persecutions were endured, to the loss of property, of liberty and often of life

The attempts of the Seljookians met with little success until by the changes just mentioned Armenia with the unimportant exception of Kars, had passed into the hands of the Greeks whose hatred of monophysitism was such, that they saw with indifference its partizans fall before the Turkish yataghan Then, with their hundreds of thousands, they carried devastation through the country year

---

* Chamcheán P 5 c 1—18.

† Such as a dish of cooked pigeons coming to life and flying away from table at the command of a monk who had unwittingly ordered such a forbidden dish to be cooked on a fast day and the current of a river reversed to convince an emperor of the orthodoxy of the Armenian mode of blessing the waters at Christmas ! Chamcheán P 5 c 9 11

after year, and in A D 1049 sacked Ardzen a city near the modern Erzroom, massacring 140.000 of its inhabitants, carrying as many into captivity and levelling its 800 churches with the ground * Toghrul died A D 1063, but the *falcon* was followed by the *conquering lion* † Alp-arslan his successor in completing the conquest and ruin of Armenia took and pillaged Ani, the capital of the Pakradian kings with such slaughter that its streets were blocked up with the bodies, and the river Akhooreán reddened with the blood of the slain ‡ The king of Kars, thinking his city no longer safe now followed the example of the kings of Ani and of Van and exchanged his kingdom A D 1064, with the emperor for a small territory in the southern part of Pontus embracing Amasia and Comana.§ From this conquest of Armenia by the Turks which was thus completed it ceased to have an individual existence Its ancient provincial divisions were obliterated, and Armenian names of places were gradually supplanted by others of Turkish origin The sons of Seljook when sultans of a vast empire retained the wandering habits of their ancestor who pitched his shepherd s tent upon the banks of the Jihon Instead of imposing upon Armenia a regular government, they alternately over-ran it with their devastating hordes and left it a prey to desolation and anarchy until by the death of Malek-shah it was given up to the undivided influence of the latter of these curses

It would be useless to attempt to thread the labyrinth of the petty undefined and often hostile principalities, into which Armenia was divided between the breaking up of the empire of the house of Seljook and the invasion of the Moghuls The southern provinces, occupying the defiles

* Chamcheán P 5 c 15 St Mart vol 2 p 201

† *Tóghrul* signifies in Turkish a falcon and *Alp-arslán* (properly pronounced Elb-arslán) signifies a heroic or strong lion

‡ St Mart vol 2 p. 224   § Chamcheán, P 5 c 16

of mount Taurus, were divided between two branches of the family of the Turkman Artuk and the relatives of the Kurd Sulah-el-deen, so renowned in the history of the crusades under the name of Saladin The slave of a Seljookian prince assuming the title of Shah armen, established and transmitted to his posterity a kingdom whose capital was Khelat on the western shore of the lake of Van Ani had been given by Alp-arslan to a family of Kurds, but after an obstinate struggle they were dispossessed by the kings of Georgia, who now at the height of their power, not only extended their sway over the northern provinces of Armenia but infringed upon the territories of the kings of Khelát and the Atabegs of Aderbaijan *

Although Armenian rule in Armenia itself had thus ceased we may, by going only to the adjoining province of Cilicia still find a small body of the nation governed by its own kings During the rule of the Pakradians, and of the governors who preceded them in fact from A D 597 the Greek emperors had made repeated attempts, by proclamations, by councils and, in that part of Armenia which belonged to them, by direct force, to bring the Armenians to a union with the Greek church But their efforts, notwithstanding some partial success at times produced no better ultimate result, than irritated obstinacy on the part of the Armenians, and overbearing contempt on that of the Greeks After the three Armenian kings with so many of their subjects, by retiring within the Greek limits had voluntarily put themselves in the power of the emperor, the same attempts were repeated in a still more objectionable form At last Kakig, the exiled king of Ani, provoked beyond endurance by the contempt which the Greek bishop of Cesarea had thrown upon his nation by calling his dog *Armen* (Armenian), cruelly murdered that prelate by tying him and his dog in a bag together, aud provoking the poor animal to

* St Mart vol 1 p 42, 377—383

tear his master to pieces * He was himself slain in consequence, but Roopen his companion and relative avenged his death by establishing, A D 1080 an independent kingdom in Cilician Taurus, which for 295 years was governed by his descendants Already were those mountainous regions occupied by a numerous Armenian population, but the standard of the Roopenians drew away still greater numbers from the cruelties of the Turks and the persecutions of the Greeks The kingdom increased from small beginnings, till it occupied the whole country from the summits of Taurus to the sea, and from the Euphrates to the western limits of Cilicia Ain zarbah, Tarsus and Sis were successively its capitals The power of the Greeks from whom it endured occasional wars and constant enmity at length fell before the lance of the crusaders But the previous capture of Nice by the same military adventurers and the consequent transfer of the court of the Seljookian sultans of Room from thence to Iconium had already planted upon the very borders of Cilicia a still more persevering and harassing enemy The crusaders themselves influenced the fortune of the Roopenian kings more by intrigue and intermarriages than by open war or confirmed friendship † The Moghuls were their least injurious neighbors When their hordes had already swept over Persia Georgia and Armenia had advanced into Mesopotamia, and had conquered the sultan of Iconium, the Armenian king was so fortunate as to arrest their march by a timely submission and obtain a treaty of friendship and alliance, which the descendants of Chingiz never failed to respect till their conversion to Mohammedanism weakened their fidelity to Christian allies But this intimacy with the great Moghul provoked the jealousy of the successors

* Chamchean P 5 c 18

† The Armenians so often mentioned in the history of the crusades were of this Cilician kingdom

of Saladin, and for nearly a century, the sultans of Egypt, occasionally aided by the Turks of Iconium, made incursions into Cilicia, destroying its cities, and carrying its inhabitants into captivity, until alarmed lest sympathy for the Armenians should bring upon them another crusade from Europe, they, with barbarities not to be described, put a final termination to Armenian royalty A D 1375, and made Cilicia a province of Egypt *

While Armenia proper was under a distinct government, whether royal or provincial, its spiritual and civil capitals were generally the same, and the incumbent of the see of St Gregory was rarely troubled with a rival The Turks at the same time that they destroyed its civil government, caused the Catholicos, as early as A D 1060, to take refuge in mount Taurus † He subsequently resided in some one of the numerous convents of the Black mountain (mount Amanus) to the west of Samosata, until A D 1125 when the office of Catholicos and a small principality in Fourth Armenia becoming united in the same person the castle of Dzovk was made the capital of both ‡ The principality however, being at length ruined by the Turks, the seat of the Catholicos was transferred A D 1147 to Hromkla a fortress on the west bank of the Euphrates below Samosata,§ where it continued till A D 1294, when, that place having been destroyed by the Egyptians, it was removed to Sis, then the capital of the Roopenian kings.‖ During this disturbed state of the nation, a number of bishops in different places assumed the dignity of Catholicos, but only one succeeded

---

* Chamcheán P vi —The sultáns of Egypt of this dynasty are called Ayoobites from Ayoob the father of Saladin (Vit Sal p 1) A family of poor Emeers in Mount Lebanon still seem to lay claim to descent through them from the great antagonist of Richard the lion-hearted and are known as Emeers of the house of Ayoob

† Chamcheán P 5 c 15   ‡ Ibid P 6 c 4.

§ Chamcheán P 6 c 6.   ‖ Ibid. 6 c 19

in creating a permanent division in the church A con
vent in Aghtamar an island in the lake of Van had ac
quired some celebrity by having been the residence of
the Catholicos for several years in the days of the Pakra
dians and now when the successors of St Gregory fixed
themselves at such a distance as the mountains of Cilicia,
its bishop A D 1114 boldly threw off their supremacy
and supported by five other prelates assumed the title and
functions of Catholicos * The excommunication, which
was immediately denounced against him, was removed
after 180 years † and the Catholicos of Aghtamar contin
ues to exercise his functions at the present day in full
communion with the other branches of the Armenian
church —During the reign of the Roopenians the convents
of the Black mountain produced many writers who took
a high rank in the monastic literature of Armenia

We must now return to Armenia proper and review the
events which it in the meantime underwent The first
effect of the advance of the Moghuls under Chingiz khan
from their distant region north of the wall of China was
to force westward the different hordes of Turks which
after accompanying Toghrul across the Jihon had fixed
themselves in the eastern part of Persia Led by Jelal el
deen son of the last king of Kharism they spread over
Armenia in their march A D 1226 subjecting its in
habitants to the evils of war and of religious persecution ‡

---

* Chamcheán P 6 c 4   † Chamcheán P 6 c 19

‡ Chamcheán P 6   c 13 —It was in the train of Jelál el deen that the
horde from which the Osmanlies sprang migrated from Meru Shah-Jihan
in Khorasán to Asia Minor Their chief Soleimán dy ng when they had
advanced as far as Erzengan his son Erdogrul conducted them into Bithynia
where he was presented with a small district by the Seljookian sultán of
Iconium Othmán his son conquered Broosa and laid the foundation of
the empire and the dynasty which have to this day retained from him the
name of Ottoman or Osmanly Mininski Lex Com § 10 Mod Trav
Syr and As Min vol 2 p 328 Id Turkey p 12

4

The Moghul generals, who followed were cruel as conquerors and oppressive as governors. Their extortions were diminished by a visit of the Armenian king of Cilicia to their distant masters and a temporary tranquility was restored to Armenia by the personal presence of Hoolakoo, who, A D 1256 as the lieutenant of his brother then the occupant of the throne of Chingiz transferred the Moghul head-quarters from the desert of Mooghan to the beautiful city of Maragha in Aderbaijan and changed the encampment of a nomadic horde into a philosophic and civilized court. The tolerant spirit of the first Moghuls or rather their partiality to the Christian religion, was but partially destroyed even after the successors of Hoolakoo embraced the Mohammedan faith and we read of but temporary and limited persecutions, even to the last days of their reign *

Timoor (Tamerlane) the greatest of earthly conquerors, about A D 1390 swept away the miserable relics of the house of Chingiz and repeatedly traced his bloody track across the mountains of Armenia. But he left behind him no efficient rulers and Turkman tribes soon effaced the footsteps of the last of the Moghuls † Hordes of Turks bearing the particular name of Turkman originally followed Toghrul to the south of Armenia they received accessions from the companions of Jelal-el deen and now divided into the two tribes of *Ak koyunly* (white sheep) and *Kara-koyunly* (black sheep) with Diarbekr and Van for their

---

* Chingiz and his successors have been exceeded by few in cruelty as conquerors but as rulers they seem to have granted toleration to every sect and protection to the citizens of every nat on During their reign the whole of the vast region between the Mediterranean and the Chinese sea was thrown open to the unrestricted investigation of travellers It gives one a sublime idea of their power and their mildness to see the Polos passing this distance in safety protected simply by the passport of a sovereign on the throne of China

† Malcolm s Hist of Persia vol I p 316 Hist of Persia in the Mo dern Travel er Pers vol 1 p 160

respective capitals they ruled over or rather over ran, the whole of Armenia But the Osmanlies of Constantinople on one side and the Sofies of Persia on the other stripped them of their power about the beginning of the sixteenth century * and they now lead a nomadic life in Cilicia and the adjacent countries †

The Turks and Persians for a long time shared the whole of Armenia between them But the Russians, by possessing themselves of Georgia at the beginning of the present century and by subsequent wars have now become large proprietors Our journals will illustrate the *effects* of so long a subjection to moslem masters and I willingly shun the painful task of tracing out through the barbarous wars of such bitter political and religious rivals and the grinding oppression of such tyrannical governments the *successive steps* of its degradation I will merely record the protest of Armenia against the eulogies that have been bestowed upon Abbas the Great one of the most unfeeling devastators that Armenia whose acquaintance with tyrants has not been small has ever known That he might defend his borders against the Turks he coolly determined to draw through Armenia a broad intrenchment of perfect desert Its unoffending inhabitants after seeing their houses and every vestige of cultivation and of home disappear were collected in the plain of Ararat and driven like so many cattle to Persia husbands and wives parents and children separated multitudes drowned in the Aras others subjected to the cruelty and lust of the soldiery and all under the very eye and influence of the monarch ‡ A part of them were indeed located with peculiar privileges in Joolfah at Isfahan but could this satisfy the nation for its country made a desert, and itself made homeless ? Or can

* Malcolm s Hist Persia vol 1 p 320

† Niebuhr Voy en Arab vol 2 p 336

‡ Chamcheán P 7 c 8 9 Chardin Voyages en Perse ed Langlès vol 2 p 304

humanity consider it an equivalent for another colony of fifty thousand, carried in the same violent manner to a province where an unhealthy climate soon swept off every soul? *

Some changes occurred in the church after the destruction of the Cilician kingdom which deserve to be noticed The Catholicos at Sis although deprived of the support of an Armenian king and court maintained his spiritual rule over the nation until A D 1441, when an assembly of seven hundred of the clergy placed another in Echmiadzin, the possession of a hand of St Gregory being supposed to give that convent superior claims † The successors of the latter have ever since been considered the principal Catholicoses but the Catholicos of Sis still governs a small branch of the Armenian church in full communion with the rest according to a treaty of peace and amity signed by the incumbents of the two sees A D 1651 ‡ Mohammed Second after taking Constantinople A D 1453, induced many Armenians to settle in that capital and removing the Armenian bishop of Broosa thither gave him authority over all the Armenians in his dominions with the title of Patriarch The patriarchate of Jerusalem which originated as early as 1311 owed its commencement much in the same way to the sultan of Egypt to whom that city was then subject § As neither of these patriarchs with the exception of that of Jerusalem for a short time || has ven

---

* Chamchean P 7 c 9 Mal Hist Pers Vol 1 p 368 —Sir John Malcolm in his valuable history of Persia and others have followed the Persian authors If we had received our accounts of Sennacherib or Nebuchadnezzar from Assyrian or Babylonian writers instead of Jewish we should probably have a very different opinion of their characters Even his admirers however cannot conceal that the domestic character of Abbas was stained with the most unnatural cruelty —He is reported to have carried no less than 500 000 Georgians and Armenians captives to Persia Chardin vol 2 p 62 Chamcheán P 7 c 9

† Chamcheán P 7 c 3   ‡ Chamcheán P 7 c 12
§ Chamchean P 6 c 21 || Chamcheán P 7 c 16

tured to ordain bishops or consecrate the *meiron* (holy oil),
two duties peculiar to a Catholicos they are considered
as merely bishops clothed with authority, and spiritual dependents rather than rivals of the head of the church at
Echmiadzin Appointments both to the office of Cathol
icos and patriarch having ever been treated by the Turks
and Persians as subject to the approbation of the civil pow
er they could not be other than sources of corruption especially when that power was Mohammedan, and influ
enced almost solely by bribery In fact, the remainder of
the ecclesiastical history of Armenia is so exclusively made
up of the intrigues and broils, and barefaced corruption of
ambitious ecclesiastics that I shall not be blamed for leav
ing it untold

The Armenians are known at the present day as a scat
tered race and one cannot rise from the perusal of their
history, without wondering, not that they are so but that
they should still be found in considerable numbers in
their own country We have already noticed their existence in the north of Mesopotamia, their emigration to Ar
menia Minor and Cilicia, their settlement in Constanti
nople and their forcible removal by Shah Abbas to Persia
We are also told that the Saracens and Greeks, while con
tending for their country each took away multitudes of
captives Toghrul and Timoor carried thousands to un
known countries, the Egyptians removed sixty thousand
to Egypt and it is known that the Persians in every war
even to the last with Russia have always carried their cap
tives into servitude Multitudes, moreover have at various
periods been induced by oppression at home to seek vol
untarily an asylum in distant countries, to say nothing of
other multitudes that commerce has enticed away We
are not surprised therefore at finding them not only in al
most every part of Turkey and Persia but in India as
well as in Russia Poland and many other parts of Europe

RESEARCHES IN ARMENIA

—◆—

LETTER I

SMYRNA AND CONSTANTINOPLE

Object of the journey—Departure from Malta—Arrival at Smyrna—The
Armenians of Smyrna—Their Academy—Papal Armenians—Departure
from Smyrna—Magnesia—Thyatira—Galembéh—Balı kesr—A dismal
night—Soo-sughurluk—Mahalúj—A Turkish coffee house—Arrival at Con
stantinople—Visit to the Armenian Patriarch—Origin of his see and
manner of his election—His rank and power—His expenses and income—
Evils attendant upon his election and upon the appointment of bishops—
Intolerant nature of his government—Patriarchate of Jerusalem—Armenian
primates of the capital—Armenian Academy—State of education—Print
ing press at Orta koy—Papal Armenians

DEAR SIR

IT was to ascertain the state of the Armenians *in their
own country* that Mr Dwight and myself were commission
ed to undertake the present journey   We were advised to
take Smyrna, or at least Constantinople, in our way, mere
ly to obtain facilities for ulterior movements   Our inquiries
therefore in those cities were specially directed to the main
field of our investigations   You will of course hardly
expect a detailed account even of their Armenian inhabi
tants   and will need such an account the less, as you have
already the reports of so many that have preceded us   I
shall present Smyrna and Constantinople merely as stages

on the high road to Armenia· and in general, as in our
journey we hasted to reach that country as speedily as possi
ble, I shall endeavor to do the same in my report·

The Instructions of the Prudential Committee· dated the
19th of January 1830, were brought to Malta by Mr
Dwight· on the 27th of February·   We both felt the impor
tance of the suggestion that the mountains of Armenia could
be travelled most easily in the summer months, and were
gratified at finding ourselves ready on the 17th of March,
to proceed to Smyrna in the vessel which brought Mr
Dwight from Boston·   In the channel of Scio· we were
overtaken by a ship, thirty four days from New York·
which brought the last intelligence that reached us from
our native country, except what we gleaned from Paris
and St Petersburg gazettes, until we arrived at Constanti
nople on our return·

We landed at Smyrna on the 26th of March· and were
welcomed by a circle of our countrymen and Christian
friends·   There is still a light burning in the "candlestick
of Smyrna·   A few are found there who love the Savior
and are ever ready to welcome the missionary· and speed
him on his way·   We were cheered by their society aided
by their Christian counsel· and encouraged by a promise of
their prayers· And being there on Easter· we commemorated
with the church at Smyrna, the dying love of our Lord —
The sixteen days of our stay passed away pleasantly in the
hospitable family of our countryman and fellow laborer, the
Rev· Mr· Brewer·

Little information could be obtained respecting regions
so far in the interior as those we proposed to visit·   No Eu
ropean mercantile establishment was found· having branch
es or correspondents in that direction· to whom we could
take letters of recommendation· or of credit·   The exten
sive internal trade of Smyrna appears to be almost exclusively in the hands of native merchants·   An Armenian of the

city was able to give us letters to Tokat Echmiadzin and Tif-
flis An Indian Armenian also recently from Bushire where
he had been treasurer to the English Residency, gave us
valuable hints respecting our route and the best mode of
travelling , and afterwards likewise kindly forwarded to
us of his own accord letters to archbishop Nerses at Tiflis
and to the Catholicos at Echmiadzin Our European friends
readily furnished us with facilities for obtaining at Constantinople all that we needed

The Armenians of Smyrna are estimated at 8 000, including those who are gone over to the papal church and are
known chiefly as thrifty merchants and active brokers
They have but one church In this twelve priests officiate
in turn at the head of whom is a bishop The present occupant of the see is Gabriel, patriarch of Jerusalem Being
too inefficient to manage the intrigues of the monks, and to
avert the extortions of the Turks he was obliged some time
ago, to leave that city and is now enjoying his ease in this
quiet flock while a more able spirit is endeavoring to extri
cate his convent from its multiplied embarrassments The
priests are uneducated with the exception of one who was
then at the head of the Armenian academy but is since dead

The Armenian academy is an interesting object It
has been in operation about thirty years, and is the
only school in the place for the Armenians the few
taught by the priests being hardly of sufficient importance
to be named The building which was erected about five
years ago is situated in the church yard and is a speci
men of Armenian taste and neatness The establishment
is said to be possessed of ample funds chiefly the result of
legacies and it being a free school any Armenian who
chooses can send his children The number of scholars
was about two hundred They occupied different apartments and were of all ages and grades of learning from
the abecedarian to the student of logic We were grat-

ified to find the New Testament in their hands   It was
introduced at the suggestion of the agent of the British and
Foreign Bible Society by Boghos the professor of gram
mar as a class-book for those whom he was teaching the
ancient Armenian   I had become acquainted with this in
teresting layman in a former visit and was sorry to find
him now in ill health and excused from his duties in the
school   He is a scholar in his own language a friend to
scriptural as well as scientific education, and would be a
useful coadjutor to a missionary at the same time that he
would himself derive advantage from such a friend   He
gave us a letter to his former master the head of a similar
school at Constantinople with a hint that we should find
him enlightened and friendly   We have since learned
that he never resumed his connection with the school at
Smyrna, but found a more eligible situation at Broosa,
from whence he has drawn upon the Bible depository at
Smyrna for two hundred New Testaments for his pupils

We heard the papal Armenians estimated at 2000 or
3000   But I can hardly persuade myself that they are so nu
merous although they have undoubtedly multiplied within
a short time   A few years ago there were none except a
few emigrants from the vicinity of Nakhchevan   They
have no church, but attend worship at the Latin chapels,
of which there are two, the Austrian and the French
Their popery gives them a partiality for Europeans for
alas ! in Turkey a European, in his influence upon the
natives at least is almost of course a papist   They are
consequently better acquainted with foreign languages
than their orthodox* countrymen   And although the

---

* I think of no better term by which to designate the members of the proper oriental Armenian church   It certainly does not become *Protestants* to
countenance the exclusiveness of Rome by calling them in her dialect
Schismatics   The papal Armenians are the real *schismatics* from their
proper church

light of Europe shines upon them through the lurid clouds of Romish bigotry they yet discern sufficient to give them a superiority in education and general intelligence over those who have no religious partialities to direct their eyes away from Turkey

On the morning of the 12th of April we found our selves in readiness to depart for Constantinople The chance of encountering a north wind at the Dardanelles, which rendered the length of a passage by sea very un certain and might prolong it several weeks determined us to go by land We could not hire caravan horses for the whole distance and even with post horses should be expos-ed to many inconveniences without a tartar so we yielded to the advice of friends and engaged the *tatar aghasy* (aga of the tartars) to furnish us with a tartar and post horses to Constantinople We had a fellow countryman and one attendant in company, so that we were four in number and our horses amounted to ten, including those of the tartar and two *suryies* (postilions) Mustafa the tartar having seen our baggage loaded and received the half of his pay according to agreement delivered to each a formidable *kumchy* (whip) and we mounted at 9 A M As we moved northward over the plain of Boornabat, the size of its olives and the extent of its vineyards made us admire its fertility, while the quince in blossom and the fig just putting forth its leaves, added to the charms of a lovely morning Numerous springs gushing out from the verdant declivities of the hills beyond were grateful to us, whose latest associations contrasted them with the naked rocks of Malta while one of our companions, having re cently learned in the deserts of Nubia to be choice of so precious an element, seemed ready to charge Providence with a blamable want of economy in suffering so much of it to be wasted But the Psalmist was taught by a better philosophy to admire the provident care of Him that ' send eth the springs into the valleys which run among the hills for '*they give drink to every beast of the field* From the highest point we enjoyed a commanding view of the plain of Magnesia and then hastened towards it by a long and rapid descent As we approached the town Mustafa, placing himself in our rear cracked his whip and crying *haideh* (go along) quickened the pace of our horses and drove us in much as if we, like them, were a herd of domestic animals

Magnesia is at the northern base of a precipitous moun tain, formerly called Sipylus the southern declivity of which is visible from Smyrna and was still striped with snow The remains of a citadel and a ruined city wall crown the summit and sweep down the steep side of a rugged hill between it and the town Report assigns to the present city a population of 80 000 but in answer to a passing inquiry we were told that the Turkish fam ilies are but 8000 the Armenians 400 and the Greeks 800 there are also 100 or 150 of Jews * The Armen ians have two churches and are none of them papists

April 13 We were on horseback again before day break, and though the cold and damp of the night soon chilled and benumbed us the sweet notes of the nightin gale, and the rattling of the stork gave interest to our ride over the battle ground of Scipio and Antiochus We crossed the Hermus by a wooden bridge while yet the darkness hid its fabled sands of gold and when the day dawned we found ourselves threading a serpentine path among the sloughs and ditches that intersect the alluvial surface of the great Lydian plain It can hardly be ex ceeded in fertility and still only a small part of it is under cultivation Five hours and a quarter in a north easterly direction led us out along the banks of the Koom-chai

* Throughout Western Asia population is customarily reckoned by fam ilies or houses instead of individuals A family or house will probably average nearly five persons

(sand river the ancient Hyllus) where it enters it on its way to the Hermus   Then crossing an undulating and uncultivated though arable tract we reached Ak hisar the ancient Thyatira at a quarter before 1 P M

Curiosity to see as much as we could of a town where once flourished one of the apocalyptic churches, made us improve to the best advantage the few hours of our delay Ak hisar occupies an eminence elevated but little above the surrounding alluvial and marshy plain   and having been reduced to ashes a year or two ago its houses were now mostly of one story and built of boards   Its population can amount to but little more than 1000 families of which 300 may be Greek and 25 or 30 Armenian   Walking through its streets   we observed many inscriptions and broken pillars and were offered numerous coins the relics of Thyatira   An ancient church now a mosk was mentioned to us among its curiosities but in vain did we solicit a number of Christians to conduct us to it   At length an old Turk offered to be our guide and we hastened with eagerness to examine it   Its foundations and some broken and fallen columns bespoke a high antiquity and a few aged cypresses threw over the precincts a gloom befitting the spot   As we entered the yard   two Turks performing their devotions in the portico looked around upon us with an expression that called us infidel intruders and made us feel that the lamp of true religion which once burnt brightly in this   candlestick '' was extinguished in the darkness of Mohammedanism   The door was locked and no arguments could obtain the key without leave of the governor, which we had not time to obtain So we reluctantly turned away from a spot which, as Christians, we felt that we had almost a sacred right to visit

After four or five hours delay we mounted again to complete our day s journey of 18 hours, or about 54 miles

5

Night soon closed upon us, and we had a chilly and cheerless ride over miry and rough roads to Galembeh We arrived a little before midnight and our supper of pilav was brought in at half past one

April 14   The sun was up before we were aware and without stopping to make inquiries or to breakfast we mounted our horses at 6 A M   I can only say that Galembéh is a market town of some 500 or 600 Turkish families situated on a small branch of the Caicus   A hungry ride over a mountainous tract, covered with stinted oaks which had not yet begun to put forth their leaves   brought us, at a quarter past 11 to a solitary khan named from an adjacent fountain Kuz-cheshmeh (virgin fountain)   It was a hovel of reeds and mud with one end planted against the side of a hill and kept by an old man who had nothing to give us but dirty coffee spoiled *yoghoort* (curdled milk) and sour milk without even a morsel of bread Our double meal of breakfast and dinner on such materials was soon finished , and continuing our ride we descended into an open valley where is the warm bath of Utelly   Its water springs from the ground of a temperature considerably above blood heat while within a few rods is another fountain pure and cold for the refreshment of the travel ler   The broad plain of Bali kesr beyond seemed larger, more beautiful and fertile than even that of Magnesia but, like that only a small part was cultivated   Bali kesr it self where we stopped for the night contains about 2000 Turkish, and 200 Armenian families and is governed by an aga who has under him forty villages including Galembeh inhabited only by Turks   Its houses, like those of almost every place on this road, are made of unburnt bricks, and have a mean appearance

April 15   We were detained for want of horses till half past 5 P M. when we got under way in a cold rain storm

Daylight forsook us before we left the plain, and we entered and crossed a mountainous region beyond, in one of the most dismal nights I have seen. In obedience to our tartar, we arranged ourselves in Indian file and as near to each other as possible, that none might lose the path. Still so great was the darkness that we were enabled to keep in each others track only by the cries of the surijies, and an occasional sight of two or three white horses in the company or perchance the sparks of a pipe, which some companion had lighted to drive away sleep. Even with these aids some one would occasionally drop behind or, instead of descending with the rest run along the side of a declivity to the no small danger of his neck. A drizzling rain wet us to the skin and a cold north wind, blowing in our faces seemed to penetrate to the heart. The *path* (it was not a *road*) could hardly have been worse sometimes passing through bushes that almost dismounted us at others descending steeps which well nigh pitched us headlong and frequently crossing ditches that could be leaped only by an effort that threw our poor animals upon their knees. Our baggage horses got completely mired more than once. On the brinks of how many frightful precipices we passed I know not, for the darkness kindly covered them. About midway a light issuing from a hovel, the only building we saw invited us to enter. Never was a fire more grateful nor coffee more refreshing. At length just as the day dawned and at the foot of the last mountain, we entered the village of Soo-sughurluk. The only warm room in the *menzil-khaneh* (post house) was filled with brawny Turks stretched upon their carpets and sleeping in the fumes of the tobacco they had smoked in the evening. Mustafa's authority procured us with some difficulty, a spot to spread out half our beds, and stripping off our drenched garments, we sought a little warm and sweet repose

April 16   When called by our tartar to proceed we found that the storm had not at all abated, and putting on our damp clothes we mounted again in the rain at half past 10 A M   The plains and mountains which we had crossed thus far run towards the Archipelago, but the plain, into the head of which we had now descended extends northward to the sea of Marmora, the direction of our route   A river of some size flows through it the whole extent, and together with the frequent marshes that intersect its low alluvial surface adapts it peculiarly to that semi amphibious animal the buffalo as the name *Soo sughurluk* (place of water cows i e buffaloes) imports   Towards evening the rain ceased, and we arrived at Mahaluj a little before sunset   Only bread and eggs could be obtained for our breakfast dinner and supper, which to the great increase of appetite the want of food during the day obliged us to crowd into one evening meal

April 17   A ride of two hours and a quarter in the morning brought us to an inlet of the sea of Mármora which serves as the port of Mahaluj   The wind was contrary and obliged us to lounge away the day in a coffee house filled with Turkish travellers, who like ourselves were waiting for a change of wind   The public room was spacious, and fitted up with enclosures six or eight feet square, arranged around its sides and in the centre like the pews of an old fashioned church except that their floors were raised some three feet from the ground and their partitions were hardly a foot in height   Each party had appropriated one of these and sitting upon a carpet, if it was so fortunate as to have one, was busy in the two favorite Turkish employments of smoking and meditation   The *kahwyy* (coffee-maker) at his fire place, a prominent spot opposite the front door, was almost the only active man, and the occasional low conversation of a party, mingled with the gurgling of *nargeehes* (water pipes) and frequent calls for fire to light a pipe or coffee to treat a friend was almost the only noise in this company of forty or fifty travellers We sought and obtained a small private apartment, not to escape from noise, but for liberty of unrestrained conversation ourselves

April 18 On entering the sea of Marmora, this morning we found the wind still strong against us It soon brought on a shower of rain, and drove us into a harbor, in the little island of Kalo limnos for the day

April 19 The south wind blowing softly in the morning we sailed at sunrise and early in the afternoon reached the capital As we passed around Seraglio point itself the perfection of beautiful scenery, and surrounded by views that entrance the beholder, we would fain have obtained a more distinct impression by the aid of a spy glass , but our Turkish companions indignantly checked the curiosity that would take a nearer view of the forbidden beauties of the palace of their Sultán, and for the sake of peace we laid down our glass

I propose not to detain you at Constantinople, any more than at Smyrna, by general descriptions Let us take a glance at the Armenians, and then move onward to their country

We made an early call upon the Armenian patriarch, and repeated our visit before we left He has so intimate a connection with the state of the Armenian church throughout the empire, that I will not only relate to you our intercourse with him, but will also present some general facts respecting his patriarchate —We were first conducted to his *wekeel* (vicar) an officer corresponding to the chief secretary of a civil governor He was a gentlemanly and intelligent ecclesiastic, about thirty five years of age

5 *

His inquiries showed that he detected our object before we had time to declare it, and he soon put the direct question whether we were to preach to the Jews, or, since there were already some missionaries for them whether we should not attend to the Armenians. The several Armenian ecclesiastics who have been connected with us at Beyroot and at Malta, immediately came under review, and no doubt remained in our minds, that the patriarch of Constantinople keeps himself constantly informed of our operations among his people. The patriarch himself, to whom we were soon introduced, betrayed even more extended information, by remarks respecting Mr Wolff's proceedings in Persia. He was a corpulent man, of about forty five remarkably kind and flattering in his address, and seemed to tax his countenance and his tongue to the utmost to make us understand how much he loved us and was delighted by our visit. In fact, we could with difficulty civilly avoid spending the night at his palace. Our conversation, at each visit, covered considerable ground and the information it elicited will be presented as it shall be called for by the introduction of the several topics, in the course of our journey.

The *origin* of this patriarchal see, as you may learn from the Introduction, dates at the capture of Constantinople by the Turks. A D 1453, and was owing to the appointment of the Sultan, Mohammed Second.—The *nomination* of its incumbent is exercised by the Armenian primates of the capital. The person whom they elect, receives from the Sultán a fermán of confirmation, and is then patriarch. His removal from office is like his appointment. Very rarely does the Sultan attempt it, unless solicited by the primates, then he deposes one and confirms another at their will.

In *rank*, the patriarch does not differ, as to spiritual matters, from the other bishops. He can no more ordain a

bishop, nor consecrate the *meiròn* (holy oil) than they
But in a more secular sense he is the head of the Armenian church in Turkey Through him alone can that
church, or its officers or members as such, communicate
with government, and only through him also, does the
government control the church establishment In a word,
he is regarded by the Sultán as the responsible head of his
sect Of course he must be clothed with considerable
powers They are defined by the most solemn fermans of
the government, which, as the office is one of its own cre-
ation for state convenience is interested in maintaining
its authority In his own diocese as bishop of Constantinople the patriarch exerts his authority over the priests
and people directly An instance occurred while we were
there of his imprisoning two priests for having turned papists One claimed Russian protection and was consequently delivered up to the Reis-effèndy and released the
other remained in the patriarchal prison till his recanta
tion opened its doors In other parts, the direct exer
cise of his power extends only to the bishops but they are
so dependent upon him that his influence in their dioceses
must be very great He appoints, recalls and even ban
ishes them to distant parts of the empire A special fermán for every such act must indeed, be issued by govern
ment but a hint from him, with a few piasters is suffi
cient to obtain it. Besides thus controlling the bishops,
he also divides or unites dioceses, so that their number
and limits are never fixed The city which had a distinct
bishop last year, may this year be subject to the bishop of
some other city, which then formed part of still another
diocese

The *extent* of the patriarch s jurisdiction is the same
with that of the empire excepting only so much as is em
braced in the patriarchate of Jerusalem The Catholicos
of Sis the history of whose see has been sketched in the

Introduction, presents the singular anomaly of a superior placed in dependence upon an inferior. In spiritual rank he is one grade above the patriarch and the other bishops, inasmuch as he can ordain bishops and consecrate the meiron. But he is regarded by government only as a high metropolitan, pays to the patriarch, instead of the Sultán direct, his annual tribute, and can only obtain through him, like other bishops the fermáns for which he has occasion. Only for his election he is not dependent. That rests with some ten or fifteen primates (of his diocese I believe,) and the bishops and monks of his convent. The Catholicos of Aghtamar is probably as independent of the patriarch as the Kurds, in whose country his see is situated, are of the Sultan. Of this whole system, indeed it ought to be remarked, that in such a despotic and unsettled government as Turkey it must be subject to many irregularities. The patriarch's power being borrowed from the Sultan wherever the latter is unable to execute his orders, there will the authority or protection of the other cease to be felt.

The *fiscal concerns* of the establishment must not be overlooked. The patriarch pays to the Sultan an annual tribute, called from its being paid at different times, *mukattaa* (installment), and it is the only regular contribution expected by the government from the Armenian church, or its officers in their ecclesiastical capacity. To obtain his ferman of confirmation, however, every new patriarch is obliged to distribute among the chief officers of the Porte a large amount in presents. Such pecuniary obligations, are sources of no small embarrassment but the patriarch will not throw them upon the primates and bishops, for he would thus lose the advantages of power and profit derived from the collection of the sums necessary to meet them.— As the see has no glebes nor funds it becomes important to inquire from whence it derives an amount equal to this tribute these presents and its current and incidental expenses As bishop of Constantinople the patriarch has, within that diocese, all the sources of episcopal income, which are common to other bishops, and will be hereafter specified From every other diocese the incumbent bishop pays him an annual mukattaa reserving to himself its collection Upon being appointed to a diocese also, every bishop gives the patriarch a present more or less liberal according to circumstances Occasionally recourse is likewise had to sources of income that are extraordinary When the patriarch gets too deeply in debt to extricate himself the wealthy Armenians of the capital sometimes contribute liberally to his relief *

Let us see how a hierarchy originated and upheld like this by a Mohammedan power operates — *The choice of a patriarch, or, as the case may be his deposition, is a fruitful source of intrigues strifes and corruption* The voice of the primates cannot always be unanimous nor nearly so Indeed, as they are not a regularly appointed body, nor

* Many of the facts upon which the account here attempted of the Armenian patriarchate of Constantinople is based were obtained during our visit to that place They have been multiplied and digested by the aid of the Armenian bishop Dionysius (commonly called Carabet,) at Malta who besides being a native of Constantinople was once for a time connected with the patriarchate The whole has been submitted for confirmation to Hagóp Abgár (usually called Yacob Aga) another uncommonly intelligent Armenian bishop in Syria who once had the business of the patriarchate in his hands as wekeel and also to the Rev Mr Goodell for some time resident upon the spot

Bishop Hagóp adds at this place the following note —The Mukáttaa when he was wekeel of the patriarch was 10,000 piastres [a thousand dollars or more] Of this sum Angora (from 36 villages) contributed about 1000 Isnikmid 1000 Kaisarieh 800 Moosh 500 Tekir-dagh 500 Smyrna 500 Sivás 500 Sis 500 Adreneh 500 Erzroom 450 Diarbekr 450 Orfah 400 Arabkir 400 Tokát 300 Kutáya 300 Baiboort 250 Amásia and Marsovan 200 Shebin-kara-hisár 200 Trebizond 150 Terján 150 Gumish kháneh 100 A few other places of minor importance made up the sum

their numbers fixed, it may easily happen that more than one candidate will claim a majority   In such a case, as the patriarchate is an object of ambition, parties must almost necessarily run too high for either to submit, except to the voice of an authoritative arbitrator   That arbitrator is of course the Porte, and the only weight that will move the balance of its decision is money   The candidate that offers the highest present for confirmation is confirmed; and as often as his unsuccessful rival offers more, the confirmation is recalled and given to him   Even the mukattaa though its amount is considered fixed does not always escape at such times without being increased Thus the highest office of a Christian church is virtually set up at auction, a moslem holds the hammer and takes the offer of the highest bidder   In this case as in most others, a quarrel among Christians becomes a direct source of income to the Turk   How can he be expected then, especially as his religious prejudices coincide entirely with the interest of his purse to check the evil ?   There is however, an important check in the fact that the primates in whose divisions the evil originates are ultimately called upon to contribute heavily from their own purses when the amount of the bribes exceeds the patriarchal resources —The actual history of the patriarchate is, in fact, little else than a history of intrigues.   During fifty years in the seventeenth century, fourteen persons were raised to the office of patriarch, one of whom was elected and deposed no less than nine times, the whole number of elections and depositions was nearly forty, and one priest held the office for six years, (including one in which he was supplanted by an individual raised directly from the humble employment of baker,) before he was ordained bishop   Four times the primates, instead of electing a patriarch, kept the office in their own hands, and on one occasion, increased the mukattaa from 100 000 to 140 000 akcheh,‡ that they might be allowed to retain it A *vartabed* (clerical monk) supplanted them by increasing it in addition to large presents to 400 000 akcheh and hired a Turkish guard for an extravagant sum to enable him to make good his claims But his rivals proved too powerful for him he was thrown into the common prison, and there shortly after perished by poison †

The appointment of bishops is also productive of much intrigue and corruption The patriarch, naturally wishing to realize a large income will generally if there are rival candidates as there cannot fail to be give the appointment to him that offers the highest present The inauguratory present too is a direct premium to the greatest possible instability of the episcopal office for the oftener one bishop is recalled and another appointed the oftener does it come into the patriarchal treasury One check upon these evil tendencies is, that the people of the diocese in question, from whom these bribes must ultimately come, will, when their purses or their feelings are tampered with too far make their complaints to be heard Another is, that most bishops take care to secure partisans among the primates upon whom the patriarch himself is dependent, and thus have authoritative advocates at hand to countermine the intrigues that may be formed against them circumstances having led them to imitate the system pur-

---

* The *ákcheh* (called aspron in Greek) was originally the only Turkish coin and denomination of money The *pará* which is equal to three ákcheh was first coined in Egypt and hence is called by the Arabs Misreeyeh (Egyptian) The *ghroosh* (piastre) equal to forty parás is of still later origin.—The value of Turkish coin has decreased so much, that it would be difficult to determine the value of the akcheh at the time here spoken of Chardin however who was at Smyrna only fourteen years later says it was worth a *demi-sol* and that 120 were equal to an *écu* Voyages en Perse vol 1 p 16

† Chamcheán P 7 c 12—19

sued by the pashas of the empire, who, as is well known, have their spies and agents in the very divan of the Sultán

Dissent also and free religious toleration is opposed The idea of government is that every sect of *rayahs*, i e subjects not Mohammedan forms a distinct nation and must have a representative and responsible head at the capital The Greeks Armenians and very recently the papal Armenians have such a head in their patriarchs, and the Jews in their chief Rabbi and are of course acknowledged as tolerated sects The Jacobite Syrians having no other representative the Armenian patriarch acts as their agent Other sects existing only in certain provinces have a local toleration, without being represented at the capital as the half independent Maronites in mount Lebanon, and the Copts in Egypt With such an idea for the basis of its legislation the government of course looks upon every new sect other than those already acknowledged and represented as an unwelcome intruder Do any of the Armenians forsake their church for such a sect? The patriarch has only to report them as insubordinate to bring them into embarrassment For the very fact that they have revolted from him makes them infractors of a fundamental principle of the empire, and they no longer rank among its protected subjects This system like every other in Turkey is liable to many irregularities and probably nowhere has so much force as at the capital To the Greek islands it hardly applied at all they being represented by islands and not by sects.

The case of the papal Armenians illustrates its operation, and is therefore full of instruction to protestant missionaries Their numbers at the capital and in other places were considerable, they were as a body, more intelligent than their countrymen, among them were men to whom uncommon wealth and official station gave great influence, and European sympathy was altogether on their side

Still they were every where obliged to rank as a part of the flock of the patriarch. They could have no churches of their own, their priests could not wear the clerical garb nor be known as such, except under the shadow of European influence and at baptisms marriages and burials they were obliged to call upon the Armenian clergy, and pay them the accustomed fees. Such very nearly was their situation even at Angora where they amounted to many thousands while the Armenians were only a few hundred. The Sultan, having been informed of the part the Persian Armenians had taken in the late war of Russia with Persia deemed it necessary, when anticipating in the beginning of 1828 a rupture with the same power himself, to remind the patriarch that he must be responsible for the good conduct of his nation. He replied that for all who belonged to his flock he would readily be responsible but that there were some who did not acknowledge his authority and for them he could not pledge himself. The names of such were demanded and he sent them in. The persecution which came upon them when thus placed in the predicament of an unacknowledged dissenting sect, is well known. The banishment of the laity seems to have been almost peculiar to the capital and its suburbs, and was ordered under the pretence that every one must return to his own city, and of course they to Angora from whence they had come * But the persecution was felt in the most distant parts and even in the Kurdish pashalik of Bayezeed their priests were searched out and banished †

* Khatti-shereef Jan 10 1828

† The punishment which the chief Rabbi was able to bring upon the Jews baptized by the Rev Mr Hartley is another illustration of the same intolerant system. Hartley's Researches in Greece and the Levant p 211—219

The papal Greeks of Syria seem at first view to form a real exception of an unrepresented dissenting sect enjoying complete toleration. But the fol-

The patriarchate of Jerusalem when the dominions of the power that created it were united to the Ottoman empire would probably itself have fallen to the share of the patriarch of Constantinople had not the primates by whom he is himself appointed taken it into their own hands In fact the question of its independence did for some time re-

lowing note kindly added here by the Rev Mr Bird of Beyroot on perusing this letter explains the anomaly

 ꞌIt appears from report that this schism owes its commencement to cer tain emissaries of the pope chiefly Jesuits and Franciscans, who came to Aleppo and began their operations about the year —— They recommend ed themselves by their learning their medical services and their alms The Greeks were found in a very neglected state and were put to shame for their lifelessness and ignorance in all things regarding religion They therefore by degrees began to embrace the new doctrines of their papal bene factors until in a few years the new converts became the stronger party and after two or three ineffectual struggles of their former brethren to pre- vent it took open possession of the Greek church The work of conver sion still went on until through shame and other inducements scarcely a family remained on the side of the Orthodox Greeks

 This was the state of things at Aleppo when there appeared among them a bishop by the name of Germanus Adam a man of uncommon talents who held some peculiar notions in regard to the words of consecration in the ser vice of the mass On this subject the new sect became divided and after much contention the party of the bishop after his decease and through the in fluence of a clever Greek bishop returned to their ancient faith and obtained a ferman from Constantinople which secured to them the church and au thorized them to bring their adversaries to their worship by coercion In consequence some of the papal party were driven away some apprehended and sent into banishment and a number murdered

 Since then the present Greek patriarch of Damascus has thought it politic to give up the persecution and to obtain the restoration of the fugitive and ban ished individuals The sect therefore remains at present in a state of per- fect toleration and in consequence of many of them being employed as scribes and agents about the local governments their power especially since the Greek insurrection in Europe is decidedly superior to that of the ortho dox When it was at first reported that the Sultan intended to appoint a common head of the three sects of popish converts viz the Armenians Greeks and Syrians and that this head was for the present an Armenian the Greeks expressed their determination sooner to return to their mother church than to yield obedience to a chief from their Armenian brethren and so they still remain as it appears nominally unknown at Constantinople

main undecided but now the two sees stand upon nearly the same footing The patriarch of Jerusalem pays his mukattaa directly to the Sultan and takes out fermans in his own name, for which and for other purposes he has an agent residing in the capital, and not only does his nomination rest with the primates of Constantinople but they also take upon themselves to control the funds and the internal government of his diocese They procured the recall of the patriarch Gabriel who is now bishop of Smyrna By mismanagement a part of which was attributed him the convent of St James (the patriarchal residence at Jerusalem) had incurred an immense debt To remedy the embarrassment the primates sent seven inspectors* to assume the whole management of its concerns leaving to the patriarch merely the physical power of putting his seal to documents of their composition He unwilling thus to be made a cypher neither acknowledged their authority nor welcomed them to his convent The primates consequently provoked by his obstinacy sent men clothed with power from the Sultan to bring the helpless prelate forth with to the capital —The patriarchate extends over Egypt, and the pashaliks of Acre Damascus and Tripoli and pays a mukattaa to Damascus as well as to Constantinople †

You will naturally wish to know more of such an important body of men as the Armenian primates of Constan-

---

* One of them was bishop Dionysius already referred to

† The sum paid to the Sultán says Bishop Hagóp is sometimes 1 500 piastres that paid to the pasha of Damascus is now fixed at 80 purses or 40,000 piastres Such was also its original amount under Jezzar pasha From his time however it was gradually increased to the enormous sum of 800 000 piastres when Bishop Hagóp was employed to obtain a khatti-shereef from the Sultan for reducing it to the original sum A ferman had been previously obtained to the same effect but through the management of the Damascus authorities it was found entirely useless The ferman cost $13,300 and the expense of the khatti shereef was $11 000 more nearly the whole of which sums was expended in presents to the officers and servants about the Sultán

tinople The church universally acknowledges to a cer
tain extent, the voice of the laity in its government In every
place, we find individuals, who stand forth and act for
their fellow citizens Such individuals in the capital
where questions of national interest are started naturally
act as representatives of the nation Hence the primates
are regarded by the government in this light We were
not able to learn that they are chosen in any other way,
than by the general consent or opinion of the public in
formally expressed Whoever by his wealth birth * or
talents, can make his influence felt as a primate is a pri
mate Their number of course cannot be fixed but it
does not vary far from twenty four They are immense
ly rich and are generally connected with government or
its officers as bankers

The Armenian academy was visited by us at the same
time that we called upon the patriarch it being within the
same precincts as his residence But before entering it,
I must say a word respecting those precincts in general,
the neatness, finish and taste of which are such as to
transfer one the moment he enters them away from Turkey They embrace a spacious palace for the patriarch,
three churches side by side sufficiently large for a congregation of several thousands and commodious apartments
for the school, besides various rooms for other purposes The whole has been built since the old church was
burnt at the destruction of the janizaries The expense
was defrayed by voluntary contribution and more than
half came from the purse of one primate named Bezjan
Harūtun who is banker to the mint I have not found
in the Mediterranean a church with so little to be objected
to, and so much to be praised, as these three In simplici
ty they even excel our own for not a pew nor a bench
breaks the evenness of their plain carpeted floors Pictures adorn the walls, but they are very few and executed
in good taste

We were received by Gregory Peshdemaljan, the principal of the academy, with a cordiality suited to the account of him, which we had received from Boghos of Smyrna. He is a layman, well acquainted with the language and literature of his nation, and himself the author of a very respectable grammar and dictionary of the ancient Armenian We found him surrounded by a company of young men fifteen or sixteen years of age possessed of the fair and ingenuous countenance, so peculiar to the young Armenians of Smyrna and Constantinople They were members of the highest department of the school The lowest, embraces the children of the poor who are taught gratuitously to read and write In the second are others of more respectable connections who are studying the same branches The members of the third now forty or fifty in number, are introduced to the elements of grammar That study they complete when advanced to the fourth under Gregory the number in which is about the same They were generally possessed of uncommonly interesting countenances, and had an appearance of great neatness and order as they sat each upon his cushion or carpet in double or triple rows around the floors The whole number of scholars was not far from 300 It has a considerable income from a fund contributed by the same primate who aided so liberally in erecting the buildings of the establishment and the remainder of its expenses are borne by the Armenian community —There are schools attached to the other Armenian churches but none of them are of much repute We were told also that private schools for girls are not uncommon, but we got admission to none of them.

It is painful to find that none of the modern improvements in primary education have been introduced, even in this most enlightened part of the Armenian nation The only thing that shows a tendency that way, is the use of a

spelling book and one or two other first books, in the
modern Armenian their vernacular dialect. Abundantly
able helps in grammar, arithmetic and some other branches
have been issued from the press at Venice, as well as
here, but they are in the ancient tongue, and accessible
only to the few who understand it   Even in geography, I
was surprised to find them so well supplied, that when
we mentioned Andover as the place to which we should
send a Persian dictionary which the Patriarch had the politeness to give us, a person present immediately referred to
a book in ancient Armenian not only describing its
position accurately but also that of the adjacent towns

The Armenians have not only no department for foreign
languages in the academy nor any distinct school for them
in the city but the number acquainted with them is ex
tremely small   As a reason we were told that the govern
ment has heretofore looked less favorably upon those who
knew the languages of the Franks   The reason is plausi
ble , but I have so often heard Christians in Turkey urge
their existence under a Mohammedan government as an
excuse for all their faults whether barbarous customs want
of education, or even immorality of conduct that I am
inclined to suspect this to be only the standing apology,
and entitled to no more weight   My suspicion is confirm
ed by the assurance of one of the oldest and most observing
of the English residents at Péra that he was not aware of the
Turks having any jealousies against the education of their
Christian subjects   The fact is that the two great motives
which direct the education as well as the conduct of men
are religion and money   Neither of these leads the Armenians to cultivate foreign languages   The religion of their
church is not contained in Latin nor in English but in Armenian and therefore only leads them to study the latter
From the Turks and not from Europeans as will be seen
when I come to speak of the papal Armenians, do they expect

employ and mercantile business and an acquaintance therefore with the dialects of Turkey is all that they need for the acquisition of money

A printing press belongs to the patriarchate and a room is still assigned to it but it is no longer in operation There is however another in one of the villages on the Bosphorus which we visited Taking a boat at Top-kha neh we were rowed to Orta koy as the village is called, in forty five minutes On entering the house we found a venerable but active old man folding paper who proved to be the head of the establishment His father he in formed us had it before him and as he was now himself eighty four years old it must have been in existence not far from a hundred years Himself his four sons and eighteen grand children form the family or little clan of Arab-oghloo who are not only the owners but do the work of the establishment Government exercises no supervision over it nor does it demand any taxes It embraces a foundery in which are cast a variety of Armeni an Greek Roman Hebrew Rabbinical Russian and Arabic types The latter they make only for the government press for which they have recently cast a new font after the model of Persian manuscript which pleases the Sultan so much that he has granted the family not a little to the gratification of the old gentleman s pride the Mohammedan privilege of wearing yellow slippers It is he assured us the only Armenian printing establishment in Turkey We found three presses in the office, and they were printing in Armenian and Hebrew Among the books printed here is the Persian dictionary already men tioned It is in Persian Armenian and Turkish and was composed by a learned Armenian who died before it was printed The same primate whose generosity I have had occasion to mention more than once already caused an edition to be printed, and placed in the hands of the patri-

arch for gratuitous distribution among his countrymen
The book is a royal octavo of 700 pages and the edition
was about 700 copies

The *papal Armenians* of Constantinople were estimated
at the time of their banishment at 27 000 and most of
them resided in Pera and Galata where they had the soci
ety and countenance of the Franks and could attend the
Latin chapels of which there are six or seven in the two
places Their condition before this event has been already alluded to They have since returned, and are now
one of the established Christian sects of the empire Like
the Christians in other parts of Turkey who have em
braced the faith of Rome they are more respectable for
wealth and intelligence than their countrymen owing
doubtless to their connection with Europeans to whom
they are decidedly partial For it is a well known part
of the policy of papal missionaries to denationalize their
converts by substituting attachment to Rome and her
children for patriotic partialites With the papal Greeks
of the Archipelago it has been carried so far that many
who are of genuine Greek descent consider it an insult to
be called Greeks The papal Armenians own the name
of Armenian still but they like the Franks better than
their countrymen Even in the interior of Turkey 900
miles from Constantinople a papal Armenian priest and
his family with whom Providence cast our lot for a night
announced themselves to us as brother Franks (supposing
us to be of course papists) and treated us with more kindness than we experienced from any other natives the whole
journey at the same time that they exhibited a bitter en
mity towards their Armenian neighbors They naturally
seek to learn the languages of their friends, and in fact
have for this purpose, a flourishing school in Pera A key
to European intelligence is thus acquired and they of
course become more enlightened than their countrymen

The partiality is mutual. Does a papal European let him be merchant consul or embassador wish to employ a native? He of course looks out for a papist. I base this remark upon the general fact, which no one acquainted can deny that in Smyrna and Constantinople and indeed throughout the Levant almost all the native Christians employed by papal Europeans are papists. Some particular cases also I have attentively watched. In an important town which in the course of events had been nearly stripped of its Christian population we found a papal gentleman possessed of influence as the mercantile and political agent of a European consul and made still more prominent by the fact that he was the only European in the place. With the proper Armenians he cultivated no friendship, they were even treated coldly when they called upon him. But his house was the home of papists. Did any one wish for his acquaintance or aid? His being a papist was urged as a prevailing plea. He knew and counted every papist that moved into town. And if he remain and his influence be sufficient he will substitute a papal community for the numerous Armenian population that once inhabited the place. The nation he represents is protestant but he has drunk deep of the party and proselyting spirit of Rome.

I am sorry that Europeans of the Romish church do not not stand alone in this thing the influence of protestants also rests in the same scale. The fact, that most of the native Christians employed by protestants in the Levant, are of the Romish persuasion is one that those gentlemen themselves will not deny. The reason of it they perhaps hardly know, it certainly does not lie in any partiality for papacy. But are they aware of the strength they thereby add to the power of Rome and the discouragements they heap upon other bodies of Christians that would be as glad as themselves to see that power abolished? There can be no doubt that their partiality for papists in deed though not in intention does actually discourage the other Christians from those attempts at education and improvement which a contrary course would foster to the great advance of their intelligence and general character And would it not be the easiest possible thing for them without trouble or injury to their own interests to withdraw the contri bution of their influence from the pope and direct it to a quarter where it would effectually weaken his antichris tian power ?

LETTER II

FROM CONSTANTINOPLE TO TOKAT

Delay at Constantinople—Preparations for the journey—Reflections at start
ing—Gébizeh—Isnikmíd—A wedding procession—Sabanjah—Buffaloes
—Khandék—Temporal influence of Mohammedanism—A Turkish saint—
Dootjeh—A night s ride—Boly—Gerideh—Turkish intemperance—Cherkesh—Mode of travelling—Karajalar—Deception of our Tartar—Rapid
travelling—Kharajulen—Koj h s r—Angora—Turkish fountains—Tósia
—Haji Hamzeh—Dangerous pass—Osmanjuk—Marsován—Turkish su
perstition—Amásia—Habits of tartars—A civil Turk—A Derbénd—
Drowsiness in riding—Toorkhal.

DEAR SIR

IT was on the morning of the 21st of May, that we took
leave of the capital of Turkey and set our faces towards
Armenia   Our detention had been longer than we had an
ticipated, but we regretted it the less as it brought our
journey through one of the most delightful countries in the
world into the most charming season of the year   We
had also the consolation of reflecting that perhaps it had
not been altogether useless as by the politeness of Mr
Rhind, who was then negotiating a treaty between the gov
ernment of the United States and the Porte we had had
an opportunity to preach every Sabbath to a large part of
the English residents who were then without a chaplain
The friends generally to whom we had been introduced by
letters from Smyrna had treated us with no little hospitality
and kindness   By their aid we had been able to fix defi
nitely our route to the farthest point which we finally reach
ed and we ever found reason to think it the best we could
have taken They had helped us, also, to many facilities

that contributed materially to the successful accomplish
ment of our journey

The same reason that made us come by land from Smyr
na increased by the fact that the north winds had now set
in for the season induced us to decline a passage by water
to Trebizond *   The tardy movements of a caravan also,
which without allowing for detentions would take at least
thirty five or forty days to Erzroom, threatened to make our
journey too long   and we therefore again put ourselves under
a tartar   For greater security we caused him to set his seal
to a written contract, in the presence of the tartar aghasy
who thus became responsible on the part of government
for our persons and property and in consideration of this
had a claim upon our tartar for ten per cent of the money
we paid him

Trunks were too frail and too awkwardly loaded for
the rapid mode of travelling we had selected   and we
therefore substituted for them two large bags fitted to be
attached to each other and slung one on each side of a
horse, two saddle bags and two valises all of thick Russian leather, made impermeable to water by a lining of
waxed cloth, and so constructed as to be fastened with a
padlock   Matresses were too bulky, and we took instead
of them a carpet and coverlet for each rolled in a piece of
painted canvass that served to defend them from the rain

---

* There seemed to be but two winds at Constantinople the north and the
south   The former prevails with occasional intermissions during summer
and combined with the strong current of the Bosphorus prevents all vessels from entering the Black sea while it blows   It is much cooler and
damper than the latter and a change of wind rarely fails to produce a de
cided change of temperature and of weather   A meteorological table kept
by Mr Dwight showed some changes while we were there of 17° and 22°
of Farenheit in six or eight hours   The lowest temperature in the open
shade at 8 o'clock A M from the 20th of April to the 20th of May was
48° and the highest 71°   the average temperature at that hour was about
57°   The lowest temperature at 8 o'clock P M was 52° and the highest
85°   the average was about 71°

by day and answered for a floor when our lot was to lie on the ground at night An ample Turkish pelisse in our valises lined throughout with *chilkufa* the fur of the Cau casian fox was at hand to impart its abundant stock of warmth by day or by night as we might need it Four copper pans fitted to each other and fastened together by bars of the same metal a mill, pot and cups for grinding making and drinking coffee with a knife fork and spoon for each and a copper drinking cup were our utensils for cooking and eating A circular piece of leather with iron rings attached to its circumference and a chain with a hook passing through them and named a *sufreh* served when open and spread upon the ground as a table and when drawn up and suspended to a horse as a bag to carry our bread and cheese The whole embracing our clothing bedding and table and kitchen furniture was comprised in a compass that enabled us to carry it on ordinary occa sions with only one extra horse so unsparingly did we lop off civilization s factitious additions to the necessaries of life in order by travelling as nearly as possible in the style of the country to proceed expeditiously economical ly and with few allurements for robbers As the Turkish post furnishes only naked horses we were obliged to add sad dles and bridles to our other accoutrements To our sad-dle-bow we attached pistols to answer their usual object in this country to make the timid appear bold and formida-ble For our own snug dress were substituted the loose robes of the Turk the European hat was exchanged for the oriental turban and our feet were encased in the enor-mous stockings and boots of the tartar such an accom-modation to the prejudices of the country being deemed expedient in order to avoid unnecessary notice expense and trouble, if not insult —With these preparations we found ourselves completely equipped for a tour in Turkey

Mr Rhind to whom we were already indebted for pro

7

curing us fermáns and tezkerehs, (government and custom-house passports,) for travelling in Turkey, and passports for entering Russia and our countryman Mr Walley, who in addition to many other favors had obligingly offered to act as our agent during our absence completed their kind attentions by accompanying us to Scutari, and bidding us farewell as we mounted our horses

It was a moment of sadness How many must be our fatigues, anxieties, perhaps sicknesses, before seeing again the face of a countryman and a friend ! Could we even expect that both would escape with life the perils from sickly climates and pestilence in the wilderness in the city and in the sea among robbers and false brethren that awaited us ? I had commenced the enterprise with a strong presentiment of never surviving to revisit my friends which was but imperfectly allayed by reflecting upon the uniform protection of Providence in former journeys.   In my companion a similar feeling was enhanced by unacquaintance with the country and its people, and greater freshness and intimacy of attachment to friends left behind   But neither of us did it lead to a moment s despondency or wavering of resolution for we doubted not that Providence had led us into the path we were pursuing nor that our object was worth all that we were risking for it and we were cheered by throwing ourselves simply upon God s parental protection

It was 10 A M when we started, and though the clouds were dropping a slight shower of rain we were still grateful that they kindly sheltered us from the sun   Our route for the day skirted the shore of the sea of Marmora, with the Prince's Islands in sight and lay across an undulating tract of country variegated with fields of grain vineyards and fruit trees   At Bostanjy bridge two hours from Scu tari our tezkereh was carefully examined and countersign ed   Leaving Maltepeh to the right we passed through the miserable villages of Kartal, and Pendik, and reached

Gebizeh the ancient Lybissa at 6 P M where we stopped for the night   It seemed larger than any village we
had passed but as the menzil khâneh was near one ex
tremity we saw little of it   For so fatigued were we by
our first day s ride, though only 9 hours * that instead of
making inquiries we speedily threw ourselves upon the
floor to sleep, not allowing even the fleas, which always
swarm in a Turkish post house, to interrupt our repose
You will perhaps accuse us of something more than fatigue when I confess that not even the mound which cov
ers the ashes of the great Hannibal at this place, attracted
our attention

May 22   We started at half past 4 A M and crossing
a considerable tract, with soil and scenery much like that
of yesterday except that the sea was not in sight we came
down at length, through orchards of cherry trees whose
fruit was just beginning to ripen upon the shore of the gulf
of Nicomedia   Although the shore and the declivity of
the swelling hills which rise up from it, seemed susceptible
of the highest cultivation we passed no village before
reaching the town, 9 hours from our night s lodgings.   We
noticed yesterday frequent flocks of sheep moving slowly
towards the capital, and to day the road was absolutely
obstructed by thousands and thousands of them. They
came from the immense pastures of Armenia, and were
attended by their Kurdish shepherds

Isnikmid (frequently pronounced Isnimid,) the Turkish
representative of Nicomedia,† is beautifully situated on the

---

* The hour by which the stages of the Turkish post and in fact all dis
tances in Turkey are measured is an hour's march of a caravan and though
it of course varies according to the nature of the ground may be estimated at
an average of three miles or just an English league   The length of stages
mentioned between this and Erzroom is not the time we were travelling
them nor our own estimate but that which is fixed by government

† It is curious to see how modern names used by the Turks betray their
ignorance of the languages of the people they conquered   The name by

declivity of a hill sloping down to the northeast corner of
the gulf to which it gives its name　Several brigs and
kayiks (boats) beating towards it in that direction, and
wooded mountains, verdant hills and fertile plains on every
other side, combined charms of marine and rural scenery,
worthy the capital of Bithynia and the favorite residence
of the imperial Diocletian　Many of its houses are of im
posing height and showy form, as if still ambitious of its
former magnificence but their frail structure and decayed
state betray its real degradation　It contains about 25,000
inhabitants, divided in the proportions of 4000 Turkish,
500 Armenian and 500 Greek and Jewish houses.

Our next stage from Isnikmid to Sabanjah a distance
of 6 hours, led us eastward through the plain that extends up from the head of the gulf　Its alluvial soil is damp,
but extremely fertile, verdant swelling hills bound it on the
left and a regular mountain range clothed throughout
with a thick and unbroken forest, stretches along on the
right　Cultivation ceased as we advanced and our solitary
path led us through thickets of trees and shrubs of almost
tropical luxuriance, the freshness of whose fragance with
the coolness of approaching evening and the music of birds
quite made us forget the fatigue of a day s ride of 45 miles
Our musing was soon interrupted by a scene as comic as
the spot was charming　It was a procession conducting
a Turkish bride from some neighboring village to her
spouse in the one which we were approaching　She and
her veiled companions of every age were stowed in six
covered carts, so narrow as barely to accommodate them
as they sat tailor like upon the bottom facing alternately

which the Greeks now commonly call Constantinople is ἡ πολις (the city)
by way of distinction　When going thither they say εἰς τὴν πολιν, and
this expression pronounced by them is *tim-bolin* the Turks have converted
into Istambool　In the same way Isnikmid is derived from εἰς Νικομηδειαν
and Isnik from εἰς Νικαιαν

the right and the left. They were drawn by buffaloes to whose yokes were attached standards ornamented with flying handkerchiefs of every color as if to add comeliness and gaiety to the most ungainly of beasts By their side walked armed men and musicians to announce, by their guns and the music of squeaking pipes and coarse drums what otherwise would certainly not have been expressed the joy of the occasion —We reached Sabanjah at half past 7 P M It is a common village, on the margin of a lake of fresh water at the foot of the mountain just men tioned, and contains 150 Turkish with 25 Armenian and 15 Greek houses

May 23 The lake of Sabanjah is some 3 or 4 miles in breadth and washes the foot of the mountain so that we could avoid ascending the latter only by wading some distance in the water In it buffaloes were bathing with little beside the mouth and nostrils projecting above the surface So essential is water to these animals, that their drivers are sometimes seen throwing it upon them from brooks that are too small to allow them to bathe They are larger and stronger than common cattle, of a dull slate color almost destitute of hair, with projecting shoulder and hip bones, and ugly in form and temper In Egypt, the Bukaa of mount Lebanon, Asia Minor and Georgia the buffalo is almost as much used as the common ox To one who is acquainted with its aquatic propensities, Pharaoh's dream of the kine *coming up out of the river* Gen 41 2, 3, seems perfectly natural After leaving the lake a ride of two hours and a half across an alluvial plain like that of yesterday, of which it is in fact a continuation conducted us to the muddy Sakharia (Sangarius or Sagarius), which we crossed by a temporary wooden bridge Beyond it, the plain retained the same features for some distance, but at length became a marsh, through which we were conducted by a long causey of logs, precisely similar

7 *

to the *corduroys* of some parts of our own country   Three hours from the river, we reached a dry and more undulating tract, but hardly any cultivation appeared the whole day, and most of the country was grown over with trees and thickets, in which the beech and the walnut predominated

We found our post-house at Khandek, 10 hours from Sábanjah   The village is surrounded by a grove or rather forest, of spreading trees in which its houses, except a few in the centre are scattered each in its separate enclosure, so as to be almost entirely concealed   Streams of water run through most of its streets to the great increase, according to Turkish taste of its beauty but according to ours of its filth   It contains about 200 houses, all inhabited by Turks   The horses in the post house were too miserable to be used and the aga of the village at the request of our tartar pressed others from the inhabitants for our service   It was so late however before they came that he determined not to leave till morning and was consequently obliged to restore them to their owners, who claimed them for to-morrow s labor

We rejoiced at this detention as it enabled us to steal an hour s quiet retirement in the woods for meditation   Sitting down under a spreading walnut by the side of a murmuring mill-stream I was led by the charming woodland scenery around, to reflect upon that mysterious providence by which so beautiful a country has been placed under such a blighting government and in the hands of so indolent and barbarous a people   By the industry and cultivation of our own countrymen it would be made 'even as the garden of the Lord ' Surely the religion of the false prophet by being allowed to spread over such fair portions of the globe, has been placed in the most advantageous circumstances to meliorate the temporal condition of man if such be its tendency   The result is found in fertile re-

gions depopulated and run to waste, and people surrounded
by nature s richest gifts debased and destitute of the comforts of civilized life   Could God have taken a better method of showing to the world that the religion is false and a
curse to man ? Skepticism itself must now admit the con
clusion

May 24   Our morning s stage was 10 hours   For the
first four we rode over a broken tract of the richest soil
covered with a thick growth of beech maple, oak, and
other forest trees that overshading the road, transported
me in imagination to the recently settled parts of the United States and in one place a cultivated field covered with
girdled trees quite completed the deception   My companion was strongly reminded by the whole aspect of the country of the western part of New York, a region endeared
to him not only by its fertility and beauty, but also by the
tender associations of home   The trees became less thick
as we advanced and in an hour and a half more crossing
the great Melan here running northward we entered an
extensive and most fertile alluvial plain partially cultivated,
and thinly shaded with large white walnuts   The hollow
trunk of one of them was the house of a Turkish saint.
By having a fire always ready to light the pipe, and a jug
of water to quench the thirst of the traveller, and by his
comic singing and gestures plainly indicative of lunacy
or foolishness he obtained in charity sufficient to sustain
a life to which the Turks attach an idea of great sanctity
I was surprised to see our tartar as a salutation seize him
rudely by the beard, but he immediately drew it to his
mouth and by kissing it turned what otherwise would
have been the most intolerable of insults into an act of
the greatest veneration   Although the mountain range
which had continued on the right from Isnikmid here exhibited upon its top some drifts of snow, this low plain,
under the rays of the sun, from which until to day the

clouds had shielded us was excessively hot, and we were not sorry to be detained at the post-house for horses some five or six hours in the heat of the day

Dootjeh, where we stopped is a Turkish village of about 200 houses much scattered and containing some hewn stones and broken columns indicative of the site of ancient buildings   The plain extends to the foot of a mountain about two hours and a half beyond   Thus far from Isnik mid, carts drawn by buffaloes, here much more numerous than the common ox were constantly passing to and fro transporting timber toward the capital   A few rice fields attracted our attention as we approached the extremity of the plain   At half past 7 P M   as the shadows of night came on we entered a defile of the mountain, and were conducted for more than two hours up a continual and difficult ascent   The thick boughs of the forest overhanging the path made the darkness intense and put our eyes in constant jeopardy, while the broken pavement of the road and the narrow bridges by which we repeated ly crossed a mountain torrent exposed us to frequent falls and bruises   One horse gave out and refused to stir and all were extremely fatigued   At the top we found a rough police guard in a dirty old *derbénd* (guard house) sleeping and smoking by a blazing fire   Placing ourselves around it we enjoyed its cheering influence for an hour while our surijies were catching a horse from a neighbor ing pasture to supply the place of the one that had failed Gradually descending hence over an open and apparently arable tract we reached Boly two hours and a half after midnight, having accomplished 10 hours from Dootjeh, and 60 miles since the morning   Fatigued and sleepy and chilled with the change of climate and the dampness of the night, we wrapped our pelisses around us, and lay down to rest upon the floor of the post-house

May 25 Boly represents the ancient Hadrianopolis, which was celebrated for its warm baths They still exist, but are several miles distant. It contains about 800 Turkish houses and a distinct suburb is inhabited by about 40 families of Armenians A Turkish bath in the morning relieved us of three evils unavoidable in our mode of travelling viz soreness dirt and vermin and by a quarter past 9 A M we were in good order for proceeding The excellent horses of this post were only two hours and a quarter in carrying us over the plain of Boly The rays of the sun though they shone through an unclouded sky, rather cheered than oppressed us and this, with the banks of snow on the mountains around testified to the elevation of the spot The plain itself is undulating and well watered, and being almost entirely under cultivation and animated with frequent villages presented a beautiful prospect. We found no tract so fully cultivated in the whole extent of Asia Minor Even the hills beyond partook of the same feature and had some villages among them Here we traced a limpid streamlet to its source and recognized the alder upon its banks, though unlike our own, it grew to the size of an apple tree with a trunk nearly a foot and a half in diameter At a derbend, which answered as a half way house we rested a moment, and devoured a roasted lamb with which our tartar had providently stocked our sufreh at Boly The latter half of our ride was over a hilly country that had little to interest us and we reached our post-house at Gerideh 12 hours from Boly, at half past 5 P M

The coolness of the air that had braced and cheered us in the afternoon increased to chillness in the evening and made a close room and fire acceptable The paper windows of the menzil khaneh helped us to one and a pot of coals in our enclosure furnished us with the other I noticed as an evidence of the coldness of the climate, that

every enclosure had a spot in the centre fitted for this con
venience in fact we were assured that the snow falls several feet deep in winter and observed that some of it was still
lying upon the mountains but a little above us Gerideh
a corruption of Gratia one of its ancient names is a mar
ket town of about 200 Turkish houses built of hewed logs
in the best back woods style of the United States

Our tartar seemed to be on good terms with the *menzilgy*
(postmaster), and as they sat drinking their *arak* (brandy) before all the comers and goers of the inn he expressed his surprise that we did not allow ourselves the same indulgence
We explained our reason but at the same time mentioned
that we had fewer objections against the use of common wine
with our meals   Contrary to our expectation in a town en
tirely Turkish, wine was offered us , though while brandy
was drunk so openly, the wine was brought carefully con
cealed under a cloke   This was the only place between
Isnikmid and Marsovan where we found wine and between
Niksar and Erzroom we found none, though we might probably have obtained arak in almost every place   The rea
son is that Turks much more readily drink the latter than
the former perhaps because the prohibition of wine in the
Koran is express while that of distilled liquors is only im
plied *   Often have they directly or indirectly solicited me
for brandy but for wine never   Both the tartar we took
from Smyrna, and the one that conducted us to Erzroom
were hardened drinkers and they were doubtless disappointed that we did not help them to the forbidden dram
Unfortunately in the one case a Greek and in the other an

* They ask you says the Korán respecting wine and the *meiser* [a
game of chance] Say that in them is great wickedness and advantages to
men but their wickedness is greater than their advantages   (Sooret-el
bokarah)   O ye that have believed ' wine and the meiser **** are an
abomination of the work of Satan   (Id Sooret-el maideh)   From the
fruit of palms and grapes ye obtain intoxicating liquor (*seker*) and good
noutriment in this there is a sign to people of understanding   Id Sooret
el-nahl

Armenian fellow traveller, carried bottles in their pockets. It is a disgrace to foreign as well as native Christians in this country that they so readily become panders to this appetite of the Turks, and help them to break a really commendable precept of their religion

May 26 We lay down with the intention of starting at midnight but soon a cry of robbers called the inhabitants to their arms, and it proved that some of the post horses were stolen The accident detained us till 3 and a quarter A M Starting then, we found the country hilly, little cultivated, and less fertile than hitherto till we came down to a little valley upon one of the branches of the Parthenius. In it were two small villages the second of which is called Hamamly Here, 7 hours from Gerideh we breakfasted and changed horses. Then crossing the river by a bridge, we ascended a mountain, and concluded that we had fairly entered Paphlagonia

At Cherkesh a small village which we reached at 1 and a quarter P M we rested half an hour It was crowded with people attending a fair which passes around the several villages of the district in rotation In the crowd were two dervishes who exhibited before us the common trick of driving a bodkin through the cheek and into the throat but they proved themselves no great adepts at legerdemain The remainder of our day's ride was over a regularly undulating table-land without a shrub and with little grass but sowed in spots with grain The coolness of the air and the patches of snow on the swelling hills that bound it on the right proved its elevation not to be small Our horses galloped over it at a rapid rate, and at 4 and a half P M we reached the post-house at the little village of Karajalar 8 hours from Hamamly

We now *travel tartar* in fine style, and I must invite you to look at us as we move over these naked plains Two horses, the first led by a surijy upon a separate ani-

mal, and the second tied by his halter to the tail of his
companion carry our baggage   Our tartar with a *kalpak*
(cap) of black lambskin upon his head some twelve or
fifteen inches in length looking much like a stove-pipe
with a yellow cushion stuffed into its upper extremity and a
heavy kumchy in his hand to give force to his frequent
exclamation of *haideh* rides by their side   We meta-
morphosed into Turks with unshaven lip and turbaned
head, bring up the rear   Every stage, often thirty miles
or more, is travelled without allowing our horses a drop
of water, and our gait is frequently a rapid gallop   in en-
during which, the loaded animals especially exhibit a
strength and hardiness that quite astonish us   Besides the
smart of the tartar s lash the weight of their load and the
swiftness of their gait they are subject to many cruel acci
dents   A false step in such rapid travelling often causes
one to stumble and the other tied as he is to him is most
ungently and unceremoniously arrested   or if the ground
is hilly one sometimes rolls down a declivity and drags his
companion reluctantly after him   Their motion is so great,
that, snugly as our baggage is packed not a stage is passed
without its turning more than once so as to bring the girt,
sustaining the whole weight of the load suddenly across
the poor animals' back often already completely excoriated
by the chafing of the saddle   Such accidents being frequently the fault of the surijy, are apt to bring him into a
quarrel with the tartar in which we have more than once
seen the yataghan instead of the kumchy, applied to his
back

At Karajalar the deception of our tartar which we had
already suspected, was fully developed   We had hired
him at Constantinople as we supposed for ourselves alone,
and although an Armenian had joined us at Scutari and
two others at Sabanjah we were not sure that any thing
was wrong   But here we overtook two Turkish merchants,

with three heavily laden horses and two surijies, equally with ourselves under his convoy, so that we were actually a minority of the party. The reason why the post houses had been found so often destitute of horses or furnished with only bad ones, was now explained for the tartar had drained them by keeping this company just before us. With this addition and embracing a second tartar as an accidental companion our caravan now consisted of nineteen horses more than most post houses could be expected to contain. It was but a specimen of the double dealing however to which one soon becomes accustomed as an every-day occurrence in Turkey and reflecting that our contract was really cheaper than the tartar could afford without additional profit from the rest of the company we determined not to complain so long as we did not suffer for good horses or lodgings.

Beyond Karajalar the same table-land continued and our party moved over it often nineteen abreast upon an almost unbroken gallop for 3 hours to Kharajulen where we stopped at 7 P M. Had you seen us loaded horses and all bounding over the plain as if for a wager the scene would have amused you, unless perchance pity for the poor animals had produced an opposite impression. We should ourselves have dealt more mercifully with the poor beasts and in fact with their riders had we been our own masters. But, with a level road and good horses the irresistible tendency of a tartar is onward and our Mohammed aga had no moderate share of the propensity of his profession. Having as usual anticipated us a little he awaited our arrival at the post house and as we drove up in good spirits after a ride of at least 60 miles since the morning exclaimed to his friends, *el hamd lillah alushdular* (thank God they have got used to it) highly gratified by such a proof that we were now able to push on as fast as he wished.—This place contains about 200 houses, all Turkish.

8

May 27. After passing, for two hours and a half, over a tract more broken than the plain of yesterday, we came upon a small tributary of the Halys, called the Derin-goz, which we followed, sometimes upon its banks and sometimes at a distance, the remainder of the day. Besides several villages upon its southern side and a few trees, now became a rarity, I noticed nothing till we reached Koj-hisar which completed a stage of 8 hours. It was a Turkish town of about 200 houses. Its shops afforded us eggs for about two cents a dozen, and bread was proportionally cheap.

We were now at our nearest approach to Angora, a place interesting to the merchant for its celebrated manufacture of goat s hair camlet (*Angora shaly*), and to the missionary for its numerous and wealthy papal Armenian population. A beautiful specimen of the cloth manufactured at this village was showed us and in the vicinity we saw some of the animals from the hair of which it is made, but we heard of no Christians of any name between Boly and Tosia.

On starting again we found the most luxuriant vegetation on the river and our road for some distance was hedged with roses. Exposed to the scorching rays of the sun in a temperature 98° however we enjoyed it but little and soon the valley became narrow and cedars were the only ornament of the hills that enclosed it. At the half way house, an airy *koshk* (kiosk) over a jetting fountain afforded us a few minutes cool repose and tempted us to a selfish admiration of that trait of the Turkish religion which leads to such acts of benevolence to the traveller. For several hundred miles on our present road we could hardly travel far enough to become thirsty, without finding some fountain, a work of supposed meritorious charity by some devout Turk, inviting us to drink of its limpid jet.

Proceeding we noticed in the alluvial of the river many fields of rice, that offspring of heat and parent of sickness

Our post-house was in Tosia at the end of a stage of 10 hours Crossing a rapid tributary of the Derin goz by a covered bridge of stone, we entered it through luxuriant gardens and pretty summer houses extending from the southern base of a precipice where it is situated down a long declivity toward the river Being by its situation, advantageously exposed it appears large as in fact it is I counted fifteen or twenty minarets and was told that it contained 3000 Turkish and 50 Greek houses It has no Armenians In this place only did we find any partisans of the janizaries They were here predominant and two or three persons had been recently killed in their broils We subsequently learned that some time after we passed along they were entirely suppressed

May 28 As we descended the river the rice fields continued along its banks but the mountains around assumed a rugged and naked aspect We crossed to its right bank by a ford in the course of the morning and five hours and three quarters from Tosia came to its junction with the Halys, at a point where that river after coming down from the east turns suddenly northward * Following up the southern bank of the latter stream called very properly from the color of its muddy water Kuzul Irmák (red river) we were led into a narrow valley shut in by precipitous mountains and heated by the closeness of the air and the concentrated rays of the sun almost to the temperature of an oven Though fainting to us its atmosphere was proved to be congenial to vegetation by the surprising luxuriance of the fruit trees and gardens which occupied it. Here at the end of a stage of 8 hours we found our post-house at the little walled town of Haji Hamzeh

* Kinneir in the map inserted in his Travels in Asia Minor Armenia, and Kurdistán has mistaken these rivers one for the other

A crowd of bearded dirty Turks were assembled at a fair and judging from their features I should say that the temperature of the spot favored the growth of human passions as much as of vegetation for they certainly seemed the most ruffian like multitude I ever saw   Even the children indicated the sinister influence of the presiding genius by hooting at us from the walls as we passed

As we rode up the river the mountains which closely hedge it in increased in height and ruggedness affording by caves and fastnesses in their precipitous fronts retreats for robbers from whom this pass is said never to be free   Three hours from Haji Hamzeh the river washes for some distance the base of a precipice three or four hundred feet high along the face of which perhaps sixty or a hundred feet above the water we had to climb a narrow path wrought out of the rock   As we entered it Mohammed who for some distance had taken care that we should not separate mustered us in a solid column and making the mountains echo with his tartar cry urged us forward with the assertion that this spot, an account of its danger is in the mind of every traveller from the moment he leaves Constantinople   The singular advantages of the place and the appearance of the people at the last town every one of whom looked more like a robber than an honest man argued that there was ground for apprehension but we saw not a living being   The valley beyond spreads into a broader and more open plain and we pursued a level road through it till 7 and half P M   Then crossing the river by an excellent bridge solidly constructed of hewn stone (said by Kinneir to be the work of Bajazet) we entered Osman juk 8 hours from Haji Hamzeh   It is at the foot of an isolated rock on which is a ruined castle and from its low situation and bad water must be very unhealthy

May 29   We started a quarter before one in the morning, and leaving the alluvial of the river to the right,

found ourselves at daybreak riding through a hilly country
After many hair-breadth escapes from falling from my
horse through drowsiness we reached an old derbend,
where I threw myself upon the floor and was instantly
asleep Minutes of such sleep are worth hours in the soft
bed of home In this case they were few however, for I was
soon roused to eat a breakfast of butter and honey with a lit
tle bread and then urged upon my horse again After a short
distance we came to a mountain ridge at a point, where a
savage chasm between impending precipices affords a passage through it to a foaming torrent on its way to the Ha
lys It was too narrow for a road, and with much fa
tigue to our animals and an occasional misgiving of our
own nerves we climbed over the top along the brink of
one of the precipices Tracing for awhile on the opposite
side the small valley of the stream here a quietly murmuring rivulet we came out upon the plain of Marsovan

Our stage was 12 hours, and coming after a night of
so little sleep we reached the town with our patience quite
exhausted at the seeming interminable extent of the plain
Its length in the direction of our route must be twenty or
thirty miles and its breadth though less is also very con
siderable Its surface is prettily undulating and though
the soil is light and but little cultivated it is watered with
frequent springs and several villages are scattered over it
It is difficult in some cases, to settle definitely the boundaries of the ancient divisions of Asia Minor and I can only
say that in the course of yesterday's ride we left Paphlagonia probably touched upon the borders of Galatia, and
entered Pontus At any rate there can be no doubt that
we are now fairly in the latter country I cannot affirm
the same of Armenia Minor though the statistics of this
place seem to say, that we are at least approaching it
Marsovan occupies the site of the ancient Phazemon, from

8 *

which it also evidently derives its name   Although not
pretending to the dignity of a city and having the form of
only a village we were credibly informed that it contains
5000 houses of which 1000 are Armenian and the rest
Turkish   From hence a post route branches off to Trebizond probably by way of Samsoon which cannot be very
distant

The excessive heat delayed us five or six hours in the
middle of the day and we did not start till a quarter after
5 P M   The light of day left us before we reached the
hills at the extremity of the plain   and some apprehension
of robbers being felt by the company our tartar, as was his
custom on such occasions rode out to examine every appearance of man or beast near the road   Once he chased
an animal which but for its fleetness I should have
taken for a sheep until he was out of sight when one of
his Turkish friends instantly started in pursuit   His anxiety was explained by his assuring us on his return, that it
was not an animal but a spirit an idea suggested probably
by the previous conversation of the tartar who, with the
extreme credulity in supernatural appearances common
among moslems had been entertaining the company with
accounts of ghostly lights that frequent this plain and lead
travellers astray by carrying them hither and thither, one of
which had once made him wander here a whole night   At
length we began to descend a mountain so steep that our
horses could scarcely go down it and so high that we
were an hour in reaching the bottom   High precipices on
each side appeared to close before us and it seemed in
the darkness of night as if we were descending into an
immense natural funnel   Here in the very bottom, we entered Amásia at 11 and a quarter P M   Our last stage
was 8 hours, making 60 miles since the morning, and
we were not long in seeking repose in the open veranda of
the post house

May 30 Dayhght showed that the obscurity of night had deceived us in the form though not in the grandeur, of this singular spot for instead of being a chasm without an outlet it is, in the language of the geographer Strabo who was born here a great and deep ravine through which runs the river Iris The city is situated on both banks of the river in the narrowest part which it com pletely fills Lofty precipices overhang it on either side, one of which in front of our window is formed by a distinct rock crowned with the walls of an old fortress In its perpendicular front appear several excavations like the cells of anchorites respecting which tradition has preserved several fables not worth relating The rays of the sun concentrated by the surrounding precipices create an excessive heat which occasions fevers in the warm months, but an abundance of fruit and other productions originating from the same cause give the place counterbalancing attractions for which man in every part of the world is ready to expose his health and life Whether Amasia has retained any relics of its regal times except its name we did not learn It now has all the features of a common Turkish city except that its houses are constructed rather better than is usual in this region An excellent bridge connects the two divisions into which it is separated by the river It contains 4000 Turkish 600 Armenian and 125 Greek houses In passing through the bazár we noticed piles of stones which on inquiry, proved to be salt It is dug from a mine not far distant and used in its native state * Among the principal productions of Amasia is silk, of which we were assured, 24 000 okas are raised annu ally †

* Probably the same that Strabo speaks of in the district of Ximena, and which he suggests may have given the river Halys its name.

† The weight of the oka differs in different places In Smyrna it is 2.78 lbs

For the sake of repose and retirement, while my companion was abroad I spent most of the day in the elevated veranda of the post house, and of course observed little besides the circumstances that occurred in its court yard. Our companions fatigued like ourselves, and lounging smoking or sleeping under the trees which overshadowed it, were its constant occupants. Tartars occasionally came changed horses smoked their nargeelies and hastened on their way saying as usual but little to others of their profession who were on the ground. They are the news-carriers of the country and generally manufacture a new rumor for every town which is eagerly caught up by the common people. But when they meet each other from a mutual understanding of the art of story making perhaps they seem to have nothing to inquire or to relate and a simple *salam* is often all they say. One however in this case gave out a report that was true and important. He announced his approach by the peculiar cry between a grunt and a whistle which is the tartar's horn as he nears a post house, and entering the yard in full speed dismounted and seated himself upon a platform near the gate as a signal for a nargeely, which was immediately brought. Not a word was said, but the hostlers saw that the horse had been driven to his very last effort, and instantly plunged a knife into his mouth to save his life. At length, after the nargeely was smoked, he let it be known that several thousand *delies*, (old troops now disbanded,) had assembled in rebellion, and were plundering the country around Sivas, the pasha of which had dispatched him with an order to the governor of Amasia to join him immediately with a thousand soldiers. Where were his dispatches I know not, but they were doubtless speedily and safely delivered, for although falsehood is more natural than truth to the mouth of a tartar, there is hardly so trusty a set of men in the world. They not only take the greatest care of papers committed to them but thousands of dollars in the valise of a tartar, without a receipt, or an obligation is as safe, danger from robbers excepted as in the vault of a bank

At the close of the day a sufficient number of horses the want of which had detained us since the morning was obtained and we continued on our way On leaving the town we passed an ancient building of an unusually venerable appearance the front wall of which surprisingly solid and thick was entire in its ancient style and formed a striking contrast to the coarseness and weakness of the other parts which were of modern origin It was doubtless an old church which we were told in the course of the day when inquiring for antiquities had once been used by the Turks as a mosk but was now shut up and deserted because they found that they could not say their prayers in it! Our road led for some distance up the narrow valley of the river being separated by a hedge of roses on the right from the luxuriant gardens and fruit trees principally the cherry now loaded with its blushing fruit which occupied its rich alluvial and having on the left a perpendicular precipice with the channel of an ancient aqueduct cut in the rock along its base The precipice ceasing at length we turned to the left from the river and passing in our ascent through a sort of natural gateway formed by two shelving rocks so near as but just to allow our loaded animals to pass we emerged *superas ad auras* The coolness of the evening air at the top revived us from the languor of the atmosphere of the city which had been heated at midday to the temperature of $92°$ in the shade As we descended again into a tolerably level tract bounded on either side at no great distance by hills the darkness of night closed our observations

Our half way house was as usual a derbend and by the time we reached it an hour s rest by a fire, and a supper

of eggs and yoghoort with bread and butter and honey,
were very acceptable   The civility of our host pleased us
even more than his fire or his fare   The Turks, even to
the lowest porter in the streets systematically regard Christians   whether natives or Europeans   as inferior to them
selves universally refusing to enter their employ as servants
and making it almost an article of their religion never to
show them respect by rising up in in their presence *
When embassadors in Constantinople tolerate such ill bred
arrogance in their own janizaries plain travellers like ourselves need expect nothing else than that, at almost every
post-house the dirtiest Turk should accommodate himself
at the expense of our convenience and that, by the land
lord himself, the slightest attentions should be paid us with
evident reluctance   Such treatment besides all the inconvenience that attends it, is harrassing to the individual and
national feelings of every man but to the Christian who
knows its true cause to lie not in a disparagement of him
self or his nation but of his religion, and sees in every
instance of it an exercise of contempt toward the holy faith
that he loves which has been practised so long as to have
become an integral part of the national feelings and customs of a whole people it is infinitely afflicting and griev
ous   It is chiefly this moslem arrogance that creates the
necessity of such an attendant as a tartar and the authority of ours generally exacted for us sufficient respect to prevent our suffering any serious inconvenience   Still it was

* Their pertinacity in this article of discourtesy was finely tested during
the late Russian war according to an account given us by an Armenian bishop who was with the army   When after the battle of Soghanly-dagh
which decided the fate of Erzroom the Russian general entered the tent of
one of the Turkish pashás   though deserted by his own troops conquered by
the Russians and plundered by the Cossacks he refused to rise, until
absolutely ordered to do so   After the capture of Akhaltsikhe, Gen Pas
kevich was obliged to issue a proclamation before he could obtain this mark
of respect from those whom he had conquered

so new and so grateful to have in this wild country and
this dark and tedious night a Turk not only give us his
own warm seat by the fire but hasten to relieve our stif-
fened limbs of our clokes and boots, and to meet every
want as soon as expressed that I cannot but record it to
his praise We readily gave him double the usual present
as he helped us to our horses and then left him under a
shower of his prayers for the prosperity of our journey He
had learned his politeness by once residing in the English
palace at Constantinople

About three hours more brought us to another derbend
Its keeper was asleep within and could with difficulty be
awaked to make us a cup of coffee But the guard was
was sitting around a large fire in the open air the blaze
of which as it shone through the branches of the overshad-
owing forest, discovered a lofty gallows at hand, as proof,
both that the vicinity is infested by robbers and that they
here find their punishment Which reminds me to say what
I ought to have told you earlier that the derbends which I
so often mention are stations of police guards appointed to
defend uninhabited parts of the public roads from robbers.
Being generally at a distance from villages they serve also
as places of refreshment to travellers The name itself
is a Turkish word that signifies a pass or defile We found
the assertion of Strabo that the district of Amásia abounds
in trees true to night somewhat to our inconvenience
For it is not very comfortable to ride through a forest in
thick darkness with the constant apprehension that a
straggling branch may find its way into one's face and
eyes Fortunately the high kalpák of our tartar who went
before us was most happily formed for detecting such intruders and whenever it encountered one the cry *dal war*
(there is a limb) from its owner, warned the company to
avoid the danger

The last two or three hours of our stage seemed of in-

terminable length, for drowsiness came upon me like an
armed man, and resistance was in vain   My utmost efforts
could but just open my senses sufficiently to external objects to give my dreams a new starting point before away
they would fly in spite of me with all the velocity of their
nature   If a nod that disturbed my balance again arrested
them, it was but to allow them to start afresh from some
new goal as speedily as before   Thus the velocity of
dreams was mistaken in my imagination for our actual
gait and we seemed to have travelled hours when we had
really advanced but a few rods   At length after day
break, we ended our stage of 12 hours at Toorkhál, and
were instantly upon the bare floor of the post house   I
thought not of a bed for I had been for sometime grudging
the naked ground to the meanest animal that lay sleeping
by the side of the road   and though the villagers had al
ready begun to collect for their morning pipe and cup of
coffee when we arrived, no company or noise disturbed my
slumbers

May 31   Toorkhal is situated in a plain at the foot
of an isolated rock crowned with the remains of a fortress,
and contains perhaps 150 miserable houses in a ruinous
state   We stopped less than three hours and then left for
Tokát   It is 8 hours distant and a plain interrupted only
by a few undulations and isolated hillocks extends the
whole way   The soil is gravelly and but little cultivated
though several villages were in sight   and, with the exception of an immense multitude of young locusts that were
stripping the ground of its verdure, we noticed nothing to
record

LETTER III

FROM TOKAT TO ERZROOM

Situation of Tokát—Its manufactures and trade—Armenian churches and schools—Papal Armenians—Tomb of Martyn—Favorable spot for a mission—Sivás—Ruins of Comana—Niksár—A pastoral scene—Kotály —Koylisár—Kara hisár—Hospitality of a menzilji—Fundukly-bel—Sheherán—Turkish post establishment—Chiftlik—Erzengán—Cross the boundary of Armenia—Kara koolak—River Euphrates—Under-ground houses—New mode of travelling—Description of a stable—Russian au thority only respected—Erganmazar—Preparation of fuel—Pretended hospitality—First view of the Russians—A hot spring—Reach Erzroom

DEAR SIR

EXTENSIVE and luxuriant gardens, occupying the banks of the river in the vicinity of Tokat and abounding with the pear the peach the cherry and other fruit trees that partially conceal by their foliage numerous small but neat country houses made our approach to the city highly pre possessing Crossing to the south side of the river we found spreading walnuts overhanging the road, and under their grateful shade, entered the town at mid-day panting under the oppressive temperature of 100 °

The moslem *Corban-bairam* (feast of sacrifice) when the pilgrims at Mecca complete their pilgrimage by offering sacrifices in the valley of Mina occurred the day after we reached Tokat and our tartar that he might keep the feast and slay a lamb in token of participating in the cere mony determined to stop two days We were not dissatis-fied with the arrrangement as it not only gave us time to repose but allowed us to examine more minutely a city that has been pronounced the largest and most commercial

9

in the interior of Asia Minor   And as we have now entered Armenia Minor, I may be allowed to give a more detailed report

The ancient name of Tokát is supposed to have been
Berisa.   Under the lower empire it was called Eudocia and
the same name is given to it by the Armenian writers
That it is not on the site of Comana Pontica, as formerly
supposed, is now quite certain   It is on the south side of
the river, anciently called Iris but now bearing the name
of the city itself and occupies a small valley, confined between a mountain on the east, a gentle hill on the south
and a perpendicular ragged rock with the ruins of a fortress
upon its top on the west   A great number of trees, either
in clusters, or scattered singly among the houses, add much
beauty to its external aspect.   But, in general, we were
disappointed in its appearance and size   It is unwalled,
and all the houses, even to that of the governor are of unburnt bricks and if its streets are paved, as has been often
mentioned in its praise, it is no more than can be said of
most towns of any magnitude in Turkey   Still some of its
edifices are of good size and parts of it are tolerably neat
for a Turkish city   It belongs to one of the sultanas, and
its governor is not subject to the pasha of Sivas

Its principal manufactures are copper, silk, and calicoes
The feast had stopped the operations of the copper foundery but we got access to it through one of its officers
It is a small establishment, carried on entirely by hand, and
simply designed to purify the copper that is extracted from
the mines of Maaden near Diarbekr   By a singular order
of government, if we may believe our informant the metal
is not allowed to be refined there nor elsewhere but must
be brought hither, a distance of more than 250 miles to
undergo the process   We saw many pigs of it in the foun
dery looking almost as impure as the ore itself   When
refined, the larger portion of it is carried elsewhere to be

manufactured A great number of shops here, however were employed in making it into vessels and various other utensils Silk like copper is not produced at Tokat but is brought in a raw state from Amasia and other places and is here manufactured into goods The calico manu factory resembles much the one in Smyrna except that it is larger and like that it is chiefly employed in stamping the coarse calicoes that are used in Turkey for handkerchiefs and women s head-dresses Every figure is stamped by hand Trade is carried on principally with the interior and with Smyrna and Constantinople With Trebizond it has hardly any intercourse The most wealthy of the Armenian merchants is said to pay taxes on his business and property to the amount to 15 000 piastres annually

According to our informant, a respectable Armenian merchant the present population of Tokat is 4000 Tur kish 1350 Armenian 500 or 600 Greek, and 70 Jewish houses A priest whom we met in the church of St Sarkis, and who appeared to be a sensible man informed us that the Armenians have 7 churches in the city and 30 priests besides a vartabed who is the bishop s wekeel and preaches The bishop himself lives in the convent of St Anna about an hour distant where he has five varta beds There is also another convent four hours distant, dedicated to St Chrisostom whose tomb was carried thith er from Comana where he died, when that city became un inhabited Its only occupants are a vartabed and a lay man *

* The priest's tradition does not contradict the ecclesiastical historians and withal confirms the supposition that Tokát is not Comana Sozomen and Socrates say that after Chrisostom had been banished for some time to Cucusus in Armenia Minor his enemies procured an order for his trans- portation still farther to Pityus But as soldiers were executing the order he died at Comana on the road After thirty five years Proclus caused his remains to be brought to Constantinople Soz L. 8 c 22 28 Socrat L 7 c 45

Within the precincts of the church of St Sarkis we found an Armenian grammar school the only one in the city Its teacher was a layman and a man of some intelligence As we entered, a class of his pupils were employed in chanting prayers as one of their regular lessons probably in order to qualify themselves for a similar service in church He informed us that he had 160 scholars and that he taught them reading writing and a little grammar Their principal class book was the Venice edition of the New Testament in ancient Armenian We afterwards learned, what he for some reason declined making known to us that these books were furnished him by Mr Barker the British and Foreign Bible Society s agent at Smyrna The Armenians here have a number of smaller schools but they never have had one for females The priest of the church of Karasoon Manoog estimated the whole number of Armenians in the city that can read at 500 besides perhaps 50 women

In the estimated number of Armenians already stated are included 80 papal Armenian families They never had any church were always obliged to pay their baptismal and other similar fees to the Armenian clergy and the two priests who formerly ministered to them were banished when their brethren were driven from Constantinople Although few, their number embraces the wealthiest merchants and it speaks loudly in their praise that before the event just mentioned, they had a female school.

The Greeks have one church but we did not visit it or them , nor did we have any intercourse with the Jews

While at Tokat we had the melancholy pleasure of visiting the tomb of the Rev Henry Martyn who died at this place in the year 1812 when on his way from Persia to England His remains lie buried in the extensive cemetery of the Armenian church of Karasoon Manoog and are covered by a monument erected by Claudius James Rich, Esq late English resident at Bagdad An appropriate Latin inscription is all that distinguishes his tomb from the tombs of the Armenians who sleep by his side *

The name of the place where the lamented Martyn closed his short but distinguished career of earthly usefulness, is already familiar to the friends of missions, and that melancholy event has thrown around it no small degree of interest In recommending it therefore as the best spot for a missionary station which we visited in Armenia Minor, we have not to introduce to notice a place entirely new Besides its own Armenian population which is not small it has a convenient situation in reference to several other places that contain many of the same people On the west are Marsovan and Amasia on the northeast Niksar, and on the southeast Sivas embracing together with Tokat itself, not far from **24,000** Armenians within a circle extending in the farthest direction not more than eighty miles from this centre without reckoning any that may be scattered in villages Whether there are many thus located, we did not ascertain by inquiry but we should expect to find them, in this their adopted country not merely in the migratory and alien character of merchants and mechanics in cities but in that of peasants cultivating the soil as if it was their nation s home In a word Tokat is the spot to be chosen as a centre of operations for the Armenians of Second Armenia as Cesarea is, probably, for those of the First and Third Armenia, and Tarsus for those of Cilicia

Whether its climate would prove to be salubrious is questionable It is hot in summer, and in the warmest months

* For a copy of this inscription and the few facts we were able to collect respecting his death the reader is referred to the late Boston edition of his Memoirs

intermittent fevers are not uncommon   but we were assured that there are not more than ten days in the year of a
higher temperature than we experienced the day that we
arrived and that disease is very easily avoided by attending to one s diet and other common precautions   Whether
the missionary would not at first find himself attracting an
undesirable degree of curiosity and have to put up with
some insults, is also questionable   For the people are entirely unused to the residence of Europeans among them,
and their would be no consular protection at hand   Still,
the inhabitants of Tokat are not worse than those of other
places in the interior of Turkey   and are we never to go
any farther from the coast than a European s hat can be
seen or a consul s arm can reach ?   European society and
protection are certainly desirable, and other things being
equal, those places where they can be enjoyed should be se
lected first   But when we come to consider them essen-
tially necessary we forget the high declaration, that ' it is
better to trust in the Lord than to put confidence in princes '

As Sivas one of the places that would fall within the
range of a missionary stationed at Tokat does not lie in
the route we are pursuing I may be allowed to say a word
respecting it here   Its name, when Mithridates made it
his royal residence was Cabira   the name of Sebaste was
given to it by his conqueror   and this has been converted
by Turkish ignorance into Sivas   It was regarded by the
Armenians as the capital of Second Armenia   and, as we
have already seen, the Ardzroonian king Senekerim in
A D 1021 transferred his residence thither from Vasboor
agán, with a large part of his subjects   His posterity became extinct in A D 1080 * and the place soon fell into
the hands of the Turks   When taken by Timoor it con
tained, we are told, 120,000 inhabitants nearly all of whom

* Chamchean P 5 c 18

were massacred with the most barbarous cruelty * Under the Ottoman government it has long been the capital of the pashalık of Room, and is now the residence of a pashá It lies eighteen hours southeast of Tokat and contains about 1800 Armenian families among whom are no papists In the village of Torkhan however an hour distant, that sect numbers about one hundred families, who have a church openly Their priests are in banishment like those of Tokat Kinneir says Sivás is dirty and ill built, and its inhabitants are a coarse and rude people

June 3 We left Tokat this morning at 8 o'clock, and instead of recrossing the river immediately continued along its southern bank about two hours in order to visit the ruins which are commonly called here old Tokát They occupy both banks of the river but principally the northern and are all coarse and modern except a few foundations These bear marks of genuine antiquity and I am inclined to believe the Armenian tradition which makes this the site of Comana But the shrine of Bellona no longer creates here the luxury and proffligacy of Corinth † nor do the remains, or even the tomb of Chrisostom, now attract hither the sympathies of christians for that persecuted man ‡ Not a human being inhabits the spot and a few uninteresting stones only distinguish it Crossing the river here we rode a few miles up its valley which is fertile and considerably cultivated Then turning to the left over a gentle eminence, we descended by the side of a noisy torrent, through a ravine thickly shaded with the oak

* Chamchean P 7 c 1 † Strabo Lib xii

‡ This allusion takes for granted the accuracy of the local tradition but I see no reason why Comana in Cappadocia may not have been the place of his death. Cucusus (now Gogison) was in its vicinity and it is as probable that he passed through there as here on his way to Pityus (now Pitsunda) in Colchis

the beech, the plane, the maple the box, the hazel wild
grape vines and roses into the valley of Niksar   Though
somewhat marshy, it is even more fertile and beautiful than
the one we had left   We crossed it nearly at right angles
and passing the river of Niksar (the ancient Lycus) by a
most bungling ferry boat, we stopped at the town for the
night though but 9 hours from Tokat

Niksar is but a corruption of Neocesarea the town in
Pontus which is known as the birth place of Gregory Thau
maturgus   It occupies a gentle eminence at the foot of a
range of mountains which forms the northern boundary of
the plain   A citadel with a strong wall and gates still
standing contains the bazars and business and forms the
nucleus of the town   the deserted ruins of another fortress
on a height above throw around it an air of antiquity and
forests of fig pomegranate pear cherry walnut and other
fruit trees, concealing the houses of the main body of its in
habitants along the sloping declivity below give to it rural
charms of the very first order   High on the north hangs
the mountain clothed with the foliage of an almost impene
trable forest , and spread out on the south lies the plain
carpeted with the verdure of the smoothest meadow   A
copious shower just after we stopped gave the highest fin
ish of freshness and life to the whole   In a word, the
scenery of Niksar united with that of many other places
in Pontus of a similar cast has stamped upon my mind an
impression of that country that would need very little aid
from monastic propensities, to induce me to take up my
residence with the shade of St Basil in its beautiful forests
The town contains 600 Turkish 120 Armenian, and 20
Greek houses, and in a distinct suburb are 40 Greek
houses more.

June 4 Our road from Niksar led us directly to the top
of the highest peak of the mountain that rises behind it

The fatigue of the ascent was forgotten in the charms which surrounded us At first small ravines wooded with walnuts wild cherries and other trees formed channels for murmuring rivulets that descended to water the town Nearer the top a forest of lofty beeches shaded a ground beautifully studded with a great variety of delicate flowers The top itself rose bare above all trees and shrubbery, and the very greenness of the sward which covered it except where a drift of unmelted snow still lingered here and there seemed only to give a finish to its baldness From this elevated position which it took us four hours to reach we could look across the whole region of the Iris and its trib utaries to the snow capped mountains that bound it on the south Sitting down by a spring to eat a morsel of bread we basked with pleasure in the rays of the sun now rai sing the thermometer to only 56° though they had so re cently scorched us in the valleys below with a temperature of 100°

Descending through a grove of pines which in the in verted position of their limbs seemed to bear marks of the weight of wintry sleet and snows we came soon into an open and beautiful grazing country Level meadows and swelling hills covered with the finest sward interspersed with here and there a woodland and intersected with rivu lets of the purest water seemed to give reality to the po etical charms of pastoral life As we approached the log village in which was our post-house a grotesque group with pipe and tambour, headed by one in the costume of a za- ny came forth to meet us and imagination instantly seiz ed them to complete the deception by adding to the scene Pan and the Satyrs in actual life engaged in their favorite amusement Poetry soon became prose however when on entering the village we found that the head man being about to take to himself wife was keeping a feast of fifteen days and these his musicians hoping to add our present to his pay, had stopped a moment from celebrating his joys to welcome our arrival

The village is named Kotaly it is 8 hours from Niksár Its houses which were few, were in the style of the best log architecture of the United States, except that they were covered with a flat terrace which extended like a portico several feet in every direction from the body of the building In one of these we were furnished with better accommodations than we had had since leaving Constantinople Our room was well floored and neatly ceiled throughout A good fireplace with jambs and hearth of hewn stone and an andiron (unfortunately there was but one) a rare article of furniture in Turkey was supplied with a cheerful fire Our modest and civil host soon furnished us with a frugal supper and for the consideration of twenty three cents provided a roasted lamb for tomorrow —There are no Armenians in this vicinity, but a village not far distant has 30 Greek houses

June 5 Apple and pear trees in blossom gave to our morning's ride the charms of early spring and an occasional glimpse of the snowy summits of the Janik mountains on our left, showed that winter still reigned not far from us Leaving the open grazing country after three or four hours and crossing a succession of exquisitely beautiful lawns enclosed in a grove of pines we were conducted at length up the long and narrow dell of Baghursak deresy, among juniper and barberry bushes, into a continuous and dense forest The prospect that burst upon us, as we unexpectedly issued from it in the afternoon arrested us immovably by its indescribable grandeur We were on the edge of the elevated plateau to which we had ascended yesterday So far below as to be but indistinctly seen the river of Niksar wound its course through a ravine whose sides were lofty mountains We stood on the top of one of them Opposite to us, mountain rose above mountain with all the roughness of crag and precipice, till the summits of the farthest were whitened with wintry snows Our stage was to end at the very bottom of the abyss We worked our way without danger though not without fatigue down to the brink of a perpendicular precipice about 100 feet directly over the town in which we were to stop Here some caution was required to avoid the serious accident of being landed in our post house sooner than we wished, but at last after a descent of two hours and a half in all, we safely reached the bottom

Koylisar, the town which we had found is 12 hours from Kotaly Its name, which as explained to us, is a contraction of *gokly hisar* and means heavenly fortress is derived from an old fortress that towers almost in the heavens above it It consists of 400 or 500 Turkish houses, all of which are hid among gardens of fruit trees We had been told that we should find fruit here as plenty as in Amasia but it proved to be only a proverbial saving to express extreme fertility No species of fruit was yet ripe

June 6 As we started this morning Mohammed informed us upon the authority of a tartar who had passed in the night five days from Constantinople, that an embassador from our country had just been received with great honor at the capital, and added as if it were news that would give us great pleasure, that the Sultán had granted us a king From previous information we understood that our commissioners had finally signed the treaty A few such wars as the last with Russia would do away the old idea of which this language is a relic, and which is even now credited in many parts of Turkey, that every sovereign of Europe receives his crown from the Sultan

For more than seven hours, we traced the course of the river up the profound ravine already described The confined air and concentrated rays of the sun, made us suffer again the heat of Amasia Dark and threatening precipices overhanging us seemed repeatedly, in the sudden turns of the valley to close up every avenue and prevent, by an adamantine barrier elevated to the clouds, the possibility of egress Sometimes our path lay along the narrow but level margin of the river which was occasionally cultivated with cotton At others projecting buttresses of the moun tain either crowded us quite into the water or forced us to climb narrow and undefended foot paths along their faces from forty to sixty feet above it In one of these perilous passages a baggage horse stumbled and fell A projecting rock just at that point providentially saved him but in at tempting to rise he threw from his back the baggage of our Armenian attendant and it was immediately hurried out of sight in the eddies of the swollen stream Issuing at length from this frightful pass we left the river to the right and came upon an open country covered with a green sward and surrounded by mountains white with snow Our horses seemed to enjoy the change almost as much as ourselves and passing rapidly over the hills we soon reached Kara hisar distant from Koylisar 12 hours

Kara hisar is situated on high ground at the foot of a dark precipitous rock crowned with a ruined fortress In the town according to one informant there are 1000 Turkish 550 Armenian and 30 Greek houses, and in a village an hour distant 500 Armenian and 70 Turkish houses but another reversed the number of Turkish and Armenian houses in town declared that there were no Greeks and made the village consist of 500 Armenian and 50 Greek houses They all both houses and inhabitants seemed miserably poor and many of the streets were fill ed with dunghills The *ser-asker* (generalissimo) of the eastern division of the Turkish army, who retreated hither before the Russians was now living upon the inhabitants, and we could hardly find enough in the market for a scanty dinner Much to our surprise however when the *siny* (a large copper tray used in Turkey for a table,) was brought in, instead of the frugal articles we had given to be cooked, it was loaded with some of the best dishes of Turkey. Our wonder was increased, by learning that our landlord would receive no pay for it, but had provided it as an act of gratuitous hospitality! To suspect a sinister motive for such kindness seems ungrateful, but really we were quite as much surprised that a tavern-keeper should give us a meal gratis in Turkey, as we should have been in America; and I strongly suspect that our tartar, thinking we should more easily swallow, by the help of a good dinner the advice he had persuaded our host to give us about going to Trebizond, paid him for it. According to his contract, he was to take us to Erzroom by way of that place which would not only lengthen the journey six or seven days, but be inconsistent with his engagements to the others that were under his convoy. He had been for several days dwelling upon the dangers and difficulties of the road, and now the menziljy joined with him in painting them in the strongest language. We finally concluded to give up the excursion, not through apprehension of danger but because we were too fatigued to think of adding 200 miles to our journey, and were anxious to reach Erzroom before the Russians should leave.

There is a tolerably good road from here to the Black sea, to the west of Trebizond of only 24 hours. A post road also branches off here for Diarbekr. It leads by Arabkir and Maaden, and is 8 stages, averaging each 12 hours. In winter it is not unsafe.

June 7. From Kara-hisár we descended into a warm valley, occupied with gardens and fruit trees, and watered by a small tributary of the river of Niksár. A long ascent beyond showed us, even thus early, that our horses would not endure a continued ride of sixteen hours that intervened between the next post-house, and our tartar was dis-

suaded only by our Armenian companions from remedying
the defect, by selecting some fresh ones from a drove that
was passing   Though allowed to recruit an hour or two
at mid-day in a tract of meadow land, they were unable to
carry us through and obliged us to spend the night in the
deserted derbend of Fundukly-bel, which we reached at
7 P M   Not expecting to sleep out we had taken only
provisions enough in the morning for a lunch at noon, and
those we shared with our companions who had even started
without their breakfast   Finding no village on the road,
our tartar forcibly seized a lamb from a flock that we
passed in the afternoon, but relinquished it at the request
of the company protesting however that he had a right
to it, as such was the custom of the country   At last one
of the surijies procured some bread and milk from a village
three or four miles distant and stayed our hunger   The
spot, we afterwards learned is a haunt for robbers and a
man was slain by them in the vicinity about the time we
passed   But a kind Providence caused us to sleep in safety —This was the limit of the advance of the Russians to
the west

June 8 We started at 2 A M and chilled and benumbed
with the cold proceeded on to Einek, which we reached
at half past 5 having made yesterday and this morning only 16 hours   With the surrounding villages it forms a *sanják* (district) of the pashalik of Erzroom called Sheheran
Together they contain about 300 houses all of which are
Turkish, with the exception of some eight or ten inhabited
by Greeks   Here and onward in our journey, a marked
improvement appeared in the civility and respectfulness of
the Turkish population, notwithstanding their former repu
tation for rudeness   Doubtless the sword of the Russians
had taught them good manners.   We readily believed them
that they have snow six months in the year, for the thermometer this morning stood at 41° 30′, and no trees for

miles around nor aught else appeared, to break the chilling
influence of vast fields of eternal snow that lay in full view
upon the Giaoor-dagh, in the immediate vicinity on the
north   For a more effectual defence from the frost their
houses were sunk under ground   It was our first introduction to this mode of architecture and we afterwards hardly
found any other   Sheheran is the last place mentioned in
the journal of Martyn   How wearisome and painful must
have been his journey of 170 miles over the mountains and
valleys that intervene between here and Tokat where his
earthly toils ceased [1]

From this place a post road branches off for Trebizond
and there are but two stages to that city one of 12 hours to
Gumish khaneh and the other from thence of 24 hours
It was also from this vicinity we were told that the Rus
sians penetrated through the mountains even to the boun
daries of the pashalik of Trebizond within 18 miles of the
sea.   These mountains are a branch of mount Caucasus
They first separate Mingreli from Georgia   in the pashalik
of Akhaltsikhe they are called Childir-dagh and give name
to one of its sanjaks , then passing between Erzroom and
the southeastern corner of the Black sea, they receive in
this vicinity the name of Giaoor-dagh   and extending west
ward, are finally named Janik-dagh to the northwest of
Kara hisar

From hence the post establishment was completely broken up by the Russian invasion   In every post town in
Turkey a number of horses belonging to an individual or
a company are attached to the post house, and at the command
of any one who brings an order from government, and pays
for them   The established price when we went was thirty paras and when we returned, one piastre the hour
The menziljy has under him a number of surijies who act
as hostlers and whenever horses are taken on a journey
accompany them to the next post to bring them back

Their name, which signifies a *puller*, is derived from the fact that a part of their business is to lead loaded horses. When the horses of the post are not sufficient, the traveller's *menzil-emry*, as the order for horses is called obliges the authorities of the place to press into his service the horses of the inhabitants for the same price As this system provides only for travelling, and not for the transportation of letters, it is imperfect, without the separate establishment of tartars, who are the official couriers Some of them are attached to every pasha, and whoever will pay them what they demand can employ them as an express They are officers of considerable rank, and travellers by post generally take one to make themselves respected and to expedite their journey But here Ottoman establishments had ceased the post-houses were stripped of their horses, the menzil-emry ceased to be regarded and the tartar himself was no longer feared By fair words and promises however, he succeeded in getting horses enough at last, and we proceeded.

A gradual descent conducted us from the high undulating ground of Sheheran into a broad and open plain where we found our post-house in the little village of Germery at the end of a stage of 6 hours. It is on a stream of some size, whose waters pass by Niksar, and which is probably the main branch of the river that bears that name A number of villages appeared upon the plain and we were assured that there are 60 in the sanjak containing in all not far from 1000 houses none of which are inhabited by rayáhs. The sanjak takes the name of Chiftlik, from the chief town about half an hour distant, which is called Kerkid-chiftlik or Bash-chiftlik, or simply Chiftlik

June 9 Immediately after starting we passed through the Chiftlik Instead of a simple villa, as its name imports it is a market town of some size Situated on a low level of extreme fertility not far from the river, it is sur

rounded with gardens, and its houses, built of stone stand
out fair above the ground Passing out of the plain along
the banks of the river, we followed it until the fifth hour
from Germery, and then left it coming down from a snowy
mountain at the south Turning to the left ourselves our
tartar stopped us at the entrance of a wooded ravine and
loaded our pistols, saying that there were four places between here and Erzroom dangerous for robbers the first of
which we were now entering We worked our way, however with no encounter other than the steepness of the ascent, to the top of a naked summit on which a snow drift
was still braving a summer s sun Here the mountain just
mentioned was near and in full view It is called Chi
mán-dagh (verdant mountain) All the way from Niksar
the same range had occasionally appeared just south of the
river Here the river takes its origin from its extreme
and most elevated part confirming what Strabo says of the
Lycus, that it rises in Armenia

On the other side of the mountain is Erzengan 12
hours from Gérmery It was an important town of an
cient Armenia proper situated on the western bank of the
Euphrates, at the confluence of the Kail with that river *
Now it is the capital of a sanjak of the same name, belong
ing to the pashalık of Erzroom The pasha of Erzroom fled
thither when the Russsrans took his capital and was still
there when we passed having never been disturbed by the
enemy

In the little green valleys below us were a few black
tents of Kurds, pasturing their flocks and herds While
hardly a traveller has preceded us without encountering
Turkmans or Kurds throughout Asia Minor these at the
very extremity of that country are almost the first nomads
of any kind we have seen encamped Descending into one
of these valleys, we stopped an hour, and dined upon a

* St Martin vol 1 p 71
10 *

roasted lamb, in the open air, under a shower of rain As
we advanced the valley opened into a broad plain covered
with luxuriant pasturage, except that here and there a few
villagers were ploughing small fields of grain In the midst
of it, about eight hours from Germery the large village of
Lori, the only one we saw, appeared upon it at some distance to the left and we crossed a considerable stream
running in that direction It passes Baiboort, and emp-
ties into the Black sea, and is without doubt, the main
branch of the Jorokh So that the ridge which we had
just crossed separates the waters of the Iris and the Akampsis, and we may now consider ourselves within the boun
dary of Armenia proper The scenery around is thor
oughly Armenian a mixture of fertility and bleakness
plains and hills clothed alike with the greenest sward but
not a tree or a shrub to adorn them A green ridge
called Otluk bely with now and then a snow drift by the
side of our path succeeded Here directly in the road
and by the side of it were several mineral springs issuing
large quantities of gas and depositing much yellow stony
matter One of them in the valley of a little tributary of
the Euphrates that rises here had apparently raised a
mound by its deposits nearly twenty five feet in height
The water of all was without scent and tasted much like
the celebrated waters of Saratoga

We stopped at Kara koolák 12 hours from Germery
At the first village in Armenia, it was very appropriate to
be first introduced to almost the only accommodations the
traveller finds in that country We slept in a stable Ka
ra koolak contains 40 or 50 houses some 8 or 10 of which
are inhabited by Armenians In the neighboring villages
the Armenians are numerous and in some there are no
Turks We had left to-day the waters of the Iris crossed those of the Jorokh, and come upon those of the Eu
phrates for a small stream runs by this place on its way
to the latter river

June 10 Two hours after starting we left the valley of Kara koolak, and ascended a naked ridge, that afforded us a bleak and wintry prospect down upon an extensive mass of dark snowy mountains to the southeast They were on the farther side of the Euphrates, in the district of Terjan, an ancient canton of Armenia and now a sanjak of the pashalik of Erzroom   Its capital, we were told is Keghe, and it contains two or three thousand Armenian families The cold wind that whistled by us from that direction hastened our descent and at the end of the fourth hour, we crossed a ravine called Sheitan deresy (Devil's dell) Its appearance and reputation are almost equal to its name   At the crossing point three profound ravines converge and unite in one   Their sudden windings and high banks of shelving craggy rocks would conceal an army in ambush till you were in its midst   And the difficulty of the path which winds over rocks and loose stones up an almost perpendicular ascent on either side would cut off the possibility of escape   It is the third of the four dangerous passes of which our tartar had warned us   and as proof that his fears were not groundless he pointed to his thumbless hand which had been maimed here fighting with robbers   We shall not be charged with unusual weak ness of nerves if we confess that we stopped but a moment to collect some curious minerals that lay in the path and took but a hasty draught of the limpid stream that runs through its bottom

We immediately came upon the northern branch of the Euphrates and after riding two or three hours along its northern bank, stopped in a small meadow to bait our fatigued horses in the grass   This river was considered the proper Euphrates by the Greek and Roman writers, but the Armenians give that honor to the Murád-chai *
It is here enclosed by uninteresting mountains, with only a

* St Martin vol 1   p 42

few stinted cedars to cover their barren rocks Not an inhabited house appears near it for more than thirty miles, and occasional tombs of travellers, one or two of whom were tartars that have been murdered by robbers excite other emotions than one would wish to indulge when first coming upon so celebrated a river While we were lounging under the trees of our meadow a thunder storm passed over us and by its tremendous peals echoing from mountain to mountain, added a terrible majesty to the already gloomy scene The delay did not restore sufficient strength to our horses to enable them to carry us through our stage of 16 hours to Ash kulaah While still four hours from it we found that they could proceed no farther Night was near it was pouring torrents of rain we had not seen an inhabi ted house since we started in the morning and did not know that there was one nearer than the post-house Provi dentially a peasant informed us that we should find a vil lage a little off the road to the left. By transferring our loads to the strongest horses and leading the weakest we succeeded in reaching it before night

Our village consisted of ten or twelve Turkish houses Its name I did not record, but I retain a most distinct im-pression of our lodgings. It was concluded that we should be more comfortable in the house of an old gentleman and lady than in the stable where the rest of our company lodged A description of it will give you an idea of the under-ground houses of Armenia in general, except that this was one of the smallest and poorest You have only to increase the number and size of the rooms and you have a picture of the best, whether Turkish or Armenian It was formed by digging into the side of a hill so as com pletely to bury in it three of the walls, and leave only enough of the fourth exposed in front to admit of a door way Upon the terrace was thrown a mound of dirt that restored the hill almost to its original shape, and gave a

front view resembling the burrow of some animal Its
walls were of rough round stones, its terrace was of un-
hewn branches of trees, blackened by being intentionally
burnt to preserve them or incidentally smoked by the
daily fire, and its floor was the naked ground It consisted of but one room eighteen or twenty feet square, around
which were scattered a variety of kitchen and dairy furniture By the side of a post was a cheese pressing between
two stones A bag of yoghoort was suspended from a
straggling stick that contributed to form the terrace. In
another part hung a cylindrical churn some six feet long
In the centre a hole in the ground did when heated, the
the service of an oven In a corner stood two calves Our
aged host having built a fire, and spread for us carpets and
cushions straightened himself and ejaculated, *la illah illa
Allah, Mohammed resool Allah,* (there is no god but God,
Mohammed is the apostle of God) in a tone that indicated
some feeling of the vanity of the world He left his house
and all its stores entirely to us for the night and thankful
even for such lodgings we slept soundly

June 11 In what way were we to proceed ? We had
been able to procure only a few fresh horses at Germery,
and at Kara koolak none, most of those which brought us
here had come from Sheheran They gave out yesterday,
and one died on the road so that we were obliged to dis-
miss them In this village there were none We resorted to the only expedient that offered and took carts Not
the large well finished ox-carts of the United States. They
would have been chariots The body of these was a slight
railing upon timbers attached to each other in the form of an
acute triangle with the base behind and the apex at the
yoke The wheels were small and of solid planks, attached firmly to an axletree which turned with them The
yoke was a straight stick, and instead of bows it had for
each ox two sticks passing through it, and tied together

under the neck by a string   A twisted cord of raw hide answered for a chain   In five such vehicles we stowed our baggage and ourselves, and started   Our old host owned the one we occupied and fortunately he took his wife along as an aid , for the little beasts that drew us were so ill trained, that both of them by going before and beating them and holding back could hardly prevent our being hurried headlong down the hills   There being no regular road, a cart would occasionally lose its equilibrium and the body only slightly attached to the axletree be sent with its contents into the mud

In order to change cattle often we went from village to village at a distance from the public road and thus saw more of the people They seemed simple and well meaning uniformly treated us with civility and respect, and exhibited none of the haughtiness of the Turk of Asia Minor   We could not resist the impression however that they were indolent , and they were according to their own confession ignorant   Only the mollah and one or two others in each village could read   Their houses were like that already described, except that many were larger   Instead of being admitted into the family room however we were uniformly showed into the stable   I will describe one of them, and you must always imagine without being told when we stop in a village hereafter that our lodging place is like it   It is under ground like the houses and perhaps connected by a door to the family room of its owner In one corner is a chimney, and before it is a square enclosure separated from the rest of the stable by a low railing and perhaps raised a step or two above it   Through the middle of this space from the chimney to the entrance in front an alley or passage of the width of the hearth and defined by two parallel sticks laid upon the ground, separates it into two long divisions of the width of a bed   In these hay or a mat, or a carpet, or perchance a matress, is spread upon the ground for the accommodation of the occupants The terrace is here raised above that of the rest of the stable in the form of an arch, by means of hewn timbers and a hole in it in front of the fire place from four to eight inches square, admits the only light that finds its way into the stable Such is the better sort of these lodgings in the poorer one or another of the circumstances, which distinguish the corner of the traveller from the accommodations of his beast is wanting while in the very best the division between them is so complete as to make distinct rooms At this season the cattle being at grass they were empty and cleared of dung so that we had no right to complain of their odor or filth

Our tartar was now completely out of his element His lash had little effect to quicken the pace of our dull beasts , and the peasant under the wing of Russian rule, was not quite so regardful of his office and his menzil emry, as the menziljies and surijies of Asia Minor In this predicament he would fain have induced us to assume a fictitious authority to expedite our progress He had on the road spread every variety of report respecting our object in travelling that entered his imagination but his favorite one to which the number of our party gave plausibility was that we were *élchies* (embassadors) going to make the Russians evacuate Erzroom To prohibit such falsehoods was in vain for his tongue was lawless and we could not always counteract their effects In Amasia our false and unasumed dignity actually without our knowledge protected an Armenian of the company from the charges of a tax gatherer We had hardly dismounted in Tokat before two Armenians approached us with great reverence and kissing our hands begged the interposition of our diplomatic authority with the governor, to relieve them from the capitation tax Encountering near Kara-hisar a party of Kurds to whose

national predatory habits Russian authority was peculiarly
obnoxious Mohammed announced our pretended object,
and ordered them to pray for our success, and then laughed
at the old robbers, as they raised their hands and heartily
entreated that our journey might be prosperous But it
was now no longer a jest. He seriously told us that his
authority had ceased, and that it belonged to us in the character he had given us to force the people by threats and
the lash to do as we wished We, of course, could not
countenance the imposition or the injustice, but were
amused to find the face of things so changed by recent
events, that in the heart of Turkey, we as Europeans had
more authority over Turks themselves, than one of their
own tartars.

We passed four villages during the day averaging 50 or
60 houses each, one of which was inhabited by Armenians,
and at 12 o clock at night, forded a broad swollen stream
that entered the bodies of our carts On its farther bank
we stopped at the village of Erganmazar Besides 20 Tur
kish houses, it contained 40 inhabited by Armenians, who
had one church and one priest but no school The villages in
the vicinity were also without schools a few boys we were
told, are taught by the priests in the winter but in the summer forget what they have learned —The departure of the
Armenians for Georgia engrossed the conversation of
every body yesterday and to-day The Russians wherever they have been have taken a census of the christian
population, and now are carrying the greater part along
with them into their own territories. The Armenians of
this and a neighboring village decided to go while we were
here, being unwilling, as they said to be left behind alone
and having some apprehension of revenge from the Turks,
after the Russians should have gone.

June 12 We entered immediately after starting, upon
the western extremity of the plain of Erzroom Its sur-

face was here undulating and soil dry, and the uncertain ty of war and the presence of a hostile army together with the removal of the Armenians having discouraged agriculture it was almost entirely uncultivated Only here and there a small field appeared sown with wheat or barley, which was even now but just above the ground The mountains around were with the exception of frequent stripes of snow some of which reached almost down to the plain green with grass to their very summits but being destitute entirely of tree or shrub their aspect had no charms for us The plain too was equally without trees not a garden was to be seen and built as the villages were under ground very few of them appeared

We changed cattle and dined at a moslem village near the Euphrates and noticed the process of preparing the fuel of this woodless region In the villages of yesterday the cow dung was merely thrown from the stables and by heaps and mire rendered the streets almost impassable Here it was spread upon the dry ground and stamped hard in a layer three or four inches deep Being left in this state until it becomes thoroughly dried in the sun it is then cut into cakes of a convenient size and is fit for the fire This with the exception of a few districts where there are trees is the fuel of all these cold and wintry regions With it ovens are heated and food is cooked and a pipe lighted with ignited cow-dung relishes as well to a native as if it derived its fire from the purest coal

We found the villagers yesterday unwilling to fix any price to the food we ate and here our host absolutely refused to take any thing under the fair pretence that what he had given us was an act of hospitality intimating how ever that we might give his son some little memento of us if we chose Our Armenian attendant who generally settled our bills took him at his word and paid him nothing We all however soon understood this mode of dealing for we found hardly any other till we were again beyond the pashalık of Erzroom on our return to Constantinople By it your host would divest the entertainment of travellers of the servile appearance of a money making business, and, while he uses the language, would appropriate to himself the credit of the most generous hospitality In reality however, he intends his language as an appeal to your own generosity, and expects by it to obtain more money than if he presented a plain bill Ask him how much he charges and he is offended at the question, the idea of remuneration had not entered his head Give him less than he expects and he is astonished that such a man as he had taken you to be, should think of presenting so small a sum declares that he certainly is not the man to receive it, and lays it again at your feet

Three or four miles from the village we forded the Euphrates, where it was about 60 or 70 yards wide and so shallow as not to enter the bodies of our carts and just at sunset reached the village of Uluja   Here we first overtook the rear guard of the Russian army for their troops were now all assembled in the vicinity of Erzroom in preparation for their departure and hitherto we had not seen a Russian   As we came in sight of them, our tartar with scorn depicted in his face and pointing at a throng assembled around a dram-shop with music and dancing exclaimed 'there look at the Roos, polluted race!   An open dram-shop, and public drunkenness in the heart of Turkey! What an unhallowed invasion of the sober customs of the country! what a false and scandalous specimen of Christianity to be exhibited among its enemies! were the thoughts that passed through my mind   Still I could not but recognize the scene as genuinely European and I felt ashamed for the moment of my Frank blood How long shall the indulgences of the cup give us just occasion to blush before the followers of Mohammed ?

The victorious arms of Russia made the Turk and the rayah exchange ranks and it was amusing to see our tartar as he approached the first sentinel take off his armor and put it upon one of our Armenian companions So strong was his abhorrence of the invaders that he would have "persuaded us to sleep in the fields rather than seek for lodgings in the village To this however we would not consent and sent a man to make us known to the commanding officer and solicit a room In the mean time we examined the warm bath for which this place is celebrated It is simply an uncovered wall enclosing a reservoir from the bottom of which a copious fountain is constantly boiling up The water is salt and bitter and of the temperature of about 100° Our messenger returned with information that at the command of the officer the *ayan* (head man) of the village had prepared us lodgings

June 13 Ashamed to enter Erzroom in carts our party procured a few horses this morning and we reached the city in about two hours The distance from Ash kulaah where we ought to have exchanged horses last is 9 hours making 262 hours, or about 786 miles from Constantinople

LETTER IV

ERZROOM AND JOURNEY THENCE TO MEJENGERD

The Russian invasion—Description of Erzroom—Its Armenian inhabitants—
Their cemetery—School—Papal Armenians—Trade of Erzroom—A Khan
—Turkish account of the emigration of the Armenians—Character of the
Turks of Erzroom—Ignorance of America—The gumrukjy—A Turkish
breakfast—Medical practice—Climate—A missionary effort—Leave Erzroom—Alavár—Hassan kúlaah—Appearance of the emigrating Armenians—The Araxes and shepherd's bridge—Desolation caused by the emigration—Villages of Erzroom—Reasons assigned by the Armenians for their
departure—Our reception at Azab—Province of Pásin—Mejengerd

DEAR SIR

WE found Erzroom in the possession of the Russians,
and the headquarters of their army   The history of their
recent invasion I need not relate   Its extent we found
to be very considerable   No parts of this pashalik escaped except Erzengán already mentioned and Ispir with a
part of Tortoom sanjaks in the mountains between Akhaltsikhe and Gumish khaneh   From Sheheran 130 miles
west of Erzroom, they marched to Gumish khaneh, and
thence pushed their advanced guard beyond the mountains,
within 18 miles of Trebizond   The pashaliks of Bayezeed
Kars, and Akhaltsikhe were entirely overrun   In fact,
every spot in Turkish Armenia to which our journey led us,
felt their ravages

We sought an early interview with General Pankratieff,
who commanded in the absence of marshal Paskevich   He
kindly warned us that the Turks were so enraged at the
departure of the Armenians, as to render it unsafe for any
European to remain after his troops should depart, which

would be on the third day, and advised us to leave with them. We ventured, however to confide in our own judgment, that a thorough chastisement rarely fails of humbling instead of irritating a Turk, and were not alarmed by his opinion A Turkish officer, who sought our acquaintance, also expressed great astonishment at it and offered us a guard and a room in his own house, if we had any apprehension from the rabble The emigration of the Armenians, however, in another way hastened our departure, by leaving us no inducement to remain So unsettled in fact was the city, that to obtain much accurate information, was almost impossible Still we did not leave till five days after the Russians were gone and most of our observations were made when their absence had left the city and us unembarrassed

Erzroom is reputed to be the largest city and the bulwark of the Armenian possessions of Turkey It is the capital of a pashalik, which is hardly exceeded in extent by any in the empire and is the residence of a pasha who bears the title of ser-asker Besides Erzroom, he commands also according to the latest arrangement the pashas of Bayezeed and Gumish khaneh who have only the rank of two tails, and the former pashalik of Kars which, since the war is governed by only a mutsellim It is situated near the foot of a mountain on the southeastern side of the plain to which it gives its name, and at nearly equal distances from its eastern and western extremities. The plain, as seen from the city, appears of great extent and is in reality not far from 40 miles long Its surface towards the west is undulating and dry but at the opposite extremity is lower, and occupied in part by marshes, which in the spring are frequented by great numbers of wild geese and ducks. Here the river Euphrates takes its rise, and running through the whole length of the plain, passes four or five miles north of the city

11 *

The city was founded by a Grecian general, about A D 415, and named by him Theodosiopolis after Theodosius the Second his master It was the strongest in the Armenian possessions of the empire The Armenians called it Garin after the ancient canton of High Armenia in which it was situated Its present name appears to be of Arabic origin, and was borrowed from the great city of Ardzen, which stood not far to the east. As there was another Ardzen in their own section of Armenia, the Saracens distinguished this, which for a long time belonged to the Greeks by the name of *Arzen-el Room,* Ardzen of the Greeks When Ardzen was destroyed with such slaughter by the Seljookians, its surviving inhabitants, its trade and its name were transferred to this place Hence by contraction we have the current name of Erzroom, written by the Armenians Arzroom *

Only the citadel which occupies a low eminence within the city is now fortified A trench and two walls once surrounded it , but the inner wall only is now entire It is solidly built of stone and does not suffer in comparison with Turkish fortresses in general Besides the bazars the principal mosks, and many private dwelling houses, it formerly enclosed the palace of the pasha but that extensive building was demolished by the Russians The houses being built of dark stone and generally of one story have a cheerless and diminutive appearance A green sward has grown over the terraces of dirt by which instead of roofs they are all covered, and gives them when viewed from an eminence above almost as much the aspect of a meadow as of a city Except now and then a poplar the environs are as destitute of trees as are the mountains and the plains around and hardly a garden adorns them

The population of Erzroom, before the severe ravages of

---

* St Mart vol 1 p 66 Moses Choren L 3 c 59 Abulfeda and Abulpharagius as quoted in the geographical index of the Life of Saladin

the plague a few years ago, was estimated at 100,000 At the time of the Russian invasion it contained we were told upon the authority of the collector of taxes at our second visit, 11 733 Turkish and 4 645 Christian houses making a population of about 80 000 souls Of the Christian inhabitants 50 houses were Greeks and 645 papal Armenians, leaving 3,950 houses or about 19 000 souls, belonging to the proper Armenian church

Nearly all the christian population had left before we arrived, and the city was so unsettled that I can do little more than give you a brief account of it as it was, reserving a description of its present state till our return The Armenians were under the spiritual government of a bishop, whose diocese embraced the whole pashalik His previous departure prevented our seeing him but we received from others an interesting account of his character He had a seminary for the education of candidates for the ministry, and would ordain none who had not enjoyed its advantages It was probably small and the studies not of a high order, but the attempt however humble, was of the highest importance We had no apportunity of personal observation, as recent events had destroyed it In all our inquiries no other school of any kind designed specially for the education of the Armenian clergy has come to our knowledge Though the Armenians were so numerous, and their city the largest in Armenia, it is a curious fact that they had but two churches. One of them was very small, and the other so irregular, dark and mean, as to resemble a stable almost as much as an edifice for divine worship The priests, however were sufficiently numerous, they amounted to 32 Not far from the city are four Armenian convents each of which was inhabited by three or four vartabéds, and had funds enough for its support, but all of them are now deserted

In the extensive cemetery of the largest church, we first

observed specimens of the singular monuments which distinguish most of the old burial places throughout Armenia. They are of stone, rudely carved in the form of a ram. The Armenians generally even in Smyrna and Constantinople are fond of engraving upon their tomb-stones symbols of the profession or trade of the deceased. A plough shows that he was a husbandman a pair of shears that he was a tailor, an anvil and hammer indicate a blacksmith, and a hammer, knife and the sole of a shoe are the insignia of a shoemaker. Upon these there was a curious addition to such hieroglyphics. Most of them were marked with a table, a bottle and a cup, and on one was a fiddle added to the group. I know not the design either of the shape of the monument or of these highly incongruous symbols, but probably in a pastoral country the one may have been as indicative of rank as a mounted horseman among a warlike people and the other may be intended to tell posterity merely that the dust beneath once possessed in abundance the good things of this life. They were evidently ancient, and we searched for inscriptions to determine by what nation they were erected. There were letters on only one, and they belonged to the Armenian alphabet. Noticing the ground under the belly of another worn smooth we inquired the reason, and were told, that if a child lives to a certain age without beginning to talk it is passed between the legs of this monumental ram and his tongue is loosed.

Owing to the patronage of the bishop perhaps, the Armenian grammar school of Erzroom was unusually large and flourishing. Its principal was a layman who had 5 or 6 assistants, and it contained 500 or 600 scholars, divided into different departments and studying all the common branches up to grammar and logic. To obtain a correct estimate of the number of persons in so large a city population that can read is extremely difficult. It was stated to us as high as one half of the males, but, although the Armenians of Erzroom were doubtless more intelligent than those of any other part of Turkish Armenia this proportion is evidently too large We did not learn that the Armenian females of the city were ever blessed with a school, yet some of them, we were assured, could read

In looking at the present state of the *papal Armenians* of these regions it is important not to lose sight of the former Jesuit missions to which they owe their existence as a sect Erzroom was the headquarters of the Jesuits for Turkish Armenia, and was selected not only for its size but because its commerce drew thither persons of other and distant nations who might also feel their influence Through the agency of the French embassador they were furnished with strong fermans of protection and took up their residence there in A D 1688 The Armenian bishop himself was among their first converts But soon other Armenian ecclesiastics raised a persecution, in which one of the Jesuits was put in irons, the rest were banished and many of their converts heavily fined The embassador s influence restored them to the field of their labors, and such success attended them, that early in the last century they were obliged to divide their mission into two branches One bearing the name of St Gregory the Illuminator, embraced Torzon (Tortoom?) Hassan-kulaah Kars, Bayezeed, Arabkice (Arabkir?) and 40 villages The other, named after St. Ignatius embraced Ispir Baiboort Akhaltsikhe, Trebizond, Gumish-khaneh, and 27 villages Each town contained more than 1500 papists * The number of papal Armenians in Erzroom, when it capitulated to the Russians has been already stated at 645 houses Two other informants estimated them at 400 and an Armenian bishop at only 200 or 300 houses They had no church their baptisms burial services, and most of their marriages were performed by the Armenian clergy ; and in apportioning taxes to the dif

* Letters Ed et Cur vol 3 p 450

ferent sects the government always included them among the Armenians Their priests were banished at the time of the persecution of the papal Armenians in Constantinople In the villages near Erzroom their number was small, a few were scattered here and there

The Greeks were all gone, and we heard little of them except that they were about 50 houses in number, and had one church —The city had no Jewish inhabitants

Erzroom was once the thoroughfare of most of the over-land commerce between Europe and the East, which was not destroyed by the discovery of the passage around the cape of Good Hope Recently it has been diminished by a variety of causes and the freedom of trade granted by the Russian emperor to Georgia, within the last ten years, has probably diverted a part of it into that channel Still the amount of goods that now pass through Erzroom annually is not small From the East are brought the shawls of Kashmeer and Persia silk cotton tobacco, rice, indigo madder and a variety of drugs, and from the West broadcloths chintses, shawls and cutlery Little is seen of them, however except at the custom-house and in the khans We solicited a list of the prices current from the first mercantile character in the place and were assured, that it would be worth little as almost every bale of goods passes unopened, and the articles bought and sold here are of small value The same was true in the days of Tournefort, who was here when commerce was most flourishing, for he says, a patient might die for the want of a dose of rhubarb, although there were bales of it in the city The appearance of the place accords with this state of trade Now, indeed, the emigration of the Christians who were its mechanics and tradesmen had almost entirely stopped all local business The hammer of the copper-smith whose trade was once a leading manufacture was silent, and a solitary Turkish merchant, here and there, sat melancholy

and silent in whole streets of shops closed and deserted
But the limited extent and meanness of its bazars show
that its retail business could never have been large,
while, to meet the wants of the carrying trade, its custom
house is an extensive establishment and it has 36 khans
many of which are large and of a solid structure

Khans in Turkey are the same as caraván-seráis in Persia, and are buildings peculiarly adapted to the convenience
of an over-land commerce, furnishing magazines for the
goods lodgings for the merchants or whoever act as the
supercargoes and stables for the horses and muleteers,
of a caravan They are generally quadrangular structures,
consisting of a series of rooms that surround an uncovered
court upon which they open and having in the back part
extensive stables In the rooms the merchants stow their
goods and themselves, the muleteers with their horses en-
camp under the open air in the court, or retire to the sta
ble as they choose, and the arched gate way, by which
alone the court and from it the rooms, can be entered,
being closed at night, all are as safe as in a prison They
are the only taverns which a Turkish city affords and ap-
prehending that in the present disturbed state of the place
private lodgings could not be easily procured we took up
our abode in one of them It was substantially built of
stone, and like the others in Erzroom had its court covered
by a terrace as a defence from the rains and snows of this
stormy climate It had its *khanyy* (landlord) with his *kakhia* (majordomo) a *kahwyy* (coffee maker), with his coffee
room a sensible though a Turkish substitute for a bar
room with its keeper, and an *oda-bashy* (chamberlain) to
attend as a general servant to the commands of all the inmates Our room was entirely unfurnished and being
lighted like many of the private houses by only a paper
sky light in the terrace was so dark that we could with
difficulty read or write Food is never furnished in these

establishments, and we hired ours cooked abroad and brought to us Coffee, however, was always to be had at a moment s warning and it being etiquette to give all visitors a cup, our coffeebill ran up fast At the end of a week we found no less than 98 cups charged to us

The Turks seemed deeply to regret the loss of their Armenian neighbors and declared that their city was ruined reflecting doubtless, not only that christian industry and enterprise had brought much trade and money to the place, but that they should no longer be relieved from the burden of taxes, by unequal exactions from the rayahs Feeling the reproof which their departure implied they roundly asserted that they had always lived together in great harmony Some said that the bishop, having extracted a large amount of money from the convents took this occasion to flee from the punishment he had reason to apprehend from the patriarch, and by persuasion and threats had induced his people to accompany him Others declared, that, while protected by the Russians they had conducted themselves haughtily worn armor cursed the Turks and their religion, and now fled to avoid the consequences they had reason to apprehend And others still, affirmed that the Russians had frightened and forced them away Many we were assured left debts unpaid , and one Turk a tartar, applied to us for advice to enable him to recover an amount of near ly 10,000 piastres He had paid it to an Armenian for a bill on a banker of Constantinople The bill was not ac cepted, and he returned to demand his money The Armenian was leaving for Georgia and would not attend to it The commanding general was applied to in vain and on our return to Erzroom, he called to inform us that he had preferred his claims in the court at Tiflis, without success The allegation of the Turks against the bishop were con firmed by the Armenians in so far that some declared that it was by his strong advice that they were induced to go. The fact that he had, under Russian protection, baptized some Mohammedans, an offence which the Turkish law could not overlook, was undoubtedly an urgent reason for him to retire with the Russians. The influence of the clergy generally must also have been on the same side, for they could hardly have failed to be aware that their power would be increased by Russian laws.

Travellers have given to the Turks of Erzroom the name of being among the worst in Turkey; the Armenians universally declared to us the same thing,, and the Persian agent affirmed that it was true. Our observation leads us to believe that they have improved under Russian chastisement. While their conquerors were present, the most perfect quietness prevailed. As soon as they were gone, and when it was expected that their vengeance would be felt by the Christians who remained, a crier passed through the streets proclaiming, by order of the pasha and Sultan, that if any should injure an Armenian, his goods would be confiscated, and his life be in danger. While we remained the pashá did not arrive, and no sentry was to be seen in the city, nor any appearance of a re-established government. And still, not a town of New England is more free from every species of disturbance than was Erzroom.

As to their deportment toward us instead of being insulted or injured, we were treated with decided attention. Indeed, we could not avoid the impression, that they were gratified, either at the confidence we reposed in them in remaining, or at seeing among them other Europeans besides the *Roos*. For no Franks were left in the city but ourselves, and any boy was physiognomist enough to perceive that we were not Russians. As we passed through the streets, many would say, ' they don't belong to them, ' (the Russians,) and some would affirm that we were English. When called to speak for ourselves, we found it difficult to make them comprehend who we were. As we

12

were the first that had travelled in any part of Turkey with fermáns as Americans, and probably the only Americans, who, under any name, had penetrated a hundred miles into the interior of Turkey eastward from Constantinople, it is hardly surprising that the Turks of Erzroom were ignorant of even the name of the western continent   They had heard of the existence of *Yengy Dunya* (the new world), but to tell them we came from thence, seemed rather to increase than diminish their embarrassment, and as soon as they learned what was our language, the discussion generally ended by their being satisfied that we were English   We took pains however here, and in almost every place that we visited, to make known, not only the name   but something of the character of our country

Among the Turks who sought our acquaintance, was the *gumrukgy*, or inspector of customs   Being accustomed to use some method of depletion in the spring as many of his countrymen are both for themselves and their horses, he informed us that he had heard of our success in the treatment of our tartar who had been sick, and wished that we would try our healing art upon himself   The presence of the Russians (who bear the blame of every thing that is wrong) had prevented him from taking his usual regimen the preceding spring and he now felt the need of a good vomit and purge   His application was accompanied with an invitation to breakfast   Thinking, from his plethoric appearance that only powerful medicines would affect him thoroughly and give him a good opinion of our medical skill, as his countrymen are apt to esteem medicines only in proportion to their strength we put a good dose of tartar-emetic and another of calomel and jalap in our pockets, and went to his house   It was a fair specimen of the better sort of Turkish dwellings   The room in which we were received, had no means of excluding the cold of this wintry climate, without excluding the light also   for it was

furnished with only shutters instead of glazed windows
Three or four feet of the side of the floor next the entrance
was depressed a step below the rest, for visitors to deposit
their shoes, and servants to stand and await the commands
of their master   The remainder was carpeted, and a sofa
or couch the only furniture, extended around the other three
sides   Its elevation from the floor was perhaps a foot, its
width was convenient for sitting or sleeping it was
spread with a continued matress, covered with figured vel
vet, and a series of cushions faced with the same material
lay upon it around against the wall   In the two corners
were placed square cushions making two seats more elevated
and honorable than the rest, upon one of which our host
seated himself and requested one of us to occupy the other

After the usual preliminary of pipes and coffee a ewer of
water and basin were brought for washing our hands as a
preparation for breakfast   The table was a copper tray
three or four feet in diameter set upon a stool perhaps a
foot in height and covered with a cloth   A servant with
a dextrous flirt of the hand, spread quite around it upon the
floor a long piece of calico which, as we seated ourselves,
we drew up into our laps for a common napkin   A separate napkin also, was thrown across the shoulder of each
and suffered to hang down diagonally over the breast   Our
breakfast consisted of eggs dried meat mushrooms cream,
yoghoort and honey, with bread filling every crevice upon
the table and scattered liberally under it   We were furnished with neither knives, nor forks nor plates, and only
a single wooden spoon for each helped us to such articles
of food as refused to be conveyed to the mouth in our fingers   Our host's emetic did its office so well as to render
him soon incapable of discharging the duties of hospitality,
and much to our surprise a beautiful little girl, eight or ten
years of age, his only child took her father s seat very
gracefully at the table, to invite us to partake of its abun
dant provisions   Pipes and coffee closed the entertainment,

and we took our leave ordering the good gumrukjy to follow his emetic with the calomel and jalap

Our patients multiplied rapidly. But we found a difficulty in learning enough of some of them to prescribe with much accuracy. One man came for medicine for his mother; but on a second application it becoming important that we should know her age we found that she was no older than himself and drew from a neighbor what his sense of propriety forbade him to tell that she was his wife. Another presented the case of his wife in plain language but he would not allow us to see her and was offended that we should think of feeling her pulse although her disease was exceedingly painful and evidently dangerous.

The climate of Erzroom is cold and stormy, as might be expected of a place elevated as has been supposed 7000 feet above the level of the sea. From the 13th to the 22d of June the thermometer ranged at midday in the open shade from 55° to 65°. We were hardly comfortable with common winter clothing it rained every day and the wind was cold and bleak. Indeed the mountain just above the town, in a shower of the 15th received an addition to its snow, and became completely white and at our second visit, a snow drift was lying in its streets the last of April. We could not learn that any species of fruit whatever is produced nearer than two or three days journey. Reflect now that fossil coal is unknown and no wood is used except pine, and that brought from a distance of three days' journey, and you will allow me to call the climate and the country inhospitable.

The only protestant missionary effort, so far as our information extends, that has ever been attempted at Erzroom, or in any part of Turkish Armenia, was made just before we arrived. The missionaries at Shoosha aware of the obstacles in the way of preaching the gospel to moslems under the Turkish government, determined to seize an opportunity of doing it, while the presence of a Russian army would afford them protection Mr Zaremba, therefore, taking a good quantity of the Scriptures in Turkish and Armenian, and a few for the Russians themselves, proceeded first to Tiflis, to make known his intentions to the governor   His excellency entered warmly into his project, and gave him letters to all the chief officers of the army, which secured him their favorable regards, and open and decided protection   His first visit was to Kars There were no more than a hundred Turks in the city, but in the house of the ayan, where he carried his books for sale, he met a room full of effendies and others   They examined the Bible and disputed, in a supercilious manner, proving themselves to be bigoted, and easily offended at having their faith questioned   He sold but one Turkish Bible, and that was on his return from Erzroom   At Bayezeed, also, he found but few moslems , and they were bigoted and inimical, and disposed to have but little to say to him   One Turk manifested some candor , but he sold no Turkish Scriptures.   At Erzroom, where there was a great number of Turks, he determined at first to say nothing, and only send his books for sale through the bazars and streets Prices were offered much below that which he had fixed, and were at first refused , but he afterwards sold at any price, and even gave gratis.   After seven or eight days, no more offers were made and the sale ceased   He then began to talk with the people wherever he had opportunity With a few encouraging exceptions they were easily incensed at any thing said against their religion, and not disposed to inquire   He heard of eight of his books being torn in pieces.   At last, after he had spoken for his passports to depart, the kády and mufty declared to the general, that so strong was the popular feeling against him if he should be killed they could not be responsible.   He still

12 *

made a parting call upon one of them, and in a religious argument before a room full of moslems boldly convicted him and them of ignorance of their own Koran in affirm ing that it contained a doctrine, which in fact it does not.

During the whole journey though he had the Scriptures in every language he was likely to meet he sold only to the amount of 17 ducats or about 40 dollars In Turkish, one Bible and 14 Testaments were sold, and 3 Bibles and 22 Testaments were given away This seems but a discourag ing report, and yet so strong is my impression of the fanatical and supercilious bigotry of the moslems of Turkey, that I am decidedly interested and encouraged by it The intolerant spirit of their religion and a thorough contempt for Christians make them so indignant at an opposing word and deprive them so completely of the least curiosity to read our sacred scriptures that I am gratified whenever they are made to hear the truth at all though it be but to gainsay and resist and if but one copy of the word of God is bought with the intention of reading it I am encourag ed The bread has been cast upon the waters and after many days it shall be found How delightful, too to see mes- sengers of peace at hand to avail themselves of even the openings made by war, to proclaim their glad tidings' Then is the wrath of man made to praise the Lord'

After a delay of several days for want of horses, in con sequence of the emigrating Armenians having taken al most every animal that could draw or carry a burden, we made up by taking a mule our number of five and left Erz- room for Kars on the 22nd of June Our direction was eastward along the foot of the mountain that rises behind the city and led us over naked and uncultivated hills, which connect it with another nearly parallel range on the north, and separate the sources of the Euphrates from the tributa ries of the Araxes From the highest point we had a view of the whole plain of Hassan-kulaah, which, at the end of

three hours, we entered   It is somewhat lower, more
level and fertile than the plain of Erzroom, but like it
is without trees and surrounded by woodless mountains
striped with snow   Grain is sowed upon it in October, and
reaped early in the succeeding August, and it is covered
with snow from the last of November to the last of March
A number of villages appear upon different parts of it   We
were overtaken by a party of five horsemen who armed
with guns pistols swords and long spears, and clothed with
a mixture of nearly all the costumes found among the retainers of a Russian army might have been taken for
robbers   They proved to be Armenians, commissioned by
the Russian general to bring up safely the rear of the emigrants that still lingered behind   They were in excellent
spirits and boasted of their feats in intimidating the Turks
who would retain the rayáhs, but we could not avoid the impression from their manner, that they were quite as likely
to intimidate the Armenians who would of their own accord remain   Keeping along the south side of the plain,
we stopped for the night at Alavár, a little village containing
6 Turkish and 16 Armenian houses, the latter of whom
commenced their departure just as we arrived

June 23   Starting at 7 A M we passed over to Hassan kulaah, a distance of one hour   Just at its gate, we
crossed by an arched stone bridge, a small river running
eastward toward the Aras   It is the Moorts of the Armenians *   On its southern bank is a warm bath, resembling that of Uluja and of the temperature of 105°   From
the rock around on both sides of the river, water and gas
bubble up at almost every step   The town is situated at
the foot of a rock, projecting from the mountain on the
north side of the plain and crowned with a fortress not
yet entirely in ruins, and being itself surrounded by a

* St Mart vol 1 p 39

wall, appears respectable at a distance   But we found many of its houses nearly all of which were under-ground cabins, broken in and deserted, in the bazar we could procure literally nothing, not even a piece of tinder   The 100 Armenian families which it formerly contained had gone, and the Turks had shut up their few shops, and were sitting as if to muse upon the desolation around them   It could hardly contain more than 400 or 500 houses   It is 6 hours distant from Erzroom

Seven or eight miles beyond, the plain narrows to a val ley that continues to follow the course of the river   Its whole length must be twenty miles and its average breadth five or six   This morning it was crowded with Armenian emigrants   If, in some respects, their departure hindered us from obtaining the information we wished in others it was favorable ¶ for we passed such numbers between Erz- room and the Georgian boundary, that it was as if the whole Christian peasantry of the country were exhibited in review before us.   These were from the villages on the plain of Erzroom   And deeply affecting it was to see the inhabitants of a whole province thus deserting the home of their fathers and bearing in all their appearance such ev ident marks of the oppression from which they were fleeing In the United States we should have taken almost every individual for a beggar   They were clothed in rags Their furniture consisted of a few dirty matresses cush- ions, coverlets and rugs a cradle, a churn, a pail or wood- en bottle, a few copper pans and kettles, and in some cases a small chest.   A few cattle and sheep accompanied them.   Mothers with infant children generally found a place in an empty cart   But in some cases, they were mounted upon a horse, a mule, or an ass, with the heads of their little ones projecting from baskets or bags upon either side of the animal, in others the tender charge was fastened alone upon the baggage in a cart, or upon the back of a beast, and not unfrequently the mother walked with it slung in a pouch upon her back   Most of the rest, men, women and children, were on foot, though the mire in some parts of the plain was deep   All had the same hardy sunburnt and coarse complexion   In none, not even in the females all of whom except the marriageable and newly married girls were unveiled, did we discover that fair and interesting countenance which distinguishes their countrymen in Smyrna and Constantinople   They were equally inferior too in form being lower in stature, and of a broader and coarser frame   Nearly all bore marks of a desponding spirit   What had brought upon them this extreme of penury?   Their country is hardly inferior to any in the world for the cultivation of grain and the raising of herds and flocks   and their sobriety and orderly conduct is acknowledged by all   It can be nothing else than the blighting influence of Mohammedan oppression that has caused them thus to wither away

Three hours from Hassan kulaah we passed the small village of Kopry-koy (Bridgeville) and reached the junction of the Moorts with the Aras, as the *Araxes* is now universally called   The principal stream is much longer and more rapid than its tributary and comes down from the mountainous region to the south, where we were told, it takes its rise at a place named Bin-gol (thousand lakes) in Khanoos a sanják of Erzroom.   A bridge is thrown over them at their junction which is a well built structure of hewed free-stone, resting upon seven unequal arches and so little decayed that it might easily be put in complete repair   It is called *choban-kopry* (shepherd bridge), from the fact, as tradition states that it was built by a wealthy shepherd   After thus expending his property for the public good he passed the remainder of his days as a hermit upon the top of a precipice that here hangs over the left bank of the river. There, his tomb, in a spot marked by a few solitary pines, is even now such an object of veneration to the neighboring peasants, that they often visit it to say their prayers

The road to Tebriz by Bayezeed and Khov, here separated from ours, and crossed the bridge to the right side of the river We continued along its left bank and at 3 P M reached the village at which we had intended to stop Its inhabitants had their goods already packed in carts for their departure The mud and dung were so deep that we could with difficulty walk from house to house Most of the terraces were broken in and would not defend us from the rain that was falling The only spot upon which we could have possibly slept was the ground of a stable and no food, not even a bit of bread could be obtained We were glad to be relieved from the necessity of taking up with such accommodations by learning of a place beyond not far from the road where some inhabitants were still remaining How many villages around were left like this, so dilapidated that the storms of a few winters will wash them even with the ground and leave not a trace of the people who once inhabited them ! By a similar process have the regions of Western Asia been desolated and the traces of thousands of its cities been erased, from the earliest wars and captivities of sacred history to the present time The river here flows through a broad tract of grazing land broken into swelling hills of a dry soil and has upon its banks but a narrow margin of alluvial Turning to the left among the hills we saw no more of it and thus escaped the Russian army which was encamped at Khorasán the next place on the direct road Azab was the village we were seeking and we reached it at 5 P M

The whole number of carts that we passed to-day was 260 We conversed with many as we went along and in the last company a man more respectably dressed than the others mounted on a horse and armed with a brace of pistols in his girdle rode up and entered into conversation

He showed himself at once to be a sensible man, and we at last discovered that he was the priest of a village near Erzroom He assured us there were no schools in the villages around that city, any farther than that the parish priest generally taught a sufficient number to read, to have the singers in the church which the Armenian service requires He once attempted to establish a more regular school in his own village but did not succeed Those who wished their children to be educated sent them to Erzroom In some villages of 15 or 20 houses not one could read, but in his which contained 50, there were 15 His statements express the result of what we learned from other sources, and to avoid repetition I gave them as such In a word the Armenian villagers of Erzroom were entirely without schools

I have already given you the reasons assigned by the Turks for the departure of the Armenians Curiosity would have prompted many inquiries of the emigrants themselves, but circumstances constrained us to the strictest caution Though more than once solicited by heads of villages for our advice we uniformly refused it, assigning as a reason our ignorance of the government and laws of Russia. Very many, whom we encountered on the road could give no other explanation of their emigration than that others were going and they followed the multitude Our friend the priest had more decided reasons They were fleeing he said from oppression Their taxes had been heavier than they could bear The Turks individually had maltreated them He had himself not unfrequently been obliged to entertain ten and fifteen horsemen, and endure their scoffs at himself and his religion The last two had made him hold a candle for them all night and otherwise treated him so shamefully, that he swore he would leave the country He was now conducting his family and his flock to Georgia, where they would at least be on a level with Russian citizens, and no longer hear their religion cursed. Others, whose feelings resembled the priest's, told us that they had no charge to bring against their sovereign, but Erzroom being distant from his capital, and inhabited by the worst people in the world, his orders were little regarded. They loved their country, and were ignorant of that to which they were going, but their oppressions had been great, and they feared they would be greater if they remained, for the expenses of the war would probably be drawn from them. Turkish travellers often used them shamefully, instead of paying their host for their food, they would take from him some article of value would curse his religion, and abuse his children.

Let me add a word of explanation to these complaints. All subjects of Turkey not Mohammedan, pay an annual *kharag* or capitation tax as the price of their head, it being the only condition upon which the Korán allows the toleration of their existence. Other taxes, also, are often so unequally apportioned that they bear the burden of them. And so universally venial and partial is justice that they are not unfrequently, on the merest pretence, stripped of every cent. Their money, in fact, commonly flows, through one channel or another, into the treasury of the government or the pockets of its officers, about as fast as they can earn it. Their name, *rayah*, literally means a flock. it is pastured for the sake of its fleece. A war generally increases their burdens, for they are made to pay for it. That any recent improvement in the Sultán's government would in this case benefit them no security was given which they could trust. The Turks of Erzroom resisted all innovations before the war, and now not even a bishop was sent from the capital to give assurance of future good treatment, as all seemed to expect. For they crowded around us at Erzroom to know if one was coming. The customary mode of entertaining travellers explains further

their complaints of personal ill treatment   The villages
of Turkish Armenia have no khans, or public houses of
any kind but the *kakhia*, as the assessor of the taxes,
and official and responsible head of a village is called,
quarters travellers upon private families   When the enter
tainer in these circumstances, is a despised Christian and
the guest a lordly Turk, abuse cannot but be frequent
The evidence of it has worked itself into the very dialect
of the country   Almost the only terms we heard used by
the Turks of Armenia for Christians Christian gentlemen,
and bishops, were *giaoor chorbajy*,* and *kara-bash*, meaning infidel soup-maker, and black head   and they seemed
to have become so common as no longer to be esteemed
contemptuous by either party

At Azab some reluctance was manifested to entertaining
us, but our muleteers soon procured us admission to a
house   On entering, we asked the owner if he could lodge
us and were answered coolly that the *bin-bashy* (colonel)
knew   Then looking at us and listening to our conversa
tion with each other a moment he declared that we were
not Russians, and it appeared that our men had endeavored to obtain for us a forced hospitality by announcing us as
officers of the army   We informed him that our language
was English, and his countenance immediately brightened
the house was at our disposal and whatever we wished
was cheerfully brought   No nation bears so good a character in Armenia as the English   A high idea is entertained of their neatness rank and liberality, and the stranger
can receive no higher compliment in the estimation of his
host, than to be called a real Englishman   It ought however, to be added, that hardly any other nation is personally known, except the Russians   The village contained 40

* I am aware that this was applied as an honorable title to a certain of
ficer of the janizaries but I do not believe the use of it here mentioned has
any connection with that

Armenian and two Turkish houses The former were to
leave the next day and were then breaking in their terraces for the timber that supported them The latter had
already joined their brethren in some other place

We passed the evening in conversation with the kakhia
and the following is the information we obtained from him,
and others, respecting this section of country The plain
of Hassan kulaah which we entered three hours from Erz
room on the 22d, is the commencement of the district of
Pásin Of course, the hills we had previously passed, separate the ancient provinces of High Armenia and Ararád,
for Pasen was the most westerly canton of the latter Pásin
is now divided into two sanjaks dependent upon Erzroom
and called Upper Pasin and Lower Pasin Hassan kulaah
is the capital of the former, and Khorasan of the latter
Khorasan lies on the Aras an hour from Azáb and is a
mere village containing 50 Armenian and 40 Turkish
houses In both sanjaks there were about 1000 Armenian
families of which 300 or 400 were in Lower Pasin The
Turks were much less numerous There were a few papal
Armenians in Hassan-kulaah and four other villages One
village also in Lower Pasin contained a few Greeks, but
they all emigrated There were no schools in the villages,
but a few children were taught by the priests ro read In
some there were no persons that could read but in Azáb
perhaps one reader might be found in half the houses No
women could read nearer than Erzroom The only crops
cultivated here are barley and wheat, and the kakhia assured us that they yield from six to ten fold

June 24 Our accommodations were not the best last
night. The corner of the stable we occupied was but im
perfectly defined, and we found a horse among us before
morning In similar circumstances we have at other
times been awaked by a calf gnawing at our saddles or
more to our discomfort, by a cow despatching the last morsel of

bread we had laid in store for our breakfast   Our visitor on this occasion, was fortunately expelled before he had trodden upon us or done any mischief, but a stable, filled as was ours with horses and cows at this season of the year could not be very fit either in the temperature or purity of its air for a sleeping room and we arose unrefreshed and feverish   The pure morning air was doubly exhilarating, and soon completely revived us   On the farther side of a hill just beyond Azab were 300 carts of emigrants just breaking up their night's encampment   They had no shel ter but the sky except that here and there a few had joined and tipping up four or five of their triangular carts around a semicircle, formed a shed resembling the vertical half of a cone   They must have lodged uncomfortably the last night, for so raw and showery had been the weather as to make us prefer a stable to the open air   We soon turned over the hills to the right toward Mejengerd, while they fol lowed a more level but longer road to Kars farther to the left where an additional number of at least 300 carts were in sight   The Russians were in motion upon the road from Khorasan to Mejengerd and as the whole Erzroom division of the army was on the march we hardly parted company with them again till we reached Kars   No cultivation ap peared to day nor indeed but very little yesterday after we left the plain of Hassan-kulaah

We stopped at Mejengerd   Two deep ravines, forming an acute angle and both shut in by precipitous ledges of rocks unite a little below the town   On the summit of the lofty tongue between them is a long and narrow rock, upon which stand the ruined walls of a fortress built of hewed stone   On the declivity just below, are three or four isolated rocks perhaps 20 feet square by 25 in height and appa- rently resting on the surface of the ground, each of which has been excavated, by the people of a former age, for an oratory or chapel with its altar and baptismal font   The town is at the bottom of the western ravine, and is a mere village of 25 houses 12 of which were Turks A few of the Armenians were papists but all of both sects had already left, and as the Russians were just arriving and encamping in the valley the Turks had carefully shut themselves in their houses   We found at last an empty room, in a deserted Cossack post-house furnished with a chair and table, articles of furniture which we had not seen this side of Constantinople except among the Russians at Erzroom. A Turkish neighbor, on learning that we were not Russians, readily supplied us with a bowl of milk and a loaf of bread   Such accommodations we were disposed to pronounce comfortable; and so long had we been obliged to write, seated upon the floor with our knee for a desk that an opportunity to sit up to a table seemed a great luxury, and tempted us to spend the evening in writing

LETTER V

PASHALIK AND CITY OF KARS

Soghánly-dagh—Battles in the late war—Sleep on a mountain—The plain of
Kars—Benkly Ahmed—Turkmáns—Greek and Armenian worship—Ar
menian fasts—Superstition respecting the cross—Tenure by which land is
held—Singular quarantine—Description of Kars—A venial Turk—Fur
ther facts respecting the emigration of the Armenians—The Armenians of
Kars—Doctrine and practice of the Armenian church respecting departed
spirits—Akhaltsikhe—Leave Kars—Jamishly—Reach the Arpa-chai

DEAR SIR

MEJENGERD is the last town in the pashalik of Erzroom
Between it and the pashalik of Kars, there is an unin
habited mountainous tract of 12 hours   We made half
of it on the 25th of June, the day after my last date
The ascent was difficult, but once upon the top we were
conducted through a succession of valleys beautiful for the
meadow-like luxuriance of the grass that clothed and the
variety of flowers that ornamented them   The declivities
of many of the hills and mountain summits too were covered
with woodlands and forests, some of which at no very distant period, had been completely prostrated by a tornado
It is from this mountain that wood is carried to Erzroom a
distance of more than 50 miles.   We observed none but pine

The highest ridge is two hours and a half from Me-
jengérd and when we reached it at 9 A M the mud
exhibited signs of having been slightly frozen in the night
It is called Soghanly-dagh (onion mountain), and is the
spot where marshal Paskevich encountered the Turkish
army which had fixed upon it as the only barrier to Erz

13 *

room His victory was an easy one, for he only made a feigned attack, while the body of his army turned them, by pursuing the more level rout, which has been already mentioned as the one taken by the Armenians with their carts The keys of Erzroom were laid at his feet without further resistance and the submission of the pashalik followed The Russians allow that the Turks gave them but two fair trials of their bravery One was at Akhaltsikhe which resisted till its fortifications were ruined, and the other at Baiboort, where a smart rencounter took place at the very close of the war Kars made a show of resistance but the citadel capitulated as soon as the defenceless part of the town was occupied, and its walls hardly exhibit the mark of a single shot On the whole the Persians have acquired a much higher character for spirit and courage, with the Russian army of the Caucasus than the Turks

A small river runs to the left just beyond the summit referred to and is probably the main branch of the river of Kars The Russians had established two military posts upon the mountain, but the second at which we would have stopped was already crowded with the officers of the army, and we were obliged to push on a little further and spread our carpets under a pine tree A neighboring grove furnished us with fuel for as large a fire as we wished and as the weather was calm we should have had no cause of complaint, had our bill of fare been a little fuller For tunately we had roasted a good lamb two days before, a part of which still lingered in our sufreh or we should have been absolutely compelled to fast For Mejengerd was too poor to furnish us with even a stock of bread and from this military post we could obtain but four little black loaves, too hard to yield to our organs of mastication

June 26 Our lodgings in the open air proved colder than we had anticipated, and we had to call in the aid of our pelisses, to obtain a comfortable degree of warmth

The thermometer stood, at day break at only 36° 30′, and snow was lying on all the hills around   Immediately after starting we left the pines behind and you must not imagine that we saw any species of trees again, until they are mentioned, for I am such a friend of the woods, and they are in this region so rare, that you may be sure none will escape my notice   After a gradual descent of no great distance, along a fertile tract of grazing land, the plain of Kars opened before us   It is an uneven tract of great width, bounded on either side by broken mountains, and extending eastward almost as far as the eye could reach   Indeed, after travelling through it we knew not where to fix its limit in that direction except at the mountains east of Gumry a distance of 80 or 90 miles   We soon found ourselves upon it and rode for hours admiring the fertility of its soil and the luxuriance of its vegetation   It was like a succession of meadows upon different levels   We were not surprised that marshal Paskevich as was reported in the army envied the Turks the possession of such a tract, and strongly advised the emperor to retain it   Its fertility in ancient times was proverbial   The grandson of Haig we are told sent hither his son Shara whose gluttony and the number of whose children had become burdensome, because its productions were sufficiently abundant for his support   From him it derived its name Shirag and from the tradition and its known fertility combined originated the proverb, 'if you have the throat of Shara we have not the granary of Shirag ' *   We crossed to the left of the river of Kars, and an hour after, stopped at the village of Benkly Ahmed

The plain here stretched off a great distance to the south, and several villages appeared upon it in that direction Among them were seven or eight, formerly inhabited by Turkmáns.   It has been often said, that the Turks of that

* Chamcheán P 1 c 2

name are numerous in Armenia, and our instructions directed us to make inquiries respecting them. We did so, and heard of none in any part of Armenia which we visited, except these. A tartar of Bayezeed did indeed affirm that there were some near Akhaltsikhe; but, as we heard of none in that region when we were here, and, as Kars is in the direction of Akhaltsikhe from Bayezeed, I suppose he had in mind the settlement of which I am now speaking; especially as his account corresponds with the character that was given of it here. The Turkmans are generally called *Turk* by the body of Osmanlies, who repel that name from themselves and appropriate the more honorable one of *musulmán*. They usually live a nomadic life, wandering from place to place with their herds and flocks. But these were cultivators of the soil and quite the opposite of their pastoral brethren were known as a quiet and orderly people. They were Mohammedans, but had neither mollahs nor mosks, nor did they keep more than three days of the Ramadan; then, however they ate nothing night or day. Whether any of their brethren resemble them in these religious peculiarities, I am unable to say from personal inquiry as we saw none. When the Russians came, all of them fled toward Sivas. It is to be hoped that geographers will no longer adhere to the old error of calling Armenia Turcomania. That name is never applied to it in Turkey itself, and there is not the shadow of a reason why foreigners should use it.

Benkly Ahmed is a common village of 50 or 60 Armenian, and 7 or 8 Greek houses. The former have four priests and one church. We attended evening prayers in the latter, and found it, like the houses, under ground, and bearing equal marks of poverty with them. I had new emotions in first attending divine service under ground. The simple fact turned my thoughts to the time when Christianity was driven by persecution into dens and caves of the

earth, and both the miserable state of the building, and the
aspect of the assembly clothed in rags, made me feel that
I was among the subjects of a persecution similar in its
ultimate effects, although milder and slower in its operation.
The services were indeed lamentably far from primitive
simplicity, but the persevering attachment to the Christian name, which has preserved them however corrupt,
could not but excite feelings of veneration How many,
I asked myself in our native land would stand the test
that has tried this people and remain as long as they have
done uncontaminated by the imposture of the prophet of
Mecca, could the hordes of Arabia and of Tartary ever
spread desolation over the fair face of the New World?
There is still at the very least, the name of Christ left,
and that is much, it is a charm which we all feel in common, a watchword to which we all answer

The Greeks, or as they were called here, from their resemblance to that nation in faith, the Georgians, had neither priest nor church of their own but worshiped at a
separate altar by the side of the one at which the Armeni
ans payed their devotions and at the same time This
evening an old man stood there making Greek bows and
crosses before a picture of St George, while the rest of the
congregation were performing Armenian prostrations at
another shrine It was a fine exhibition of the only difference that is much thought of by the common people between the worship of the two sects. The language of the
prayers is of minor importance it may be Greek, or Armenian, or any other unknown tongue, only let each have
his favorite shrine and go through with his own distinctive
evolutions of the body and all is right Not often however, are they willing to worship in the same building; and
we should have given the good people of Benkly Ahmed
credit for unusual harmony had we not known that they
were forced to it by poverty, and felt that the continuance

of sectarian distinctions at all under such circumstances, was a stronger evidence of mutual prejudices than the jux taposition of their altars was of fraternal union.—These are the only Greeks that the pashalik contains

At the close of the service we entered into conversation with the priests who had officiated   They were ignorant in the extreme   From our European dress they could con ceive us to be none other than Russians for they knew not that any other people wear it   They were indeed in formed of the existence of several European nations but of America they had never heard under any name   Their first question on learning that we were from an unknown world, was to ascertain whether we were Christians mos-lems, or heathen or in their form of asking it, whether we were *khachabashd*, adorers of the cross a term synony mous, in an Armenian s vocabulary with Christian   Our answer led to other questions designed to ascertain to what Christian sect we belonged   The first resp   our times and mode of fasting a test to their minds mo decisive for it would in fact distinguish between any sects they knew We replied, that we believed it to be the duty of Christians to fast, but as the Bible had fixed no definite time we left it with particular churches, or individuals to fast whenever they might deem it for their edification , but that we knew nothing of a distinction of meats and our fasting was a total abstinence from food   This was so strange a kind of Christianity to them that they pronounced us at once to be like the Turks.   We informed them that we acknowledged only the Bible as our guide and that said nothing of a dis-tinction of days or meats , while they had learned these distinctions from subsequent canons and councils of men, which we did not receive   They were not disposed for con troversy, and slurred over the difference between us by the charitable proposition, that if we believed in the same God it was enough   To which we assented, after amending it by adding the necessity of believing in the same Savior Having succeeded so badly in this test, they resorted to another to ascertain where to class us It was respecting our mode of making the cross, for while non-protestant Christians make the cross as a sign of Christianity, they do it in different ways as a sign of their sect. This was less successful than the other for we plainly told them that we did not make it at all At such a heresy they were amazed our claim to the name of Christian was of course immediately doubted, and they asked if we did not believe in Christ We explained how essential a part of our religion such a belief is and closed the conversation by remarking upon the fraternal affection which ought to exist between all Christians to whatever sect they may belong

This is but a specimen of frequent conversations that took place in our journey For fasting and the cross are among the most prominent of the superstitions of the Armenians, and neither we nor any protestant missionaries, could fail to be brought often to a declaration of our practice in these respects and to be set down immediately if not for the wildest of heretics at least for very strange Christians I cannot do better therefore then to state briefly the Armenian rules and doctrines on both these points In distinction from the papists who keep Friday and Saturday the Armenians like the Greeks and in fact all the oriental churches, fast on Wednesday and Friday which days, some say, were appointed by the apostles in reference to the fact, that on the first Christ foretold that one of them would betray him to be crucified, and on the other the deed was actually done They have other fasts of a week and still longer, preceding most of their great festivals so that out of 365 days in a year, 156 are days of fasting I ought to remark however, that I apply this term by way of accommodation for not one of them is properly a fast nor do the Armenians call them so. Instead of dram, which means a fast they name them only *bahk*, or vigils. They confess that the prophets Jesus Christ and the apostles speak only of proper fasting, that that is most acceptable to God; and that vigils have been instituted on account of our inability through spiritual coldness, to fast. Still we have not been able to learn that they have any law that appoints any day or a part of any day to strict fasting nor any practice to that effect, except in individual cases and in particular convents *

In their fasts the Armenians unlike the papists, forbid fish and white meats, they are even stricter than the Greeks

* The following statement of the fasts of the Armenian church was drawn up by bishop Dionysius with the help of the Armenian Almanac

For 40 days from the Resurrection to the Ascension of Christ there is no fast at all any common food may be eaten So likewise for 8 days from Christmas common food may be eaten Except that in certain years, the festival of St Basil being (according to their reckoning) near, there is a fast of a week which since they deem it impossible to break it, they have to keep in the eight days of Christmas

The fasts are 1st. *Arachavór* the one just mentioned in January or February 5 days.—2d *Agovhats* salt and bread the quadragesimal lent till holy week 40 days —3d *Avák-shapát* great week holy week from Saturday to Saturday though on the evening of the last Saturday or Easter eve after mass every thing is eaten excepting meat and it is called *navaga-dik* or rejoicing 8 days.—4th Vigil of the festival of *Eghia* Elijah, which is always whitsun-week 5 days.—5th Vigil of *Loosavorich*, the Enlightener 5 days.—6th Vigil of *Vartavár* the Transfiguration, with the sixth day navagadik as above explained 5 days —7th Vigil of *Astvadzadzin*, the Parent of God with the sixth day navagadik (some like the Greeks keep 15 days) 5 days.—8th Vigil of *Khachveráts*, the Elevation of the cross, with the sixth day navagadik 5 days.—9th Vigil of *Varaka-khach* the cross of Varák or according to some the Vigil of the festival of *Soorp Keórk* St George 5 days —10th *Hisnág* the little fifty when some keep fifty days till Christmas 5 days.—11th Vigil of *Soorp Hagóp* St. James, which some keep with great strictness for fear of the plague, as he is the defender from that disease 5 days —12th Vigil of *Dsnount*, Christmas, the evening of the last day of which or Christmas eve, is navagadik as on Easter eve 6 days —13th Wednesdays in the year not included in the above fasts 28 days.—14th Fridays likewise not included 29 days. Making in all 156 fasting days.

in their strictest days, for they make no exception of snails, shell fish, or the spawn of fish In a word no animal food of any kind is allowed Even farther than this, olive-oil, oil of sesame wine, and distilled spirits are forbidden Every fast-day is equally subject to these rigid rules. Does any one ask why so heavy a burden is imposed upon him? he is warned that even the question is sinful For the Fathers ordered all by the command of God, and his duty is to obey, or if he be unable, he must still think the laws to be good and blameless, and the fault to be all his own * The more intelligent and thoughtful of the people are aware, that sinful conduct as well as particular kinds of food must be avoided, and that the soul must be humble and devout, in order that the fasts may be acceptable, still labor is no where forbidden nor discouraged, nor are any more religious services appointed on these days than on any other I am sorry to add, that while, with the exception of oil, the prohibited articles of food are still abstained from with much strictness, intoxicating liquors have now overflowed all the barriers that distinguish different days But I will leave the present mode of observing the fasts, and their effects upon the character, to be developed in the course of our journey

The Armenians have an extreme veneration for the original cross, on which our Savior was crucified, attributing to it powers of intercession with God, and of defending from evil, and believing it to be the sign of the Son of man that, at the judgment, will appear in the heavens coming out of the east, and shining even unto the west † In imi

* See Armeno-Turkish Catechism printed at Constantinople with the sanction of the patriarch Boghos in 1829 p. 92—100

† The following are quotations from the *Jamakirk* (church book) which contains the daily prayers of the church   Through the supplications of the holy cross, the silent intercessor ***** O merciful Lord have compassion upon the spirits of our dead."   Let us supplicate from the Lord the great and

14

tation of it many crosses are made of metal and other materials, to be used in churches and elsewhere   To consecrate them, they are washed in water and wine, in imitation of the water and the blood that flowed from our Savior's side, and anointed with meiron in token of the Spirit that descended and rested upon him, suitable passages are read from the Psalms, the Prophets, the Epistles and the Gospels, and then the priest prays, 'that God may give to this cross the power of that to which he was himself nailed, so that it may cast out devils, may heal the diseases of men, and appease the wrath that descends from heaven on account of our sins, to remain upon it himself always as upon his original cross, and make it his temple and throne and the weapon of his power, so that our worship before it may be offered not to created matter but to Him, the only invisible God'   After a cross has undergone this ceremony, it may be set up toward the east, as an object of worship and prayer, while to treat an unconsecrated one thus would be idolatry and a downright breach of the second commandment   For by the act of consecration, Christ is inseparably united to it and it becomes his 'throne his chariot, and his 'weapon for the conquest of Satan so that, though it is honored on these accounts the worship is not given to it, but to Him who is on it   The bodily eye sees the material cross but the spiritual eye sees the divine power that is united with it   ' Therefore " says a distinguished Armenian writer " thou believer in God when thou seest the cross, know and believe that thou seest Christ reclining upon it, and when thou prayest before the cross, believe that thou art talking with Christ, and not with dumb matter For it is Christ that accepts the worship which thou offerest to the cross, and it is he that hears the prayer of thy mouth,

mighty power of the holy cross for the benefit of our souls.   When the trumpet shall sound the Levitical letter shall appear the rays of the holy cross from the east shall radiate and shine

and fulfils the petitions of thy heart, which thou askest in faith *

Besides these images of the cross, they also like all non protestant Christians frequently make the sign of the cross, and to this the priest referred in the conversation I have reported Crossing one s self they are taught to believe, is the mark of a Christian in such a sense, that, as a shepherd knows his sheep by their mark, so Christ knows the sheep of his flock by their crossing themselves The apostles first introduced this ceremony they say, and parents are urged to teach it to their children the first thing, lest the greater part of the sin of their making it incorrectly through life fall upon them † By it they profess to signify, first a belief in the Trinity, as the three persons of it are

---

* See *Kirk Unthanragán* or the Catholic Book of Nerses Shnorháli p 95 259—262.—Nerses Shnorháli or the Graceful was great grandson of Gregory Makisdros whose name often occurs in the history of the last of the Pakradians and brother of the Gregory whose election to the office of Cath olicos when he was but twenty years of age caused the bishop of Aghtamár to secede and who made the castle of Dzovk his paternal inheritance the seat of his see Nerses was himself elected Catholicos in A D 1166, and exercised his office in Hromcla whence he is also called Clajensis High birth office and talents gave him great influence in his day many parts of the book of common prayer (*Jamakirk*) were composed by him and his works are now regarded universally as among the highest authorities of the Armenian church He holds the rank of a saint in its calendar Chamcheán P 6 c 4, 7

† Still a little instruction on this head even at your age will I suspect be new The rule for making the cross is this —to carry the hand but to four places the first of which is the forehead the second the bottom of the breast, the third above the left breast, and the fourth above the right breast. As the arms of the cross are four so the words to be said in making it are four one for each arm viz In nomine Patris | et Filii | et Spiritus | Sancti Life of Loosavorich p. 88 89

The Armenians and papists perform this ceremony alike but the Greeks though guilty of the absurdity of putting the hand upon the right breast before the left show a superior trinitarian orthodoxy by making it with three fingers while the Jacobites Copts and Abyssinians give an offensive prom inence to their monophysitism by making it with one

named, and second the mediatorial work of Christ, as bringing the hand from the forehead to the stomach represents his descent from heaven to earth and bringing it from the left to the right breast, that he delivered the souls that were in hades, and made them worthy of heaven They make it at every falling and rising in time of prayer, and on many other occasions such as beginning an important business going to bed at night, rising in the morning dressing, washing eating, drinking, going out at night or entering any dangerous place The benefits they expect from it are, that it will make their prayers acceptable, and their work easy, that it will defend them from the wiles of evil spirits and give them strength to war against sin *

In regard to education the priests assured us that there was no school in Benkly Ahmed nor in any of the villages nearer than Kars Each of them was accustomed to teach two or three children, and there might be eight or ten people in the village who could read. They thought the same proportion might answer for other places Among the rest some females could read, in fact, if a father himself knew how, he taught both sons and daughters without distinction

We made occasional inquiries respecting the tenure by which the Christian peasants in this part of Turkey hold the lands which they occupy, but learned little that was satisfactory Near Erzroom, we were assured, some of them were freeholders and those who were not if they stocked their farms themselves, paid their landlord one half of the produce, otherwise they paid him two thirds. But here the poor people seemed not to know what freehold estate was. Each one sowed, they said, where he pleased, without considering any particular spot as his by right of possession, or tenancy, and paid only the regular tenth of what he reaped to government Still they spoke of the lord of their village, and said, what was afterwards confirmed,

* Catechism p 40—45

that many of the Turks in town when they fled at the time of its capture, sold their villages to Armenians, under the expectation that the Russians would retain possession of the country. In fact, we were told at Kars that none of the Armenians in this pashalik were freeholders before the war.

June 27. Between Benkly Ahmed and Kars, a distance estimated at 3 hours, but which we were five in travelling, the plain is more level and fertile than what we passed yesterday, but not a single cultivated spot, nor an inhabited village, did we see. On coming again in sight of the road from Azáb, which we had left three days before, we found it crowded for a long distance with carts, and that on which we were travelling, also, was after a while filled with the Armenians of Khanoos. We had elsewhere been informed that the Armenians in that sanják were more numerous than the moslems, and amounted to 700 houses, and we were now told that all had left. They seemed more uncivilized than any company we had passed, as might be expected from their vicinity to the Kürds. Among them we first observed the custom, that afterwards became so familiar to us, of using oxen and buffaloes as beasts of burden. Most of them were on foot, and it was disgusting, and at the same time pitiful, to see the females, many of them with children slung in bags upon their backs, wading through mud and brooks, up to their knees and deeper. An hour from the city we crossed again to the right bank of the river by a stone bridge.

At the gate of Kars, a Russian sentry stopped us, and demanded our passports. After an hour's delay, they were returned, with an order for us to be admitted, and a hint that we must report that we had been made to perform quarantine. So we were carefully conducted to a dark smoke-house, and locked up with a pot of fumigating matter. But, after a minute, and before the smell of brimstone

14 *

had reached our clothes or even our nostrils, the door was opened, and our quarantine was ended. Our baggage, in the mean time, had remained without, and one muleteer to guard it At this ridiculous farce even the health officers themselves laughed, but the reason of it was obvious The Armenian emigrants were arriving in too great numbers to be freely admitted to the town without embarrassment and quarantine offered a good pretence for excluding them, especially as it had existed with some strictness in the former part of the campaign In fact the ground before the city was covered with them, while we were not only admitted thus easily but afterwards went out to them and returned without hindrance

Kars is situated on the north side of the plain at a point where the river flowing into the mountain through a deep and narrow ravine cuts off a piece of it convenient for a citadel On the back side towards the river this hill is perpendicular but is commanded by still higher parts of the mountain across the stream. A fort crowns its summit and its southern side which is covered with the principal buildings of the city is enclosed by a wall that sweeps down each end and runs along its base The largest portion of the town lies in front of the citadel, and is itself partly surrounded by a wall now in ruins A large suburb however occupies the face of the mountain itself across the river to the west and is connected by two substantial stone bridges with the town and the citadel From the river the inhabitants supply themselves with water The houses of the citadel are tolerably large and well built for Turkey, but those of the town are of the under-ground architecture of the villages The terraces of many had been broken in for the wood which supports them and the work of destruction was going on while we were there For Kars is as destitute of wood as Erzroom, and obtains it from the same mountain, and its climate too seemed to be no milder, for from the 27th

of June to the 2d of July, the thermometer in our room at
midday ranged only from 55° to 65°   It is 36 hours from
Erzroom, and 44 from Tiflis   The snowy summit of mount
Ararat can just be seen from it, bearing S 65° E

The most interesting facts in the ancient history of Kars
have been alluded to in the Introduction   Under the Turks,
it was until taken by the Russians in July of 1828 the cap-
ital of a small pashalik and the residence of a pasha   It is
now governed by only a mutsellim subject to the pashá of
Erzroom   Among the sanjáks into which the pashalik is
divided we heard mentioned Zarishád in the direction of
Akhaltsikhe Kaghezmán in the direction of Erivan and
Kars or as it is also called Takht in the direction of
Erzroom   which probably correspond nearly with Vanánt,
Apegheank and Shirag cantons of the ancient province of
Ararad , for the whole pashalik was embraced in that pro-
vince

The Turkish population of the city and I believe also
of the pashalik was formerly more numerous than that of
the Armenians , but nearly all fled before the Russians,
and we saw very few of them   The ayán Aboo Aga,
received us with civility and furnished us with lodgings But
a more mercenary man I have rarely met   He held his office as head of the Turks and had regular pay from the
Russians, and was of course a great admirer of them to
their face   Indeed he liked them so much that he promised
never to separate from them but to accompany them when
they should leave   *Us*, as we were of the English race,
he warned on our arrival that they were all thieves , that
we must never step from our door without locking it lest we
should be robbed, as such accidents were occurring every
day and that they had ruined the city   But neither his
opinions nor his attentions did he intend to give us gratis,
for hardly an article that a traveller ever puts in his trunk
failed of being mentioned, with a declaration that it would

be a most gratifying memento of the pleasure he had derived from our acquaintance. To his *countrymen* he declared, that only the presence of the Russians prevented him from making the holy pilgrimage to Mecca, and that he had every thing in readiness to start the moment they were gone. The fact was, that being yet fearful that he should be obliged to flee into Russia for his life, he had packed his goods to be in readiness, and hoping still to compromise with his country for his treason, he took every measure to make his countrymen view his conduct favorably. He even imagined that we might exert an influence to get him appointed pashá of Kars, declaring that the Turks of the place all desired that he might fill that office. The scale ultimately turned in favor of remaining, and on our second visit to Erzroom, we were amused to learn that he was actually at the head of the pashalik with the title of mutsellim.

We were prevented from seeing much of the Armenians, not, as at Erzroom, because they had gone, but because they were going, and had their thoughts too much engrossed in that way to allow of their being profitably directed to other subjects. Besides they were always ready to ask our advice, and we were not yet sufficiently acquainted with our situation to feel free from embarrassment in either giving or withholding it. For, that the Russians, the rear of whose army was now concentrated here were deeply interested in the matter, was evident. The fact that, in retiring from Persia at the close of a former war they had taken with them nearly all the Christian population of Aderbaijan, was well known. In the treaty of Adrianople with Turkey, they had caused an article to be inserted, that "there should be granted to the respective subjects of the two powers, established in the territories restored to the sublime Porte, or ceded to the imperial court of Russia, the term of eighteen months from the ratification of the treaty, to dispose, if they should think proper, of their property, acquired either before or since the war, and to retire with their capital, their goods, furniture, &c. from the states of one of the contracting powers into those of the other and reciprocally * And wherever their army marched, a census of the Christians had been taken, whether they expressed a wish to leave or not.

None of the Armenians would allow that flattering promises had been held out to induce them to emigrate, and many declared the contrary The offers really made them were, to the inhabitants of cities, lots for their houses and shops to the peasants as much land as they could cultivate, an exemption of all from taxes for six years and an appropriation of 1,000 000 of roubles (250,000 silver roubles,) and of a large quantity of grain for the poor But, though none allowed that they were allured away, many said they were frightened and they were about as likely to assign fear of the Russians as fear of the Turks, as a reason for going The morning we entered Erzroom, a well dressed Armenian gentleman, mounted and armed, came out to meet our company, and declared that for refusing to go, he had been confined two or three days in prison, from which he had obtained his release only by changing his mind His high spirits, however, exhibited in curvetting his charger and firing his pistols convinced us that he was quite as glad to get rid of Turkish vassalage, as of a Russian prison At Kars we had a singular visit from another Armenian of Erzroom, who was a gentleman both in his dress and his manners Having heard, he said, that we were not Russians, he had come to ask our candid opinion whether they would injure him if he should return to his city We were awake to the suspicion that he might be a spy, but did not hesitate to declare our conviction that he had no reason for the least apprehension He left us affirming that he should certainly go back, and that were

* Treaty of Adrianople 13th Art

the rest of his countrymen persuaded of the truth of what
we had said half of them would follow his example

The extent of the country whose inhabitants emigrated
is the same with that of the Russian conquests mentioned
in the beginning of the preceding letter except that the
troops remained so short a time in Gumish khaneh and
Baiboort that few had time to leave those places and from
Terjan, we were told only forty or fifty families left al
though all had the offer The real number of emigrants
was stated to us by an intelligent bishop who was with the
army and said he had his information directly from Gen
Pankratieff, at 7000 families from the pashalik of Erz
room, 4000 from that of Kars and 4000 from that of Bayezeed making in all 15,000 families or about 75 000 souls
When we were at Erzroom the second time however, a
young man in the service of the collector of taxes assured
us on the authority of his master that 97,000 souls left
that pashalik alone They are all located in the part of the
pashalik of Akhaltsikhe which was retained by the Russians and in the adjacent parts of Georgia except those
from Bayezeed, who settled not far from the lake of Sevàn

The Armenians of Kars had one church, which was on
the same hill as the citadel but outside of its walls Our
first visit to it was at evening prayers Its interior resem
bled that of the church of Erzroom in dirt and darkness,
except that a profusion of old silver lamps were suspended
from the roof and a silver cross thickly set with jewels
adorned an altar covered with a cloth glittering with span
gles Three priests who were present estimated the Armenian population of the city at 600 houses, said they
had seventeen priests and two vartabeds, with a bishop at
their head whose jurisdiction extended over the whole
pashalik, and that there were three vartabéds more in the
convent of St. John, nine hours distant towards Erivàn
There was formerly another large convent only an hour

from the city, but it is now in ruins, and no longer in habited

One of our informants was teacher of the only Armenian school in town   It contained he said about fifty lads, who learned to read and write, but were not advanced so far as grammar   The Psalms, the Gospels the Acts, and a work called Narek were the principal books used   It was the first and only school we found in Turkish Armenia and Mr Zaremba, in his journey, heard of none except in Erzroom, Bayezeed and Kars   The two former were broken up before we reached those places, and as the Armenians left Kars soon after we were there, we may conclude, that when we returned there was not one school in all this region

Our next visit to the church was in the morning and for the purpose of attending mass   At the close we had an opportunity of hearing prayers for the dead , for a vartabéd had died two or three days before, and prayers were now read over his grave at the door of the church   A minute description of the ceremony would be useless   Suffice it to say that the bishop one or two vartabeds, and a number of priests assisted and the service was very long   In fact the Armenians have a distinct set of prayers for dead clergy men of all orders which make quite a book and require an hour or two to be repeated   They are said on each of the first seven days after death, earth being at every time thrown upon the grave as if the burial was still going on and also on the fifteenth, and the fortieth days and at the end of a year

It has been repeatedly asserted that the Armenians believe departed spirits to be in a state of insensibility from death till the judgment   But the assertion is untrue   Some, and probably most, may say that neither the reward of the righteous nor the punishment of the wicked, is complete till the soul is reunited to the body , yet the general belief certainly is that the former are in a state of enjoyment, and the latter of misery, and that they are separated from each other   An Armenian bishop declared to us, that those who die guilty of mortal sins unconfessed go directly to hell , that those who are guilty of only venial sins and have confessed, com muned, and done penance go directly to heaven , and that those who have confessed and communed, but not done sufficient penance, will go to heaven if the church prays for them   When asked what would become of them if the church did not pray, he said, with some embarrassment,

Why if they have no mortal sins they must go to heaven of course, but so the church explains it   A statement of a council of high clergy (of whom the Catholicos of Sis was one) held at Constantinople not many years ago, is still more explicit , and the state of departed spirits is so im portant an article of faith that I cannot refrain from making a full extract.

The retribution,   it says, "of separate spirits, when they bid adieu to the world is, according to the doctrine of St Gregory Loosavorich as follows   Saints shall be near to Christ, for where I am says he, there shall also my ser vant be   John 12 26   Again, ' when earthly life is completed by the command of death, the spirit is sent to God who gave it, and the body returns to the dust from which it was made by the Creator   Angels and the spirits of saints come forth to meet the spirits of the holy and just, and with psalms, and hymns and spiritual songs, conduct them before God, praising the mighty glory and majesty of the holy Trinity, and thanking his benificent goodness, for transferring those who are called, into his own kingdom and glory, from earthly things to heavenly, from dishonor to honor,' (Hajakhabadoom, p 152, 153) And again in the same book p 171, he says, ' they, who, being firm in the holy love of Christ, gave their own souls to death, **** are saved

And by the mercy of the Holy Ghost, the gates of the life of favor, the mansions above, where the assembly of the saints are at rest, shall be opened' But for those who die in venial sin, and for those who have not completed here the penance of mortal sins that have been pardoned, [absolved by the priest,] we pray saying, 'grant them mercy, pardon and remission of sins.' (Vid Jamakirk) And in the churches we cry, 'God, giver of pardons, forgive ours that sleep,' [our dead friends] (Sharagán p. 117) 'and comfort them in thy royal pavilion of rest.' (Id p 121)"
' Wherefore the priest in the holy mass prays saying ' O Lord, remember the spirits of them that rest, and enlighten, and rank them with thy saints in thy heavenly kingdom.' For thus St Loosavorich taught, saying but as to believers who have committed sin, and confessed and done penance and received the sacrament that procures salvation [communed], and bid farewell to the world, let them be remembered in the sacrifice of Christ [the mass], and in prayer, and in charity to the poor, and in other good works that by the good deeds of those that survive, they that rest may gain the victory of eternal life (Hajakh p. 160) Wherefore the place in which the departed spirits are who need the prayers of the church is called by us *gayan* [mansion] but by others *kavaran* [place of penance] or *makraran* [place of purification] But we understand that impenitent, irreligious, and unbelieving sinners, are from this moment abandoned and condemned in hell In the words of St. Loosavorich, we say, 'different is the mansion of those who despised His law, and served grievous lusts and divers sins, for they shall inherit the outer darkness. Darkness here is outer evil, for them whose thoughts and senses are darkened, and who have wandered far from life *** And there they are in the fire of hell where there is weeping and gnashing of teeth' (Hajakh

15

p. 153.)"* Another authority adds, that " the wicked must be burned in unquenchable fire, for as there is no end to the glory of the righteous, so there is none to the torments of the wicked "†—Wherein now does this doctrine differ from that of the papal church ? The *name* of purgatory is wanting indeed, and the Armenians reject it as universally and as obstinately as the Greeks, but the *thing* is here ‡ I am well aware that the council whose language I have used was rejected by the popular voice for having been partial to papacy, but its quotations are from universally received authorities, and are certainly sufficiently explicit.

In the practice of the church, the same doctrine is most fully acted upon *Prayers* and *masses* are said, and *charity* given continually for the benefit of the dead The *prayers* are found in nearly all the offices of the church The daily service is full of them In addition to the specimens contained in the above extract, I cannot withhold the following Through the entreaties of the holy cross, the silent intercessor and of the mother of God, and of John the forerunner, and of St Stephen the protomartyr, and of St Loosavorich the patriarch of Armenia, and of the holy

---

* Hraver Siroy p 23—28　　　　　† Catechism p 9

‡ Compare the following which is the third decree of the 16th general council of the papists held at Florence A D 1438 1439　　If they decease truly penitent in the love of God before they have satisfied for commissions and omissions by fruits meet for repentance their souls shall be purified by the pains of purgatory And to release them from such pains the aids of believing survivors contribute such as the sacrifices of mass prayers alms and other acts of piety which are customarily performed by believers for other believers according to the rules of the church But the souls of those who after baptism have incurred no stain of sin and those also who after having contracted the guilt of sin have been either in their own bodies or when stripped of those bodies purified are received immediately to heaven and clearly behold the triune God as he is but one more perfectly than another according to the diversity of merits But the souls of those who decease in mortal actual or only in original sin descend immediately to hell but to be punished with different degrees of punishment

apostles, and of all the martyrs O merciful Lord have compassion upon the spirits of our dead. Prayers are also frequently said and incense burned over the graves of the deceased, particularly on Saturday evening which is the special season for remembering the dead in prayers and alms

Mass is said for the souls of the departed on the day of the burial on the seventh the fifteenth and the fortieth days, and at the end of the first year and also at other times as often as the survivors will [pay the priests for mentioning their names For you must understand that the whole ceremony of mass is not performed extra for the occasion but the priest, when he comes to the proper place in the common morning mass besides praying for all the dead in general as above quoted merely names also in particular the person or persons requested Such are the private masses of the Armenians whether for the dead or the living, for the latter obtain the benefit in the same way What this benefit is you will learn from the following words of an Armenian writer already quoted The sacrifice of Christ [the mass] which the holy priests perform with true faith in the name of the dead is in greatness far above thought and language For if Christ, by being once offered a sacrifice on the cross put away the sin of men's nature derived from Adam when he is offered many times in the name of a Christian that sleeps [is dead] what sin can it be that the heavenly Father will not pardon on account of the sacrifice of his only begotten Son? And to the believer, that which Christ offered, and that which the priests offer is the same sacrifice Only let him that sleeps have been in his last hour, in the true faith and penitent for sin ' *

Charity is given by surviving friends to the poor in the

* Unthanragán of Nerses Shnorháli p 252

name of the dead, with the hope that its merit will be credited to them as if they had done it in person. And the merit of charity is supposed to be great. It procures pardon both for the living and the dead, it gives a pleasing sensation to departed spirits before the judgment, and at that day will cause the righteous whether performed by them in person, or in their name by surviving friends, to stand at the right hand and hear the joyful sentence of approbation * Besides gifts of money and other modes of charity common to papists the Armenians have one that is peculiar It is the sacrifice of an animal   The victim may be an ox, or a sheep, or any clean beast or fowl The priests having brought it to the door of the church, and placed salt before the altar, read the Scripture lessons selected for such occasions, and pray, mentioning the name of the person deceased, and entreating the forgiveness of his sins   Then they give the salt to the animal, and slay it A portion belongs to the priest other portions are distributed to the poor, and of the remainder a feast is made for the friends   None may remain till the morrow   These sacrifices are not regarded as propitiatory like those of the Jews for the Armenians hold that they were abolished by the death of Christ   but as a meritorious charity to the needy They have always at least in modern times a special reference to the dead and are generally though not necessarily made on the day that a mass is said for the same object. The other most common occasions are the great festivals of the saints, and what are called the Lord's festivals   At Easter especially one or more is always sacrificed, the whole congregation frequently contributing to the expense and then dividing the victim or victims among them   But even this is in memory of the dead   Its origin we are told by Nerses Shnorhali, on the authority of

* Unthanragán p 252

the Catholicos Isaac the Great, was as follows. When the
nation embraced Christianity under the preaching of St
Gregory Loosavorích, the converted pagan priests came
to him and begged that he would provide for them some
means of support, as the sacrifices on which they formerly
lived were now abolished He accordingly ordered that a
tenth of the produce of the fields should be theirs, and that
the people, instead of their former offerings to idols, should
now make sacrifices to God in the name of the dead, as a
charity to the hungry *

Kars was one of the stations of the Jesuit missions in
Armenia, at which they numbered many converts,† but
now there is not a papist in the city, nor even in the
pashalik

We wished to take Akhaltsikhe in our way to Tiflis, especially as it was the rendezvous of the Armenian emi
grants But that route would have increased the distance,
and interfered with the quarantine regulations on entering
Georgia so much, that we soon saw its inexpediency I
will therefore say a word respecting that place before leaving
Kars Akhaltsikhe (or Akhiskhah) is situated in the mountains which were called by the Greeks Moschici, and gave to
the region the name of Meschia They now bear the name of
Childir-dagh evidently related to the *Chaldæi*, who once
occupied those parts. It is the only place of importance
now existing in the ancient Armenian province of Daik,
and was before the war, the capital of a small pashalik
No other place that came within the range of our inquiry
in Turkish Armenia contains any Jews Here they number about 60 families in the city and as many in the surrounding villages They have been in the country from
time immemorial, and speak no language but Turkish and

---

* Uathaaragán p. 242—252.   † Lett. Ed et Cur vol 8 p. 463

15 *

Georgian There are also in the pashalik many people of the Georgian race The Turks seem to have inherited much of the bravery of its ancient Armenian inhabitants, but they were a bad people. Besides giving an asylum to the discontented subjects of the Georgian provinces, they carried on according to information given us by Turks themselves in Kars a clandestine slave trade with their neighbors of Colchis introducing the victims of their traffick through a convenient pass in the mountains In fact, being like Poty and Anapa situated in the vicinity of people given from the earliest times to selling their children and serfs and from which the harems of Turkey have procured their favorites and its palaces their mamlooks for ages the Turks made use of it for the same inhuman purpose as they did those fortresses It is not therefore surprising that at the close of the late war, the Russians should together with them, have retained it also and the neighboring fortresses of Azghoor and Akhalkalaki Most of its Turkish inhabitants have retired to Erzroom and other parts of Turkey It is 36 hours from Kars and 34 from Tiflis, and I suppose the road from the former passes near Gumry as we did not part company with the emigrating Armenians till we crossed the Arpa-chai near that place

The Russians as they advanced into Turkey, left behind them in order to facilitate the transmission of dispatches a line of Cossack posts which in fact was but an extension of the system of posts that exist throughout the trans-Caucasian provinces From this establishment the commandant of Kars, who treated us with much civility here, and when we afterwards met him at another place increased our obligations by additional attentions, politely offered to accommodate us with horses Unable to procure other means of conveyance, we accepted his offer, and, receiving

an order from the acting commander-in chief for as many
as we needed from every post we started at 1 o clock
P M on the 2nd of July   Five large fat beasts carried
our baggage and ourselves and a hardy Cossack preceded
us, in the capacity of guide guard and surijy   The plain
of Kars the same broad and fertile but entirely uncultivated tract continued to ascend gradually till we reached
Khalfeh-oghloo 22 versts from the city *   It was a miserable ruined spot of only 12 houses, half of which belonged
to Armenians who had left   We stopped from 4 to 5
o clock and then mounted on a new set of horses and
headed by a new Cossack, proceeded on our way   The
plain beyond was covered with a fine growth of grass, but
no where did any cultivation appear   We passed but one
village, and that was uninhabited   Every feature of these
great Armenian plains gives them a dreary aspect   With
not a tree, not a fence hardly a ploughed field, and a village only at long intervals they present one wide waste of
greenness almost like the ocean and penetrate the mind
with the deepest feelings of solitude   The melancholy is
increased by the reflection that the wickedness of man, ex
hibited in exterminating wars and barbarous bloodthirsty
and avaricious governments has thus turned the most fruitful fields into deserts   We think that our own country is
thinly peopled but where can such a tract as the plain of
Kars be found with so few to cultivate it ?   Hardly one is
so solitary and naked short of the buffalo plains of Missouri
Our road as darkness came on was lined with encamp-
ments of emigrating Armenians   At 9 and a half P M
we forded the river of Kars and stopped at the village of
Jamishly on its left bank, having made 30 versts from our
last post   It was an Armenian village of 30 families, but
all had left for Georgia

* The common Russian verst is equal to two thirds of an English mile

July 3. Immediately after starting, we left the river of Kars, running to the right towards the Aras, and saw no more of it. It is the same that was called Akhoorean by the Armenians, and the ruins of Ani are still found upon it, not many miles below After an hour, another small river crossed our path, running also to the right, through lands on which appeared several villages In three hours more we forded the Arpa-chai, and were on Russian soil

LETTER VI

FROM THE TURKISH FRONTIER TO TIFLIS

Enter the Russian possessions—Gümry—Valley and village of Pernikákh—
A Sabbath—Village church—Number of the Armenian services—Their
nature and spirit—Want of education—Hamamly—Intemperance—Quar-
antine—Russian army—Cossacks—Gérger—Lóri—Enter Georgia—
Change of climate—Russian post establishment—Great Shoolaver—
Greeks in Georgia—Post carriages—Reach Tiflis

DEAR SIR,

WE had changed empires almost before we were aware
of it For both banks of the Arpa chai have the same
features of plain and gentle undulation, and the river itself
is easily forded Yet one side looks to Constantinople for
its governors and owns obedience to the laws and successors of Mohammed while the other is ruled according to
the maxims of Peter the Great, by one of his descendants,
on the shores of the Baltic The Arpa-chai has been the
boundary of the two empires from the first subjection of
Georgia to Russia, and is a most convenient one for the
designs of an ambitious power for it opposes not the shadow of a barrier to the advance of her armies. Waving
fields of barley on its eastern bank, interspersed with
meadows now bowing before the sythe of the mower attracted our attention before we knew that they were in an
other empire and, at our first introduction to Russia, pre-
possessed us in favor of the protecting and meliorating
influence of her laws As we approached Gumry about
two miles from the river, an officer of a regiment encamped
by the path, rode up and examined our passports a mo-

ment, and this was the only police or custom-house in
spection we underwent on entering the territories of the
Czar

Gumry is a small Armenian village, 30 versts from Jamishly   Unfortunately it was too far from the Cossack
encampment to allow us to visit it   The under ground
houses of the Cossacks were so dirty that we preferred
spreading our carpets on the open ground   notwithstanding
the midday sun was somewhat oppressive, to entering them,
and as nothing could be obtained to eat, we improved the
two or three hours of our delay by endeavoring to sleep
The highest peak of a snowy mountain, that had bounded
our prospect at some distance to the right during the morn
ing bore, from this spot southeast   It is now called Ala-
gez and both its position and its name show it to be the
same that Armenian history often mentions under the name
of Arakádz

Passing for three hours over the level and fertile plain
of Gumry, we reached a low mountain that connects the
one just mentioned with others on the left, and easily ascended it by a carriage road   It forms the natural bound
ary of the territory of Kars and was formerly the dividing
line between the provinces of Ararad and Kookark   It actually separates the waters of the Aras from those of the
Koor   Beyond it lay the little valley of Pernikakh, the beginning of the district of Pembek the ancient Pampegi
dzor   Long fields of barley meadows and ploughed lots
lying side by side unseparated by hedge or fence decked it
with the variegated colors of a beautiful carpet. The barley
was in blossom companies of mowers were cutting the
thick grass of the meadows, and teams of ten and twelve
pairs of cattle were turning up the black loam of the
ploughed fields   The ploughs were of astonishing size and
weight but of the form common in Turkey consisting of
a straight billet of wood, pointed with a sharp iron the

more easily to penetrate the ground having a beam attached to it by which to be drawn, and a handle for the plough-
man Enormous as it was, however, and moved by so
great a power it was far from fathoming the depth of the
soil The costume of the peasants gave us additional evidence that we were no longer in Turkey Instead of the
Osmánly turban flowing *caftan* (gown) and ample *shalwar* (trowsers), nothing appeared but the conical sheepskin cap, the snug frock and frock-coat and wide pàntaloons
of Georgia A ride of four or five miles across the valley,
in the course of which we passed a brook running through
it on its way to the Koor, brought us to the village of Pernikákh called also Beykend 27 versts from Gumry

July 4 I awoke with strong feverish sensations, arising
from exposure to the sun and wind of yesterday, and still
more from the confined air and horrible stench of our room
in the night It was a stable entered by a passage so dark,
that even in the day time we could hardly find our way
through it and ventilated only by a hole in the terrace hardly
four inches square In it horses calves and hens herded
with us and dirt was constantly falling from the terrace in
the night to the great danger of our eyes It being Sabbath,
we gave notice at the post house that we should remain until
to-morrow and walked out to breathe The weather was de-
lightfully pleasant and the fresh morning air soon dissipated
my head ache and calmed my feverish pulse None of the bustle of industry that was witnessed yesterday although it was
the festival of Loosavorich a high holiday of the church now
appeared In the village however lamentable evidence was
afforded us that though labor was suspended, nothing was
thought of the sacredness of the day Some were going to
a distant village on business others were meeting with
their friends to amuse themselves with music and carouse
over a bowl of punch and others still were lounging away
their time with their pipes or in sleep How lamentable

their condition! Without the Bible, and unable to read if they had it, without early instruction, or the ministrations of the pulpit, what means have they, on this day of rest, of feeding the appetite of the soul for action, but to indulge in amusements and sin?

We attended evening prayers in the church. Hitherto we had seen no village in Armenia possessed of a church, that was distinguished from the common houses, by form or size or any external mark that could inform the traveller that it was a church, and the same is true of the parts of Turkish Armenia which we afterwards visited. But within the Russian limits, most Christian villages showed us a church, in some cases ancient and well built, as far as they could themselves be seen. The church of Pernikákh was built of stone, and stood fairly above the ground, in the most elevated part of the village. A bell, too, that insufferable abomination to the Turk, called the people to the worship of God. The sun was shining clearly without, but the darkness within was so great that we could with difficulty distinguish a single individual. For, even were it in the open sunshine the service could not be read without lighted candles, symbolical of the " seven lamps of fire burning before the throne which are the seven spirits of God, ' and indicating the need of the Spirit to aid in divine worship. The villagers here, therefore, as in many other places which we visited, had concluded, that, as the necessity of daylight was superseded they were at liberty to make an economical saving of window-glass and of their own animal heat, by substituting for windows crevices hardly more than an inch wide, and thus almost entirely excluding it. How perfectly descriptive of the present state of their religion! In the public celebration of a worship that has substituted the doctrines and commands of men for the word of God, and the mediation of saints and angels for that of the only Mediator between God and man, the light of a taper is well substituted for the light of the sun!

Reserving for another place a description of the Armenian forms of worship permit me to inform you here of what that worship consists The Armenian ritual designates nine distinct hours every day for public worship, and contains the services for them viz *midnight* the hour of Christ's resurrection, the *dawn of day* when he appeared to the two Marys at the sepulchre *sunrise* when he appeared to his disciples, *three o'clock* (reckoning from sunrise) or the first canonical hour, when he was nailed to the cross *six o'clock*, or the second canonical hour, when the dark ness over all the earth commenced, *nine o'clock*, or the third canonical hour when he gave up the ghost, *evening*, when he was taken from the cross and buried *after the latter* when he descended to hades to deliver the spirits in prison, and *on going to bed* But never except perhaps in the case of some ascetics are religious services performed so often. All but the ninth are usually said at twice viz at matins and vespers, which are performed daily in every place that has a priest, the former commencing at the dawn of day and embracing the first six services and the latter commencing about an hour before sunset, and embracing the seventh and eighth On the Sabbath and on some of the principal holidays instead of one there are frequently two assemblies in the morning the first at the dawn embracing the first three services and the other not far from nine o'clock – embracing the second three Mass is as distinct from these services as the communion service of the church of England is from the morning prayer Whenever it is said which is generally every day it follows the sixth service, so that if there are two assemblies in the morning, it finishes the second The ninth service, when it is performed at all except in some convents, is said by individuals at home *

* The books which are used in these daily devotions of the church, are the *Jamakirk* (church-book), containing the nine services just enumerated

At the beginning of the first service in the morning, or rather, before it begins, the priest, standing with his face to the west, says, ' we renounce the devil and all his arts and wiles, his counsel, his ways his evil angels his evil ministers the evil executors of his will and all his evil power renouncing we renounce " Then turning toward the east,* he repeats the following creed, which, as it is peculiar to the Armenian church and is appealed to by papists and others as evidence of her heresy I give verbatim omitting a few expressions which decency forbids to be published   We confess and believe with the whole heart in God the Father uncreated unbegotten and without beginning, both begetter of the Son and sender [literally *proceeder*] of the Holy Ghost. We believe in God the Word uncreated begotten and begun of the Father before all eternity, not posterior nor younger but as long as the Father [is] Father the Son [is] Son with him   We believe in God the Holy Ghost uncreated eter nal unbegotten but proceeding from the Father, par taking of the Fathers essence and of the Son's glory We believe in the Holy Trinity one substance one divin ity, not three Gods but one God one will one kingdom one dominion Creator of things visible and invisible   We believe in the forgiveness of sins in the holy church with the communion of saints   We believe that one of the three Persons God the Word was before all eternity begotten of the Father in time descended **** and perfect God became perfect man with spirit, soul and body, one

---

the *Sharagán* containing hymns or anthems   the *Saghmós* or Psalms of David   the *Jashóts* containing select lessons from the Prophets Gospels and Epistles   and the *Hawmavórk* containing legends of the saints arranged in the order of the calendar   Besides which, there is also the *Khorhurtadéder* for the mass   and the *Mashtóts* for the other sacraments and rites of the church

  * He holds his hands open at the height of his breast with the palms downward and the fore fingers in contact   this being the sign of the Chris tian faith   as placing the fore-fingers alone in contact is of the Mohamme dan faith

person one attribute and one united nature God become man without change and without variation **** As there is no beginning of his divinity so there is no end of his humanity (for Jesus Christ is the same, yesterday to-day and forever) We believe that our Lord Jesus Christ dwelt upon the earth, after thirty years he came to baptism the Father testified from above, this is my beloved Son the Holy Ghost like a dove descended upon him, he was tempted of the devil and overcame him, he preached salvation to men, was fatigued and wearied in body, hungered and thirsted, afterwards voluntarily came to suffering, was crucified and dead in body, and alive in divinity his body was placed in the grave with the divinity united and in spirit he descended to hades with the divinity unseparated preached to the spirits destroyed hades and delivered the spirits after three days arose from the dead and appeared to the disciples. We believe that our Lord Jesus Christ with that same body ascended to heaven and sat down at the right hand of the Father he is also to come with the same body and with the Father s glory to judge the quick and the dead Which is likewise a resurrection to all men We believe also in the reward of works to the righteous everlasting life and to the wicked everlasting punishment After this creed some of the peculiarities of which will come under review hereafter an abominable form of confession and absolution is said for the congregation which I neglect to quote here as it will come up again when we have occasion to speak of the sacrament of penance *

You would be little interested or profited were I to enumerate the exhortations supplications prayers responses, psalms lessons hymns and anthems which follow in order They are varied to suit different festivals fasts, days of the month and other special occasions The Psalms of

* Jamakirk p 3—10

David, hymns and anthems constitute much more than half of the services, but they are not in metre and regular tunes are unknown, only chants being sung according to tones marked by a variety of curious signs attached to the words in the service books The lessons are chiefly taken from the canonical books of the Bible and are of course good But aside from them and the psalms there is a lamentable dearth of matter to gratify an evangelical and scriptural taste and very much that is positively and radically objectionable. The book of legends, parts of which are generally read at least once a day is an enormous bundle of the grossest fabrications that were ever laid upon the shoulders of the saints * The apocryphal prayer of the Three Children and that of king Manasseh form prominent and essential parts of the second morning service. Besides prayers, lessons anthems and the like specially for the dead which are very numerous single petitions for the same object are interspersed through almost every other part of the services

Other mediators are adopted so entirely to the exclusion of the only Mediator between God and man that aided even by bishop Dionysius I have been unable to find a trace of the intercession of Christ His promise whatsoever ye shall ask the Father in my name he will give it you ' seems to be entirely forgotten Instead of his name, we hear on the saints' days the following " through the intercession of the holy mother of God and of John the Baptist and of St Stephen the protomartyr and of St. Gregory Loosavorich through the memory and prayer of the saints this day commemorated and for the sake of thy precious cross, O Lord accept our entreaties and make us live " To the Virgin petitions like the following are directly addressed O holy mother of God thee do we supplicate intercede with Christ to save his people whom

* It is a folio of about 2 000 pages

he has bought with his own blood ' Mother of God, immaculate mother of the Lord and holy virgin, intercede with thine only born son that he may save us from the threatening of hell, and grant us the kingdom of heaven, and may give peace to the spirits of our dead Nor are we to suppose, that the saints are considered only as secondary mediators between us and the Son, while he alone still intercedes with the Father, for such expressions as the following forbid it Let us make the holy mother of God and all the saints intercessors with the Father in heaven, that he will be pleased to have mercy, and pitying, will give life to his creatures ' ' O Lord through the intercession of the immaculate parent of thine only begotten Son the holy mother of God and the entreaties of all thy saints and of those who are commemorated this day accept our prayers '

Many prayers are indeed addressed directly to the Son, but by what arguments are they supported? Take the following O gracious Lord, for the sake of thy holy, immaculate and virgin mother, and of thy precious cross, accept our prayer and make us live Other strange language respecting the cross has been already quoted I have turned for something more grateful to the prayer of Nerses Shnorháli which forms a prominent part of the ninth service and is probably more highly esteemed than any other prayer in the offices of the Armenian church, *
but how chilling is the following termination ! "O gracious Lord accept the supplication of me, thy servant, and fulfil my petitions for my good, through the intercession of the holy mother of God and John the Baptist and St Stephen the proto martyr, and St Gregory Loosavorich and the holy apostles, and prophets and preachers, and martyrs, and patriarchs, and hermits, and virgins, and all the saints in

* It has been beautifully printed at Venice in twenty-four different languages

16 *

heaven and on earth " I shall be gratified should other
inquiries more successful than mine, prove that the offices
of the church do sometimes recognize the fact that Christ
is even at the right hand of God, making intercession for
us

I am unwilling to take leave of the Armenian prayer
book without allowing it a chance to exhibit by the side
of such vital errors and defects some real excellencies
The following prayer is from the midnight service, and is
probably one of the oldest in the Jamakirk "O Lord of
heaven and earth Creator of all existences visible and invisible to thee do we always pray for thy dominion is in
every place, and thy kingdom ruleth over all Grant us
grace, to rise early for thy service with fear to love thee
with the whole heart and mind to keep thy commands
with our whole strength , to raise our hands with holiness
unto thee without wrath and doubting and to find grace
and mercy with thee and success in virtuous deeds For
thou art the Lord of life and the God of mercies and to
thee belong glory and dominion and honor now and al
ways and forever and ever Amen (Peace be to all
let us worship God)* To thy mighty and powerful dominion all bow the knee and worship and thy majesty is
glorified by all Behold our worship, and teach us to do
the righteousness of truth For thou art the God of peace,
who hast taken the enmity away and made peace in heav
en and on earth and published to them that are afar off
and to them that are nigh the new gifts of thy goodness.
Make us also worthy of that thy great grace ranking us
among thy sincere worshipers, O our God our Lord and
our Savior Jesus Christ Thou who with the Father,
and the Holy Ghost art glorious now and always, and forever and ever Amen '

* This expression occurs in the middle of all prayers of any length, and is
uttered by the priest turning round and waving the cross over the congregation

We stopped after service was ended, to converse awhile with the priests. As usual we found much difficulty in introducing ourselves intelligibly for although they had heard of the New World, they had not the least information respecting it not even of its situation. For they supposed it to be near Constantinople, that being the *ultima Thule* of their geographical knowledge and knew not whether it was inhabited by Christians, Turks or pagans. Their curiosity however, prompted but few questions, and soon left us at liberty to direct the conversation as we pleased. For schools they referred us to Tiflis and declared that there were none either here or in the neighboring villages. They however themselves taught some two or three children each but when asked how many in the village could read and write their only answer was that there were no writers. In fact the art of writing hardly comes within the scope of the education which appears to be given by the priests of most villages to a few individuals, for its object is merely to provide readers for the church and candidates for the ministry and these offices can be discharged by those who are merely able to read. The few children thus taught are never regarded as forming a school. We urged the utility of schools and gave an account of our own both for males and females. They seemed unable to conceive how they could be useful to any but those who intended to be priests, and finally excused themselves by saying their nation had no king. We told them that neither had our own and that kings did not always make schools. The subject was evidently irksome and the first opportunity was seized to change it.

Pernikákh is inhabited entirely by Armenians, and contains about 100 houses, with one church and four priests. It enjoys great quiet under the Russian government being never visited by Kurds nor any other disturbers of public security, especially since Erivan has passed into the hands of the emperor.

July 5   A ride of 15 versts brought us to our next post at Hamamly, a village in an open cultivated valley which is separated by hills from the plain of Pernikakh   It is composed of about 80 Armenian houses   Near the post-house, was an establishment, which we were at a loss whether to name a dram-shop or a victualing house   Whichever it might be, it was equally a new sight for an Armenian village, but soon became familiar   We succeeded tolerably at this in satisfying our hunger, but in similar establishments afterward we found the other appetite almost exclusively provided for   In fact I may here remark in general, that the Armenians of these provinces wherever their situation gives them access to strong drink frequently indulge in it to excess and though sottish drunkenness is not common instances of it do occur   In their feasts, which, being given at births marriages masses for the dead, and other similar occasions frequently occur, they almost invariably both eat and drink to excess and the quantity of wine that is swallowed is perfectly incredible   Public opinion does indeed stamp a drunkard as a vicious man, but to drink for the sake of merriment is considered a privilege of the Christian religion, and an important advantage which it has over Mohammedanism

After an hour s delay in changing horses we proceeded, following over a broken surface the course of the stream we had first crossed in the valley of Pernikakh   Our next post 17 versts from the last, consisted of only a few Cossack cabins, and I shall not trouble you with its name   One or two villages, however, were in sight   The mountains which enclose the valley of the river we had been following, lost at Hamamly their smooth and swelling form, and began to exhibit on their sides, and in their ravines, a few clumps of bushes. Here many trees appeared upon them, and their height too was become considerable   That on the right, where the river passes off through an intricate ravine

on its way to the Koor had its top covered with snow
Bears, wolves deer wild goats, and wild sheep range over
them

We turned to the left to pass over a mountain into the
valley of another branch of the same stream A little
church on an isolated hill reminds me to tell you, that the
Armenians have desert churches in mountains and retired
places distant from any habitations but not so many as
the Greeks and Georgians This was the second we had noticed Service is performed in them only on festival occasions when those who attend frequently sacrifice an ani
mal for a feast, and spend the day in carousing among the
rocks On entering a ravine about two miles from the post,
we observed a copious mineral spring in the middle of the
path from which issued a large quantity of gas It was
surrounded by old foundations of hewn stone The ravine
was rendered refreshing by its coolness and beautiful by a
forest of maple ash oak elm and other trees which clothed,
and a great variety of charming flowers which ornamented
its sides We had not seen a forest tree for the last 120
miles. Following the ravine we were conducted finally by
a steep ascent to the top of the mountain which bounds in
this direction the district of Pembek On the opposite side
was the district of Lori presenting a mountainous prospect,
with the little valley of Gerger directly below us We descended toward it, and at the foot of the mountain, were
arrested by a sanitary cordon to perform fifteen days of
quarantine before proceeding farther in the Russian territories Our last stage was 16 versts.

Gumry is the place where quarantine is usually performed on entering Georgia but, for the accommodation of the
army which was at this time returing from Turkey the
sanitary establishment was now removed to this place
The change was a most agreeable one for us Instead of
a naked and peculiarly uninteresting spot where we could

hardly have got even wood for kitchen purposes, we were located in the midst of scenery of peculiar beauty   It was a dell connected with the valley of Gerger on the north bounded on either side by high hills, and terminating in the thick forests of the mountain to the south, from whence flowed through it three rivulets of the purest water   The atmosphere was purified by frequent thunder showers, vegetation was in its most thriving state   and so cool was the climate that the thermometer ranged at midday in the open shade from 60° to 75° and at sunset was often down to 53°   In it were encamped from eight to ten thousand of the army to undergo the same purgatorial imprisonment as ourselves   Their presence caused us to be provided with comfortable accommodations and means of subsistence For the Russian quarantine establishments on the side of Turkey and Persia are furnished with no lazaretto buildings and make little or no provision for the table of the travel ler   It is almost as if he were set down in an open field, and left to manage as best he can for shelter and for food We have found persons sentenced to a quarantine of ten days or a fortnight where they assured us, they could with difficulty procure a piece of bread   At this place there was no village nor lazaretto nor but for the pres ence of the army would there have been any market   As it was however we found a shop open at which all neces sary provisions could be procured and after being the first day reduced almost to the alternative of fasting, or do ing the duties of the kitchen ourselves we succeeded in converting an Armenian blacksmith into a cook, and had no farther ground of complaint on the score of food

For our lodgings we were indebted to the politeness of Gen R who was the commanding officer on the ground and for whom we had without knowing it brought a letter from Gen Pankratieff at Kars   From our first interview with the latter, he had discovered no disposition to show us attentions and it was not without surprise, that, on the morning we left Kars, we received a letter from the hand of a soldier with the information that it was from the general to an officer at Gérger whom we should find of use to us The soldier we took to be one of those gentlemen of distinction who were condemned to the ranks by the emperor Nicolas for the insurrection that occurred at his accession Many of them are in the army of the Caucasus, and, when they happen to be under the command of liberal minded officers are treated with some indulgence We had previously met him at the lodgings of the commandant of Kars and were after all left in doubt whether the parcel was not from himself However that may be, it contained letters to two officers from both of whom we received many civilities and one of whom was Gen R He called upon us repeatedly with his staff and gave us a large tent which was already pitched in a quiet and central position with a fine arbor before it and formed the most eligible lodgings in the camp We shall have more than one occasion to speak of Gen R s kind attentions after leaving Gerger and it gives me pleasure to add, that though a papist, we found him well known at Shoosha as a friend of the missionaries He was a Pole

Our quarantine unlike the one in Kars, was in sober earnest All our baggage was on the second day suspended piece by piece in a smoke house for eight hours to be fumigated, the clothes we had on were then left to undergo the same process during the night, and at the end the doctor would not give us pratique until he had actually examined our bodies to find if they exhibited no symptoms of the plague! Common people were almost daily made to undergo the same *visit* in the open air before his lodgings! The principal reliance however seemed to be on the fumigation and the final visit, for we were left the whole time without a guardian Persons of a different quarantine repeatedly came into our tent, and we could wander over the mountains as far as we chose with none to *guard* us Such liberty enabled us to pass away our fortnight very agreeably but it certainly destroyed all effective quarantine I ought to add, that if our quarantine was worth nothing, it cost nothing except time, for on asking for the bill of charges at the end we were told that there were none

Our camp life and other intercourse with the army gave us considerable acquaintance with the Russian soldiery. Their coarse dress leathery face and clownish manners, stood out in strong contrast to the gentlemanly appearance of the English garrison at Malta from which my first and latest ideas of military life had been derived Their treatment by their superiors partook largely of servitude and barbarism When conversing with or passing an officer their head was invariably completely uncovered while his hat remained untouched and when smoking their clothes at the commencement of their quarantine whole companies were marched perfectly naked a quarter of a mile before the encampment

With the Cossacks we had much to do in the course of our journey, and our opinion of them continued to the last to improve Their name will always recall the impression made upon me by the first I ever saw He met us the morning we reached Erzroom as we were making our way through a dense fog In a clear atmosphere large as he really was, and mounted upon a tall and stately horse, with a spear at least twelve feet long projecting on one side, a rifle slung upon his back on the other a heavy sword by his side, and a brace of pistols in his girdle he would have appeared sufficiently formidable but magnified by the mist to a gigantic size, he seemed almost like Mars himself Though they speak the same language and profess the same religion as the Russians, they are a distinct nation, with their own peculiar institutions and rights, for they pay no taxes to the emperor, and in their territories on the Don no Russian holds an office or exercises authority. But the emperor claims from them a military service, which obliges every man to alternate three years at home and three years in the field, and in fact converts the whole nation of more than 300,000 individuals into a standing army. They are perfectly undisciplined; we never saw a Cossack drilling. In their marches they have none but vocal music, led by singers in front, and more thrilling notes are rarely formed by voice or instrument, than those that compose Cossack airs. With the exception of some half a dozen supernumerary horses to a regiment, which carry the effects of the superior officers, there is no lumber of baggage. Every man has his own, which is little more than a coat and a pot with a sieve, or a fiddle, or some other implement of utility or amusement, hung to his saddle. We loved to contrast this truly military contempt of encumbering conveniencies, with the baggage of the regular regiments, in which was found a coach, or a phaeton, for almost every officer. The cavalry of this army consisted entirely of Cossacks, and we were amused to see how soon, after a body of them came upon the quarantine ground, they were all provided with shelters. Low arbors, formed of the boughs of trees, were covered with earth, and in one day every mess had a hut. For his soldier-like character exclusively some might admire the Cossack, but his sobriety and independence, tempered with real kindness of heart, and a sense of what is just and right, were the traits that interested us. Our interest was increased by learning, that, though the nation is encumbered with the ceremonies of the Greek church, it exhibits frequent individual instances of a simplicity of religious feeling, that is rare among others of the same communion.

July 20. For the last few days, frequent showers had thoroughly wetted our tent every night, and reduced the tem perature of the atmosphere to an almost uncomfortable degree, but this morning the sky was clear, and, though the thermometer stood at 39° the weather was fine for resuming our journey. At the village of Gérger, perhaps half a mile from the encampment, a sufficient number of horses were not to be had and finally the Cossack who was to be our guide, consented to walk the whole stage rather than detain us. The village contained a small Russian barrack, and seemed chiefly composed of persons attached to the army. Several others are scattered through the valley and inhabited exclusively by Armenians. After tracing the valley for a short distance to the west, we crossed a hill that separates it from the valley of Lori on the north, and came to our next post at Jelal-oghloo after riding only 12 versts. Its population resembled that of Gérger, though the proportion of Russians and military men seemed greater. The valley follows the course of a river that passes near the village, and not far below, unites with that of Gérger. About a mile to the east, and on the banks of the same stream, appeared the ruins of Lori, a fortress often mentioned in the history of Armenia, especially during the reign of the Pakradians, and the invasions of the Seljookians and Moghúls. It was the chief place of the canton of Dashir, and in fact of the province of Kookárk, and when the Gorigian branch of the Pakradian family assumed, in the tenth century, the independent government of this region, under the title of kings of the Aghováns, it became their capital * Its name still remains, and is given also to the whole district.

On starting again we found it a business of labor and time to cross the river mentioned above. For although the land on both sides is nearly a perfect plain, it runs through a profound ravine formed of precipitous ledges of rocks, to be descended and ascended in crossing it. Its water was extremely transparent, and rolled rapidly over a rocky

* St Mart vol 1 p 80 85 222 365 vol 2 p 79

bed, furnishing a retreat doubtless to multitudes of trout, of some of which we had had a taste during our quarantine imprisonment It is the principal branch of the river of which the brook of Pernikakh is a tributary Some distance farther down in its course toward the Koor, it passes near the two convents of Sanahin and Haghpad, both much distinguished in the ecclesiastical history of Armenia and the latter of which will be again referred to as still an important establishment We took a northward direction over a rich meadow-land, among the thick grass and variegated flowers of which, a regiment of Cossacks were gathering strawberries It was the first fruit we had seen growing, in travelling 300 miles, since we entered Armenia, and this was yet hardly ripe Two or three hours from Jelál-oghloo, were two villages at a small distance from the road inhabited like most in this district by Armenians and in each the remains of an ancient church rose high above all the other buildings Around them were extensive tracts cultivated with grain which was not yet in the ear, an indication of an extremely cold climate We found our post after a stage of 20 versts, at a distance from any village But though a mere Cossack station it furnished us with a better dinner than we could have procured at the last village for that had offered nothing for our refreshment but inebriating liquors and salt fish Our room, too, was uncommonly decent having at least one regular paper window, and what was the greatest rarity, a bedstead, though unfortunately the only bed upon it was a handful of loose hay It was a Russian luxury, we had seen nothing of the kind since leaving Constantinople

July 21 We arose chilled with the cold, and getting under way at 6 A M found ourselves, after an hour s ride, on the northern verge of the mountains over which we had been travelling from Gumry Extending to the right they fill the space between the Aras and the Koor, nearly to their junction, in which vicinity we shall take another view of them on our way to Nakhcheván. It was not simply these, however, that we had now to descend; for the prospect before us showed that we were to bid adieu entirely to the elevated plateau whose cool climate and verdant plains and mountains we had enjoyed since long before crossing the western boundary of Armenia. From our elevated position we looked down upon a broad, and indeed to our limited vision, boundless valley brown throughout with sunburnt fields, giving us no very pleasing anticipations of the climate from which they had derived their color. It was the valley of the Koor. Beyond it a long line of bright clouds in the horizon marked out the position, as we supposed, of mount Caucasus; but not a point of it was visible.

Such was our first view of Georgia, for the declivity of the mountain before us was once the boundary between that country and Armenia. Though it presented no very inviting distant prospect our introduction to it was most delightful. Extensive and luxuriant forests reached the whole distance from us to the plain below. Guided by a Georgian surijy, the first of that nation we had found, and following along the ravine of a mountain torrent, the carriage road on which we had travelled from Gümry, we glided rapidly downward under the shade first of the beech, maple, elm and sumach and after a while, also of the oak wild pear and hawthorn forming an almost unbroken forest to our next post a distance of 15 versts. It was called Samiski but no village was near and only a shop was at hand to offer us the usual variety of spirits, wine and coarse bread. Our next post was at the foot of the mountain 18 versts distant and we reached it at half past 1 P M. How great the change of climate since 6 o'clock in the morning! Less than seven hours ride over a distance of 22 miles had transferred us, almost from a frosty spring morning into a midday summer's sun and every thing around showed that the increase of temperature which we felt was not an accidental variation that might happen any where, but a real change of climate In the morning the fields were covered with verdure kept continually fresh by frequent thunder showers, now every spire of grass was as withered and brown as if there had been no rain for months. There the ears of grain had hardly begun to appear, here we were in the midst of harvest

July 22 We were detained until 10 A M for want of horses I have mentioned that we left Kars with the horses of Cossacks, and had Cossacks for guides. On advancing farther into the Russian territories we found at each station a separate set of horses for post purposes immediately superintended, and perhaps owned by a native of the country Instead of a Cossack, too, a native acted as guide and surijy Still every post-house was a station of Cossacks, who were its responsible directors, and bound, in case of need to furnish their own horses Such an exigency occurred to-day, for though the post horses were gone, those of the Cossacks were in the stable We could hardly blame their masters, however for withholding them as they were their private property it being a condition of their military service that they furnish their own horses Besides being thus connected with the posts in every part of these provinces, the Cossacks form stations of police guards, and in that capacity are obliged to accompany travellers wherev er there is danger For it is a singular part of the Russian post system, that no one who avails himself of it, is allowed to expose himself to robbers or enemies without a competent guard.

A Russian post, as it usually appears here is a quadrangular wattled enclosure entered by a wide gate with a row of Cossack spears standing near it in front, and hav ing two long buildings for the Cossacks on either side, with

17 *

another for their horses on the back   Sometimes, however, the beasts alone are decently provided for, while the men have only little huts sunk completely under ground   The traveller will generally find a room furnished with at least a platform of loose slabs, a foot or two from the ground, instead of a bed   With all its imperfections we found the Russian post a more eligible mode of travelling than any other that we tried in our journey   It was sufficiently expeditious, and still allowed us to stop as often and as long as we chose, and withal was cheap   We paid only two copecks or about a cent and a half, the verst, for each horse, nothing being charged for the Cossack and surju or their horses   I ought to add, to the praise of the former, that no Cossack ever solicited us for a present or seemed to expect one, nor indeed did the surijies till to-day   The greatest inconvenience we found was, that the posts never furnished provisions and were often so far from any village as to oblige us to fast longer than was agreeable, unless we carried our own food   To-day, we could not procure even a morsel of bread nearer than two versts.

I know not how long we should have been detained had not Gen R with the same politeness that we experienced from him at Gérger, helped us onward   Happening to pass with a division of the army and seeing us at the door, he rode up to inquire the cause of our detention   The Cossacks were immediately ordered to furnish their own horses for our service, and in a few minutes we were moving at a rapid rate toward Tiflis.   A ride of two versts brought us to Great Shoolaver, a village of perhaps 150 houses, and the chief place of the district.   It was surrounded by extensive vineyards and gardens of fruit trees , an additional testimony that we had left the cold climate of Armenia   The Armenians themselves, however, we had not yet left, for most of its inhabitants were of that nation   Its houses too, like those of Armenia, were under ground

Near Great Shoolaver there is a village of Greeks, and I will stop a moment to record what we heard of the few of that nation which are to be found in the trans-Caucasian provinces east of Imireti We saw none, except a few mer chants at Tiflis The following are all that we heard of viz one village named Simskár between Elizabeththal and Katherinenfeld, two German colonies southwest of Tiflis , another near Great Shoolaver a third between Jelal-oghloo and Haghpád , a fourth at the copper mines near Haghpád , and a fifth, named Baindoor near Gumry on the Arpa chai They speak a dialect of modern Greek much corrupted by Turkish and write Greco-Turkish, i e Turkish with the Greek letters Their liturgy is in ancient Greek, but they use the Venice edition of the Greco-Turkish New Testament and Psalter of which however, they have but very few copies At the request of Mr Zeremba the gentleman who gave us this information we have taken measures to have them supplied with the British and Foreign Bible Society's edition To their number may now be added the former Greek population of Erzroom whom the Russians have located in the little district of Trialeti, near Akhal tsikhe

One extensive plain, of a somewhat undulating surface interrupted by only a few small hills reaches from Great Shoolaver to the Koor in the direction of our route, and stretches off to the right as far as the eye can see It is intersected by several rivers running toward the Koor, the largest of which the Khram or Ktsia, we forded ten versts from our post Almost the whole of it was one vast field of wheat which the peasants were now harvesting , and the uncommon height of the stalk and weight of the ear showed that a fruitful soil had well repaid their labor Many villages appeared in different directions, and were generally surrounded with vineyards fruit trees and poplars, the rich verdure of which, presenting a strong contrast to the uni versally sunburnt fields around, gave them, at a distance, a most inviting appearance   They proved however, upon a nearer inspection to be small and poorly built

At one of them named Kote we found our post-house, after a stage of 27 versts , and from thence took post wagons.   We had found the first of these vehicles at Samiski, two stages back , but they seemed so uncomfortable and awkward that we preferred to continue on horse-back and took only one for our baggage   Indeed I am not sure but shame contributed more than any thing to this decision, for we felt, that mounted in such clumsy machines, we should be a fair laughing-stock for a whole regiment of Russians that were encamped near   Familiarity with the sight how ever and especially the rapidity with which we could thus travel had, at the end of two stages overcome all our scru ples and we now took one for ourselves, as well as for our baggage.   They consisted of a rough semi-cylindrical body, hardly more than six feet long by three in diameter attach ed without springs to the wheels and drawn by three or four horses abreast, the middle one of which had a bow project ing high above his head with a bell suspended from the centre of the arch   With such accommodations than which we were assured the posts in Russia itself rarely furnish better we proceeded on as fast as the horses guided by a rough Russian driver could carry us over hills and stones, till our eyes were too nearly jolted from their sockets for us to see with much accuracy what we passed   Yet, even in this outlandish situation, a meadow covered with hay-cocks and a regular load of hay the first I had seen for four years, brought up before us for a moment the sweet associations of home   We observed too a short distance from Kote a small pond with what seemed a thick incrustation of salt upon its shore but we had no time to examine it   After a stage of only 11 versts, we changed again at Telet, an iso-lated post-house 14 versts from Tiflis.   Four versts beyond, we came upon the bank of the Koor and then, following up its stream to the left along the valley through which it here runs the remainder of the way we reached the city at dark A bare examination of our bill of health from Gérger satisfied the quarantine guard our assertion that we had nothing but our own travelling baggage was all that was demanded by the inspector of customs, the keeper of the gate if a single pole thrown across the path may be so named, merely demanded our names and nation, and thus easily we found ourselves fairly introduced into the capital of Georgia

LETTER VII

TIFLIS

Description of the city—Its taverns—River Koor—Climate—Different costumes—Police—Provinces of the Government of the Caucasus—Nature of the government—Influence of the Russians upon the intelligence and morals of the natives—Population of the city—Commercial character of the Armenians—Trade of these provinces—Intemperance—Archbishop Nérses—His Armenian academy—Printing press—Armenian diocese of Georgia—Interview with bishop Serope—Armenian gymnasium at Moscow—Armenian churches and forms of worship—Image worship—Protestant worship at New Tiflis—Observance of the Sabbath

DEAR SIR

TIFLIS occupies the right bank of the Koor in a contracted valley formed by irregular mountains parallel with the stream on the side of the city, and hills coming down in a point quite to the water s edge on the other A circular fort covers this point and together with a small suburb, is united to the city by a bridge of a single wooden arch, thrown over the river, here confined to a narrow channel while the ruined walls of an old citadel crown the top, and extend down the side of a part of the opposite mountain The mountains and hills around exhibit only the cheerless prospect of perfectly naked rocks and the only lookout they afford is toward the north where the valley opens and discloses at a distance of at least sixty miles, the snowy summit of mount Cazbek one of the highest peaks of the Caucasus The old and native part of the city is built upon the truly oriental plan of irregular narrow lanes, and still more irregular and diminutive houses thrown together in all the endless combinations of accident Here and

there, European taste aided by Russian power, has worked
out a passable road for carriages, or built a decent house
overlooking and putting to shame all its mud-walled and
dirty neighbors   A line of bazárs, too, extending along
the river and branching out into several streets, together
with much bustle and business, displays some neatness and
taste, and is connected with two or three caravanserais,
one of which is the largest and best we have seen
Several old and substantial churches displaying their cu-
polas and belfries in different parts, complete the promin
ent features of this part of the city   In the northern, or
Russian quarter officers palaces government offices and
private houses lining broad streets and open squares, have
a decidedly European aspect, and exhibit in their pillared
fronts something of that taste for showy architecture which
the edifices of their capital have taught the Russians to
admire

In a city possessed so long by Europeans, we had hoped
for convenient accommodations and had anticipated with
some pleasure the luxury of a good bed at least after having slept in our clothes every night since leaving Constan
tinople   The name of a tavern also was associated with
ideas of travelling comforts which had not been awakened
before   There were two in town one with a French, and
the other with a German landlord   We selected the former on the night of our arrival as the most conveniently
situated   Its dirty floors looking as if they had never felt
the effects of water gave us at our entrance, no very prom
ising earnest of the rest of its conveniences, but extreme
fatigue and the lateness of the hour made us hope that the
beds would be better and induced us soon to try them.
Hardly was I snugly laid in mine, however before it
seemed more like a bed of nettles than of down   A whole
army of blood-thirsty enemies attacked every assailable
point, and forced me immediately to seek for quarters on

the centre of the floor, the only place of refuge. Our rooms proved, in fact absolutely uninhabitable, and we were obliged to seek new lodgings The only alternative was the German inn There indeed, were none of our late enemy, but two others, which not even German neatness could exclude annoyed us almost as much Myriads of fleas swarmed in every corner and constantly peopled our clothes with animated company; and a still greater number of flies, like another Egyptian plague, annoyed our faces and eyes every moment of the day In the night we obtained some respite, for the darkness put the flies to sleep, and their more wakeful allies were avoided, in my case in part by carefully allowing none of the covering of my bed by resting upon the floor to serve as a ladder to conduct them to me, and entirely in that of my companion, who was less hardened to such annoyances by securing himself in a night-dress sewed up at the hands and feet into a close bag We should have preferred private rooms, not only for convenience, but also for economy, for our lodgings and board were exceedingly dear But the same cause which had ruined the taverns by depriving them of patronage, had filled every disposable room and none could be procured For the police takes upon itself the authority of quartering strangers, especially if they are officers, as most Europeans in the place are, in any house which it chooses, and as the army from Turkey was now fast assembling here, every nook was occupied Indeed the city is generally very crowded, as is evidenced by the high rent of houses Some, which would no more than decently accommodate a respectable family, were pointed out to us as commanding a rent of six or seven hundred dollars.

Our lodgings were on the opposite side of the Koor from the city and nearly on a level with its stream. That river, the ancient Cyrus, is here very muddy and rapid. Its rapidity is turned to a curious advantage as a moving power to floating mills five of which, not far above our house we had the curiosity to examine A chain carried up the stream and a timber resting against the bank moored each of them safe ly at a distance from the shore Three log canoes fastened firmly to each other upheld the building and its machine ry, while a fourth supported the outer axle of the water wheel which played between it and the third They seem ed to be moved by a sufficient power and besides the ex treme simplicity of their structure had the great advan tage of being above danger from floods Not far below several wheels were turned in the same way for watering gardens the very buckets which raised the water being so constructed as to form also the paddles by which the wheels were turned The turbidness of the river does not destroy its utility to the town for every fountain and well partakes so strongly of the offensive mineral properties of the hot springs that the water of the Koor alone can be used and like that of the Nile at Cairo it is carried about the streets in skins on animals for sale From its warm baths Tiflis is said to have taken its name as *Tpilis kalaki* means in Georgian the *warm city* and they are so uniformly no ticed by every ancient and modern traveller that curiosity alone would have induced us to try them We of course had little chance to judge of the effect of their mineral prop erties except upon the olfactory nerves which indicated with sufficient distinctness the presence of not a little sul phureted hydrogen The water as admitted into our apart ment was as far above blood heat as could be comfortably borne

I should as soon suppose the name of Tiflis to be derived from its situation as from its hot springs For surrounded as it is by naked mountains and hills which cut off almost every wind reflect the rays of the sun and become them selves radiators of no small portion of caloric, its atmosphere

18

is always heated   In the winter, although in the latitude
of New Haven in Connecticut Reaumeur s thermometer
does not descend lower than 3° or 4°, and in the summer
the air is excessively sultry   We did not learn, however
that bilious affections are decidedly among its endemical
diseases , but inflamatory fevers, especially in the form
which is commonly called a stroke of the sun were said to
be common   The absence of the former is doubtless owing
to the extreme dryness of the soil and climate   For there
is not a particle of stagnant water nor any rank vegetation
in the vicinity, and it rains on an average no more than
thirty or forty days in a year   As an exception however,
to these remarks which, according to the information we
gathered, accurately describe the usual climate of Tiflis I
ought to state that we did not find the weather intole-
rably hot and during our stay there were several falls of
rain one of which continued without intermission for twen
ty four hours and raised the Koor seven or eight feet   To
this may perhaps be attributed the unusual virulence of the
cholera, which broke out shortly after *

Tiflis has the appearance of an excessively busy and
populous place   Its streets present not only a crowded
but, unlike many oriental cities a lively scene   Every
person seems hurried by business   Nor is the variety of
costumes representing different nations and tongues many
of which are curious and strange the least noticeable fea
ture of the scene   The Russian soldier stands sentry at
the corners of the streets in a coarse great coat concealing
the want of a better uniform and even of decent clothing

---

* Mr Dwight s meteorological table during our stay from July 22d to
Aug 4th made the highest temperature in the open shade at 7 A M to be
78° the lowest 61° and the average 73°   The highest temperature at 3
P M during the same time was 87° the lowest 66° and the average 79°
At 10 P M the highest was 83° the lowest 61° and the average 74°   On
six days out of fourteen there were showers of rain accompanied usually with
strong northerly winds

The Russian subaltern jostles carelessly along in a little cloth cap narrow-skirted coat and tight pantaloons with epaulettes dangling in front of naturally round shoulders In perfect contrast to him stands the stately Turk if not in person yet represented by some emigrant Armenian with turbaned head and bagging shalwar The Georgian priest appears cane in hand with a green gown long hair and broad brimmed hat while black flowing robes and a cylindrical lambskin cap mark his clerical brother of the Armenian church The dark Lesgy with the two-edged *kama* (short sword), the most deadly of all instruments of death dangling at his side seems prowling for his victim as an avenger of blood The city bred Armenian merchant waits upon his customers snugly dressed in an embroidered frock-coat gay calico frock red silk shirt and ample green trowsers also of silk The tall lank Georgian peasant with an upright conical sheepskin cap and scantily clothed looks as independent in his *yapanjy* (cloke of felt) as Diogenes in his tub His old oppressor the Persian is known by more flowing robes smoothly combed beard and nicely dinted cap In the midst of his swine appears the half clad Mingrelian with a bonnet like a tortoise shell tied loosely upon his head And in a drove of spirited horses is a hardy mountaineer whose round cap with a shaggy flounce of sheepskin dangling over his eyes and the breast of his coat wrought into a cartridge box show him to be a Circassian

Of all this heterogeneous crowd the Russian, being lord of the rest demands our attention first in the narrative, as he did also in the journey For the morning after we arrived our host, having already sent in our names to the authorities, informed us, that in obedience to the laws of the country it was his duty to conduct us immediately to the police office Fortunately we had provided ourselves with passports from the Russian embassador at Constantinople or we might have been embarrassed For we learned here that the emperor Alexander in granting free trade to Georgia had ordered that to prevent persons suspected of bad principles from introducing themselves un der the name of merchants all foreigners should furnish themselves with passports from the foreign ministers of Russia With the sight of these passports the police was immediately satisfied we were only asked how long we intended to stop and whither we were going next, and our passports were detained Neither here nor in any other place within the Russian territory were our American passports inquired for It was annoying to have police officers taking notes of us at every turn and stopping place in our journey but they never showed us any other than civil treatment and as their services were unasked they were as they ought to be gratis We were never charged a cent at any public office

We made an early call upon general Strekaloff the military governor for whom we had a letter from the Russian minister at the Porte He was the second in rank of the Russian authorities and we were not informed of the exact extent of his jurisdiction though at the time of our visit he was acting in the place of his superior marshal Paske vich the commander in chief of the Government of the Caucasus who was absent at St Petersburg The Government of the Caucasus has its capital at Tiflis but extends also to the north of the mountain from which it takes its name and embraces there a tract reaching from the Caspi an to the Black sea So that its commander in-chief besides the internal affairs of the Government itself has charge of the whole line of frontier posts with which Russia has completely surrounded the mountain to check the predatory incursions of its unsubdued and barbarous tribes Our in quiries extended only to that part of the Government which lies south of the Caucasus, and is called by the Russians the *Trans-Caucasian Provinces* These provinces are *Imreti*, embracing, I believe, the supervision of Gooriel and Mingreli, and thus including the whole of ancient Colchis *Georgia* subdivided into its three provinces of Kartalini Kakheti and Somkheti and embracing also all the other cantons that lie west of Sheky Kara bagh and Erivan the *Mussulman Provinces*, which are Sheky, Shirwan and Kara bagh , *Daghistan* including Derbend, Kooba and Bakoo, and *Armenia* embracing Erivan and Nakhchevan * At the head of each of these five provinces there is a governor responsible to the commander in-chief and having the requisite sub governors of districts and commandants of towns under him

The government of the trans-Caucasian provinces par takes largely of a military nature Many civilians and natives are indeed employed, but their offices are either in themselves of no responsibility or are made so by the close supervision of some higher authority while all stations of power and trust are occupied by military officers with a field marshal at their head whose orders are backed by an army which amounted when we were there to about 60 000 men A government supported by so many bayonets can afford to allow its subjects some ensigns of liberty , and accordingly with the exception of one or two districts which notwithstanding the fearful odds against them have dared to revolt, the whole population is allowed to wear arms and you hardly meet a man without the horrid kama at his side That liberty itself however at least of speech has been banished, may be naturally suspected from the fact that with one or two rare exceptions every person when circumstances called for an expression of opinion

---

* Talish was not mentioned in the list that was given us and I am not sure where it should be classed Probably it is one of the Mussulman Provinces

was careful to say nothing anti Russian, unless the unparalleled phenomenon may be supposed to exist, of a conquered people s being unanimously attached to their conquerors Still however military and absolute Russian despotism may be it certainly in disclaiming all religious tests sets an example to some other governments whose boast is liberty   The question of their religious creed seems never to be asked candidates for office civil or military and the commander-in chief of these provinces is about as likely to be of the papal or protestant, as of the Greek faith   In fact it was reported that general Strekaloff was soon to be succeeded by a gentleman who was a protestant

In our observations of the rulers of Georgia a chief regard was had to the influence which during thirty years, they have exerted upon the *intelligence* and *morals* of their subjects   That they have as yet done nothing in favor of *education* beyond the precincts of Tiflis was affirmed by all   Their apologists said that they were desirous of doing so and had been prevented only by want of time But if the matter had lain very near their hearts they could certainly have found a few moments for it, before a whole generation had gone off the stage   In Tiflis, a school of one or two hundred scholars has existed some time, for Georgians and Russians at least under the patronage and perhaps partly supported by government   This, when we were there they were about to re-organize into a gymnasium and enlarge into the head of a system with branches in all the provincial towns   It was supposed that in Tiflis as many as 140 and in other places 60 would be admitted all to be taught and in the city one half to be supported gratis   Russians Georgians Armenians and moslems would be admitted and instruction would be given in their respective languages (considering Persian as the language of the latter,) together with geography, civil and ecclesiastical history and some other branches   But after all the whole was to be merely a military institution , open only to the sons of noblemen and persons of distinction and introductory to military academies, in such a sense that whoever had completed his studies in it would be admissible to the rank of cadet   We did not learn that government had any intentions to provide for the education of the common people

If in the term *morals* we include the grosser criminal offences against the peace of society such as murder and robbery no one can deny that in this respect they have been much improved by Russian authority   For almost perfect security has been introduced into every corner, unless it be too near the mountains from the Caspian to the Black sea   If we include in it manners and customs the question of their improvement in this respect will turn upon the decision of another whether Persian or Russian manners be the most eligible standard for imitation   a decision after all hardly worth our time to settle so little interchange of society do the Russians have with the natives and so little do they care to make them imitate their own standard   But if by morals we refer to the social vices infamous as the Georgians have always been known to be for unchastity it must be confessed that they have deteriorated   The devotees of lust have multiplied   So great was the incontinence of the soldiery that even Georgians in the province of Kakheti were goaded by it, in 1812 to an open and desperate rebellion

The number of Russians in Tiflis it is both difficult and of very little consequence to ascertain for nearly all are connected with the army and constantly fluctuating   The native population consisted in 1825 of 2500 Armenian 1500 Georgian and 500 moslem families   It has increased rapidly since and the Armenian bishop told us that the present number of Armenian families was 4000   This es-

timate is probably too high and the whole number of natives when we were there was undoubtedly somewhat less
than 30 000 souls

The large proportion of Armenians in this population allows us to suppose ourselves virtually though not really,
still in Armenia and authorizes me to consider our observa
tions upon them as an integral part of the general view I
am endeavoring to give of their nation in their own country
With the exception of one Georgian two or three Greeks
and a Swiss firm that commenced business while we were
there every merchant in Tiflis is Armenian and nearly the
same is true of the mechanics In this fact is exhibited
the natural disposition of the nation —Some have given to
Shah Abbas all the credit of originating Armenian com
merce And that the facilities for trade granted by him to
the colony he so cruelly tore from their homes and settled
in the suburb of Joolfah at Isfahan gave it the first im
pulse there can be no doubt But that impulse was successful then and has continued to be felt extensively to the
present day only because the genius of the nation is com
mercial Once detach an Armenian from his native soil,
and the magnetic needle points toward the pole with hard
ly more regularity than his taste toward merchandize The
thousands whom war has forcibly carried into captivity
may have pursued long the labors of servitude and the
still other thousands, which migrate every year voluntarily
from their native mountains to the large cities of Turkey
(some crowds of whom met us on their way to Constanti
nople) may practise for years the humble occupations
of porters and water-carriers but almost invariably do
they either in their own persons or in that of their children
work their way into some of the ranks of trade , beginning
with the initiatory grade of mechanic ascending gradually
to that of merchant, and finally the more able or fortunate
reaching that of banker, the acme of their ambition Fond

of attending to the purchase and sale of their goods in person, however distant the one may be made from the other they become great travellers and almost every important fair or mart, from Leipsic and London to Bombay and Calcutta, is visited by them From this view of their character some have asserted that they resemble the Jews The comparison seems invidious and still I cannot but feel that in some respects it is just For if there is one trait more prominent than any other and common to the whole nation from Constantinople to Tebriz it is love of money They urge a plausible excuse for it if so much may be said of an excuse for ' the root of all evil from the people and governments where they live the one being so ignorant and poor that nothing but money will procure respect and the other so corrupt that the same means only will secure justice or protection Such a view of their situation is doubtless just for in a state of society like that of Turkey and Persia, wealth and brutal force are almost the only means of acquiring influence In this alternative their national taste would not allow them to hesitate We have not learned that an Armenian rebel or robber exists

An Armenian merchant differs materially from a Greek As in his national character there is more sense and less wit so in his trade there is more respectability and less trickery Not that he is an honest man for cheating at least in the part of the nation of which I am now speaking is universal and is regarded only as an authorized art of trade Conscience it is true allows it to be sinful, but they say are we in a convent that we should be able to live without it? Indeed such is the state of things that for a perfectly upright and honest man to gain a livelihood, is generally and thoroughly believed to be impossible But a distinction must be made between cheating and bad faith. A Turk will cheat all that he can in making a bargain and yet he is proverbial for good faith in keeping it when

made I recollect an instance where one who had perhaps
told half a dozen lies to obtain the highest price for an ar
ticle we bought called us a day or two after to receive from
him a para that had been overlooked in the reckoning
The Armenians are certainly less remarkable for good
faith and yet notwithstanding all their cheating they are
not destitute of it   Their disposition to monopolize is un
commonly overbearing   A rich merchant will if possible
crush every one whose trade interferes with his   Indeed I
think I am authorized to make the remark general that it
is in the character of the nation to be peculiarly intolerant
of competition and overbearing toward a conquered rival
And the history of their civil broils when they had a polit
ical existence as well as the villanies to which their eccle
siastical rivalries now frequently lead incline me to the
opinion of a very acute observer of character that when
the bad passions of an Armenian are fully awake no deed
is too base or too dark for him to do   The merchants of
Tiflis are said also to be very clanish in their trade
ready by every means to injure a foreigner who may attempt
to establish himself among them   An instance was men
tioned to us of a European s being ruined and forced to
leave the place by their combining to undersell him in the
articles with which he commenced business

The trade of the trans-Caucasian provinces has been
fostered by the Russian government By a Ukase dated
the 20th of Oct 1821 the emperor Alexander granted special privileges to native and foreign merchants and reduced the duties upon all merchandize to five per cent for
ten years from the first of July 1822 This franchise of
trade was granted we were told in consequence of the rep-
resentations of the Chevalier le Gamba consul of France
the only European consul whom we found at Tiflis   He
had travelled extensively in these regions and we are
indebted to him for many civilities and for much informa-

tion * He considered Tiflis to be favorably situated for
trade and expected that enjoying a protecting govern
ment and lying at nearly equal distances from the Black and
Caspian seas it will again become as in the days of Jus-
tinian the thoroughfare of the over land commerce of Asia
By the one sea the merchandize of Europe is easily brought
to the neighboring port of Redoot kulaah and the other
shortens the distance of the drug-growing steppes of Tar
tary, and even of the rich valley of the Indus while superior
security tends to attract hither the trade of Tebriz from its
old channel by Erzroom Communication with Europe
through either Odessa Moscow or St Petersburg is
easy by means of the Russian post which leaves weekly
and reaches the capital a distance of 2627 versts (1751
miles) in about fifteen days The consul confessed that
though the trade of Tiflis had considerably increased his
sanguine expectations had not yet been realized The Per
sian and Turkish wars by interrupting trade and the mil
itary genius of the government leading it to bestow all its
attention upon the profession of arms and lightly esteem
that of commerce had contributed to his disappointment
He hoped however to obtain a prolongation of the fran
chise

You may suppose that we were gratified to meet the productions of our own country in this commercial market
But not every countryman s face is welcome even at the
distance of Asiatic Georgia In the first caravanserai we
entered the day after reaching Tiflis we stumbled upon a
hogshead of New England rum ! What a harbinger
thought we have our countrymen sent before their mission

---

* Besides answering our questions verbally he lent us his Travels in
Southern Russia and the Trans Caucasian Provinces which he had published
Having been unable since to procure this work from Paris I cannot refer to
it as an authority for the facts which we borrowed from it the few notes
we took not enabling me to mention the pages

aries ! What a reproof to the Christians of America that, in finding fields of labor for their missionaries they should allow themselves to be anticipated by her merchants in finding a market for their poisons ! When shall the love of souls cease to be a less powerful motive of enterprise than the love of gain ? I had before wondered where in Mohammedan countries a market could be found for the large quantities of rum that have been sent to the Archipelago, especially since temperance has checked the consumption of it at home, but have since been assured that about a third of what reaches Constantinople is bought by Georgian merchants That the people of Georgia are among the hardest drinkers in the world is well known Their country especially the province of Kakheti (the others produce principally grain) is extremely fertile in the vine It grows to an enormous size running upon trees like the wild grape and requiring little more cultivation The wine which it produces is not bad and is so abundant that the best is but about four cents the bottle while the common is less than a cent The ordinary day s ration for an inhabitant of Tiflis from the mechanic to the prince is said to be a *tonk* measuring between five and six bottles of Bordeaux ! and the quantity drunk at their revels is perfectly incredible Neither bottles nor any kind of casks however are used, and skins of goats and cattle with the hair inward and smeared with naphtha supply their place

We had hoped to find in operation at Tiflis an extensive and efficient system of education for the Armenians under the direction of archbishop Nerses the ornament and boast of the Armenian church But our first inquiries showed us that we were to be disappointed Nerses was no longer here So long ago as when the Rev Henry Martyn was at Echmiadzin he had as president of the synod and wekeel of the Catholicos the complete control of affairs at that establishment Subsequently he resided at Tiflis as

bishop of the province of Georgia, but still retained his
former office, and was universally regarded as destined to
succeed the present Catholicos, in his office as head of the
Armenian church. His name was known wherever the
nation is scattered, and though many an ambitious ecclesiastic envied his elevation and disliked his authority, the
more intelligent of the laity regarded him with great respect, as the most enlightened sensible and patriotic of
their clergy   His measures showed a mind bent upon im
proving the civil and intellectual condition of his nation,
nor did he fail to make some innovations of a religious na
ture   That he might diminish the number of priests pre-
paratory to new regulations respecting them, he determined to ordain none in his diocese for a certain number
of years, he openly discouraged pilgrimages, and forbade
the book of legends to be read any longer in the churches
under his jurisdiction   His efforts in favor of education
will appear, when I speak of his academy   As might be
expected of a man not evangelically enlightened they look
ed no farther than to the cultivation of the intellect as a
path to worldly advantages   Of his political views we obtained no information, nor did we learn the precise cause
of his removal from Tiflis   We were told in general
terms, that he incurred the displeasure of marshal Paskevich, and was at once transferred, or rather banished, to
Bessarabia   Perhaps his enlightened and independent
mind was leading him to views respecting his nation that
crossed the plans of government and, combined with his
great influence made him regarded as a dangerous subject in so distant a portion of the empire   or, more probably was likely to prove a formidable obstacle to the plans
of government respecting the Armenian *church*, whatever
they may be   Though thus arbitrarily disposed of, and
consequently cut off from the hope of succeeding to the
chair of the Catholicos, he was not entirely deprived of of

19

fice, but still is bishop of a see that embraces all the Armenians in the western part of Russia, from the Black sea to St Petersburg   So many of the Armenian colony at Camimec in Poland, as have not embraced the faith of Rome, are probably under his jurisdiction, and perhaps that is the origin of his see *

Nerses left behind him an interesting monument of his desire to enlighten his countrymen, in the academy that was built by him here   A sight of it in its best days would doubtless have gratified us much, but it has declined since his departure, and during our visit, was closed entirely, in consequence of the vacation which occurs during dog days Merely the building however is a strong testimony to his patriotism   It is a brick structure, two stories high, white-washed without, and ornamented on both sides with a row of columns and was built at an expense of sixty or seventy thousand roubles, all of which, with the exception of a few legacies was drawn from Nérses s own resources. The Russians helped in no other way, than that the general security introduced by their government encouraged individual benevolence thus to exert itself for the public good   In this solitary instance only has it produced such an effect upon education and as if even for this they would have some compensation, they were actually occupying a

---

* This colony was originally formed by Armenians who fled from the devastators of their country but at what time I have not learned   The site of their city is exceedingly strong and even down nearly to our own times, they have enjoyed a semi independence having their own officers, who were clothed with the power of life and death   In 1624 the Catholicos Melkiseti being forced in the persecutions of Shah Abbas to flee from Echmiádzin took up his residence at Leopol another Armenian colony in Poland of a similar origin and then consisting of 1000 families   After a year he removed to Camimec where he died   In 1666 the archbishop, or as he is also called the patriarch of Camimec was converted to the Romish faith by a Theatin monk and the books of his church were purged of their heresies Mukhitár's Dict Arts Gamenits and Ilov Chamchean P 7 c 10 Tournefort, vol 2   p 403

great part of the building, when we visited it, as an arsenal for the army The rooms of the part to which we had access, differed in no respect from our own academies being furnished with benches and desks in European style To erect the building, when the money was provided, was easy, but to procure competent instructors was a more difficult task One was brought from Paris, a second from Moscow, and a third from Isfahan The number finally amounted to ten or eleven, of which three taught Armenian two Russian one Persian, one French, one mathematics, and one drawing

Nerses originally designed that it should rank high as a gymnasium but after he ceased to direct it became merely a grammar school for teaching Armenian, Russian and French and is now fast dwindling into a common school None of the modern improvements in education were ever tried in it except an ineffectual attempt at the Lancasterian system Though in the study of languages the New Testament is used as a class-book, it is not and never was adapted to exert any moral or religious influence upon the nation, and probably that work was selected merely in consequence of the facility with which it could be procured A vartabed, named Harutun however who, under Nerses and since, has been its director is a useful man, and in his devotedness to the enlightening of his nation seems to look a little farther than the improvement of the intellect. He has published archbishop Plato s catechism in Armenian. The present number of scholars was about 200 and as there are no funds, we were assured that the current expenses, amounting to 3000 roubles per annum, are borne by this episcopal see

Whether this establishment was connected in the intentions of Nerses with an extensive system of schools we are not informed He never, in fact, built any other, nor is there another Armenian school within the limits of the modern province of Georgia, as already defined, with the exception of one containing about thirty scholars in Gan jeh Compared with the Georgians, the Armenians of Tiflis are said to be intelligent but in reality they can have but little education Their females have not, and never had the advantages of a school still some of them are privately taught to read And, strange as it may seem the language they are taught is not their own, but Georgian, a fact that shows the influence of the Georgians here to be greater than from their small number might be supposed, and accounts for what we were assured is true that the Armenians of Tiflis know Georgian better than their own tongue

Nerses found, in commencing his school quite as great a deficiency of books as of teachers and that without a press which would enable him to supply it, the establish ment would be incomplete, and its operations embarrassed Having heard at Constantinople that even a newspaper was issued from this press, we had expected to find it in efficient operation, and one of our first demands on visiting the school, was to be directed to it In search of it, we wandered into the precincts of the Armenian cathedral, where it is now located A bishop named Simeon Nes moonean who then occupied Nerses s place espying us, politely invited us to his apartments In his civilities, how ever, the press was forgotten, although we reminded him repeatedly of our desire to see it We learned that, though still in operation, it does very little for want of funds Only a spelling book the catechism already mentioned, an edition of the Venice Armenian grammar, and another of the Psalter, have been printed No newspaper has been attempted and the report probably referred to the govern ment gazette, a paper of little value, in Russian and Georgian, that is issued once in about twenty days, from a press

owned by government The same press has also attempted to print in Persian, but appears not to have succeeded

The bishop's politeness extended to an invitation to tea,
and we accordingly spent an hour or two with him in the
evening Tea, with which, according to a custom not un
common here, brandy was offered us in the place of milk,
was served up around a *jet d'eau* in his garden, in the
midst of vines and rare vegetables and a variety of flower-
ing and fruit trees His vines he assured us, needed no
covering in the winter, so mild is the climate It was the
hour of evening prayer in the church but he seemed to
feel under no obligation to attend, and we were interrupt
ed only by his being called to say a prayer upon the
occasion of a sacrifice It took but a moment and was
said on the spot, without any solemnity or ceremony He
manifested a perfect readiness to answer our questions respecting his diocese, and seemed indeed better acquainted
with it than with his Bible for he committed the mistake,
unpardonable in a bishop of attributing the destruction of
Jerusalem to Cyrus instead of Nebuchadnezzar

From him and from other sources we obtained the fol
lowing information The only Armenian convent in the
city is the one that is attached to this church, it contains
only the bishop nd three or four vartabeds There is also
a nunnery, with eight or ten inmates, but the diocese
contains no other In the city there are eight Armenian
churches, not including one belonging to the nunnery, and
another not used, and four or five in the suburbs, which are
served by sixty priests * The churches, like all that belong to the Armenians in these parts are without glebes or
funds The priests are uneducated, some indeed can
barely read the church services, and know not how to

* So said the bishop Langlès in his edition of Chardin gives a list
on the authority of Guldenstadt of twenty churches twelve of which he
says are in the city and eight in the suburbs Chardin vol 2; p 7

write, and out of all hardly more than two or three can be said to be at all enlightened The diocese has two suffragan bishops, one of whom, however, is now dead it embraces the whole of the province that is now called Georgia, and contains exclusive of the inhabitants of Tiflis 8000 Armenian families some of whom are serfs like the Georgian peasants Bishop Simeon is not the regular incumbent of the see, but merely acts *pro tempore* A bishop Hovhannes, who succeeded Nerses as president of the synod of Echmiadzin is to succeed him also in his bishopric

Three or four days after we reached Tiflis, a friend proposed to introduce us to an Armenian bishop who having heard of our arrival was desirous of being acquainted with us It proved to be Serope who is mentioned by Martyn in his visit to Echmiadzin He was born at Erzroom, and educated a papist in the college of the Propaganda at Rome but has since returned to his native faith French and Italian were familiar to him and he knew something of English being in this respect he assured us distinguished from almost every other ecclesiastic of his church We had two interviews with him, and found him possessed of much information and of more correct views than any other Armenian prelate whom we saw We were sorry to learn subsequently however that he is really an inefficient man He talked with us much as he did with Martyn twenty years ago and yet during those twenty years, he has effected little toward enlightening and reforming his nation Thinking probably, that it would gratify our missionary feelings he informed us, that since the capture of Akhaltsikhe 200 families of Georgians who, with some others residing there had embraced the religion of Mohammed, have been induced to return to the bosom of the Greek church As the territory of the Ingalos also another body of some 1500 families of Georgian renegadoes subject to the Lesgies, had been recently taken, they were likewise at liberty again to embrace the faith of their fathers for which they were known still to retain a strong partiality He hoped, too, that the general war which was about to be made upon the mountaineers would by subduing them to Russia, facilitate their conversion 'Though said he, 'we have all lost the spirit of missions and shall find the work a difficult one, while, if we had only the zeal of the early papal mission aries, to say nothing of the apostles, it would soon be done The Russians have had for several years, a bishop and a number of priests among the Oset (Ossetians) as mission aries, still their church is ignorant and wanting in zeal, and that is its only mission * They have indeed succeed ed by money and caresses in baptizing a few, but that is all they remain the same people as before and none of them are cordially Christians He expressed his regret, that both Georgians and Armenians here have now hardly any preaching and what they have resembles legends more than sermons For said he, so long as the clergy do nothing but read service the religion of the people must necessarily be superficial consisting only in forms and hav ing no connection with the heart as is now lamentably the case They are very strict in their fasts but their religion has almost no influence upon their morals In speaking of the education of the clergy we suggested that it ought al- ways to keep along with that of the people, or the latter will be in danger of infidelity, to which he assented, and confessed that the reverse was true among the Armenians, the people were ahead of the clergy in knowledge —He had been recently appointed bishop of Astrakhan, the only Armenian episcopal see in Russia north of the Caucasus,

* The Russian church has also had a mission among the Samoiedes at Archangel since 1825 which reports that 3510 have been converted and only 680 remain pagans The Russian embassy at Pekin is likewise a religious mission consisting of an archbishop and a number of inferior clergy

besides that of Bessarabia already mentioned Astrakhán is about 700 versts from Tiflis by the pass of Dariel, and reckons among its forty or forty five thousand inhabitants, 4000 Armenians A printing press belongs to the episcopate, but it is in a very bad condition

Serope was for several years rector of the Armenian gymnasium at Moscow, and from him and other sources we have gathered the following information respecting that institution, in compliance with an article in our Instructions It originated in the benevolence of a native of Isfahan, of the Armenian family of Eleazar now one of the richest in the Russian empire, and was opened in 1816. The legacy left by its founder not only sufficed for erecting the buildings and putting it in operation, but a permanent fund of 200,000 roubles remained,* and thirty two of its students are now fed, clothed and instructed gratis The whole number of Armenian students is about 60 and the number of graduates up to 1829 was 69 It is not how ever an exclusively Armenian institution and the Russian branch is much the largest Most of its Armenian students are from places north of the Caucasus though a few go from these provinces. They are taught the Russian, French, German, and Armenian languages, history differ ent branches of the mathematics, philosophy &c But their attention to all is somewhat superficial There is no department appropriated to any particular profession but a general foundation is laid for all hardly the right kind, however, Serope himself confessed, for theology, and none of its graduates have yet entered the sacred profession So that even here we look in vain for what is indeed no where to be found, an institution for the education of the Armenian clergy The present rector is a vartabéd, named

---

* I have taken this sum from Avdall See his account of this institution in the supplement to his translation of Chamcheán's history of Armenia Vol 2 p 527

Michael Salamteán who was born at Constantinople, and educated a papist in the papal Armenian convent of Bzummar in Mount Lebanon but has since renounced allegiance to the pope   He is much devoted to enlightening his nation and is enlightened himself   But there is reason to fear that he is secretly inclining to the principles of German neology   His religious influence of course, cannot be good , and the consequence is, that the graduates are generally irreligious   They learn Russian levity and love of honor, and come out no longer Armenians, but prejudiced against them as semi barbarian Asiatics   Instead of going to their country with the patriotic intention of reforming their nation, in the prevalent spirit of Russia they seek only for promotion, and disperse through different parts of the empire in the employment of government   Only a few have found their way south of the Caucasus   The only encouraging hope is, that the institution may in time give the nation some valuable authors   Connected with it there is an Armenian press, which was formerly at St Petersburg   The rector has kindly caused two or three religious tracts to be printed at it for the missionaries at Shoosha. There is also another Armenian press at Moscow which is the private property of a Frenchman   But neither of them accomplishes much

The first sabbath we were in Tiflis we attended divine service in the Armenian cathedral and the second in the church of a German colony in the vicinity of the city When stating in a preceding letter, of what the church services of the Armenians consist, I reserved for this place a description of their forms of worship as they appear to an observer   But so much do they differ from any thing known among us that I have little hope of giving one that shall be intelligible   The *church* itself, when built in the style common to the oldest and best in Armenia, of which the cathedral at Tiflis is a pretty good specimen, has the

form of a cross, sometimes externally, by means of short
wings attached to each side and generally internally, by
means of a lateral arch crossing the main longitudinal one
at right angles The nave or centre of the cross, is sur-
mounted by a species of dome quite peculiar to these regions but here common to old churches and sepulchral
monuments, and evidently very ancient It consists of an
upright cylindrical base capped with an acute cone The
altar, for which we have no substitute but the communion
table occupies the eastern extremity of the main longitudinal arch of the building the Armenians holding that
divine worship should be directed only toward the east.
From the back part of it rise up several steps or shelves
occupied by candlesticks crosses small pictures and other
ornaments It stands upon a platform three or four feet
high, which projects far enough in front, to allow the
priests and deacons to stand upon it to say mass, the only
time when it or the altar is used A section of the body
of the church next in front of the altar extending from
side to side of the building is appropriated to the priests
and their assistants, and is often raised a step above the
rest of the floor, and separated from it by a railing
Here the common daily prayers are said The male part
of the congregation occupy without order the remainder
of the floor, which is entirely without seats The females
are crowded into an orchestra at the western end (the only
gallery there is,) and are there screened by lattice-work
from the gaze of the men In some cases also, a similar space is appropriated to them under the orchestra,
and only enclosed by a simple railing A pulpit that
prominent and essential part of our places of worship, we
did not find in Armenia ! A church thus fitted up, however awkward it might be to us corresponds precisely with
the ideas entertained by the Armenians of public worship.
Mass is the principal thing, and the altar is raised so that

every one can easily witness its celebration Prayers are less important, and no provision is made for the readers of them to be distinctly seen or heard Preaching is hardly thought of and the pulpit is excluded

Go into one of these churches in time of prayers, (*mass* will be considered elsewhere,) and you will find a number of lamps suspended from the roof, endeavoring to shed their dim light upon the congregation, though the sun be shining with noonday brightness In the enclosure before the altar will be two or three priests, surrounded by a crowd of boys from eight to twelve years old *performing* prayers, some swinging a smoking censer, others taper in hand, reading first from one book and then from another and all changing places and positions according to rule The monotonous inarticulate singsong of the youthful officiators, with voices often discordant and stretched to their highest pitch will grate upon your ear and start the inquiry, can such prayers enter into the ears of the Lord of Sabaoth? You will be surrounded by a barefooted congregation, standing wherever each can find a place upon a sheepskin, or bit of rug, (unless the church is rich enough to have a carpet) uttering responses without order and frequently prostrating themselves and kissing the ground with a sign of the cross at every fall and rise The whole will seem to you a mummery and an abomination and you will probably hasten away wishing to hear and see no more of it

In entering the church barefoot, and in prostrating themselves to the ground, the Armenians have doubtless retained relics of genuine orientalism Abraham when he ran to meet the angels, bowed himself to the earth and Moses, when standing on holy ground, took his shoes from off his feet Why so large a part of the service has been suffered to pass into the hands of boys is exceedingly strange They fill the four ecclesiastical grades below the subdeacon, to which are attached the duties of clerks, or more commonly are substitutes for their occupants, having themselves no rank at all in the church Of the first 158 pages of the Jamakírk, containing the whole of the midnight service with all its variations for feasts and other special occasions more than 130, consisting of psalms hymns, &c are réad or chanted by them under the direction of the priests Well may the priests in view of having such important helps in their duties, find motive enough in most places to teach a few children to read ' Of the remaining pages, some half a dozen belong to the deacons, if there are any, and the remainder consisting simply of prayers and lessons from the gospel, are read by the priests All the service, with few other exceptions than the lessons, and that the priest in the middle of every prayer of any length turns round to wave a cross before the people and say, ' peace be to all let us worship God is perfomed with the back to the congregation Add to this that the whole, with the unfortunate exception of the book of legends is in a language not understood often by the priests themselves, and much less by the congregation, and if it were not is read or chanted with so little articulation as would render it perfectly unintelligible and you will hardly need any other answer to the question, whether there is any spirituality in the worship of the Armenian church The priests go through it as if it were a daily task of the lips, as a joiner s work is of his hands and are apparently as much relieved when it is over If a boy makes a mistake, he is reproved or even chastised, on the spot, though a prayer be interrupted for the purpose The people, too, are constantly coming and going or moving about, and often engaged in conversation To say that a real reverence for sacred things is unknown among the clergy, and that nei ther they nor the people have any idea of spiritual worship, seems too broad an assertion and still, in making it, we are supported, not only by our own observation, but by that of others to whose testimony we attribute great weight.

I ought not to leave this subject without a word upon image-worship. Going to Armenia, as I did, almost immediately after a visit to Greece, I could not but feel at first, that this error is not very prominent in the Armenian church. Some churches have been already mentioned that had but few pictures. As we advanced into Armenia, however, we found them multiplying, and image-worship does exist to a considerable extent. Indeed the adoration of the cross, already explained, is a most striking instance of it. Before pictures, also, tapers are burned, votive offerings are suspended, and prayers are offered, especially on the festivals of the saints they represent. The same author who so exalts the cross, gives to the image of Christ as high a rank. We, says he, 'and our sect hold and preach that, as in looking toward the God-bearing cross, we offer worship not to the visible matter, but to the invisible God who is in it, so we worship the image of the Savior, not the matter and the colors, but Christ by means of it, who is the image of the invisible God the Father. And as a name and an image are equally symbols of a thing, only that one is addressed to the ear, and the other to the eye, it is as much the meaning of the apostle that every knee in heaven, and in earth, and under the earth should bow to the image, as to the name of Jesus * But as neither a name nor an image without the substance is to be worshiped, and the saints are not every where present to dwell in their images as Christ in his, their images are not to be worshiped. But we honor and reverence the images of the saints, holding them as mediators and intercessors with

* How can those who understand the apostle literally avoid Nerses's argument?

God, and offering the worship of God by their hands For the image of the Creator only, and not that of the creature, is to be worshiped "* In a word, though the Armenians are less devoted to image-worship than the Greeks, they are more so than the papists Not, however, that they have carved images like the latter, for, like the former, they have only pictures, and I here use the word image in the latter sense

Let us turn from these heartless forms of solemn mockery to a different scene—simple and devout protestant worship in the heart of Georgia! Of the seven German colonies in these provinces, whose history and present condition will be related hereafter, one, named New Tiflis, is about two versts from the city It consists of two rows of neatly white-washed houses of one story, at moderate distances from each other, along a broad and straight street, and contains not far from 200 inhabitants who have the regular instructions of a minister of the gospel We had already become acquainted with pastor Saltet, and found him an intelligent and extremely devout man We felt at our first interview, that he was ripe for heaven, but knew not that he would so soon be there Within a month, he was brought by the cholera, in less than twenty-four hours, from perfect health to the grave He was the general spiritual inspector of all the colonies, and informed us that some at least of his charge were excellent Christians As we entered his church the worshipers were dropping in one by one, and quietly taking their seats, while the devotion in their countenances showed that they felt the solemnity of the duties in which they were about to engage, and the books in their hands testified that they had been instructed to understand, as well as to perform them The prayers of the pastor seemed to breathe the united and heartfelt devo-

* Nerses Shnorháli Unthanragán p 132 133

tion of all, his sermon was a direct, affectionate and earnest address to every hearer, and the singing, which affected me more than all, was in good German taste simple, solemn and touching I shall not attempt to describe the feelings awakened by this scene, refreshing as an oasis in a boundless desert, though in spite of me at the time, they expressed themselves in tears Since first setting foot in Asia, I had deeply felt, that a consistent Christian life and a devout simple worship, exhibited by a few truly governed by the fear of God, and shining like a candle into all the surrounding darkness, was the great desideratum needed by a missionary to give intelligibleness to his instructions, and force to his arguments How often without it, had I seemed to myself like an inhabitant of some other planet, vainly endeavoring to model my hearers after characters whom I had seen there, and of whom they could form no conception, or whose existence they could hardly believe ! Here, at last I seemed to have found the desideratum supplied, and was encouraged to hope, that this example of pure religion would be like leaven to all the corrupt and backsliding churches around

We took some pains to notice how the Sabbath was observed by the inhabitants of Tiflis The bazars and shops were all closed except those of the venders of provisions, including (if such a classification may be allowed,) the re tailers of wine and ardent spirits The number of attendants at public worship in the morning seemed but small, for the two or three churches which we entered contained but few worshipers In the afternoon the whole male population of the city seemed to be poured out into the streets and esplanades, to indulge in relaxation every one conversing of his merchandise or his pleasures, and all exhibiting a scene of gaiety and amusement While the ladies with all the famed charms of Georgian beauty, which, I may be allowed to say, has not been overrated, (for I have never seen a city, so large a proportion of whose females were beautiful in form, features and complexion, as Tiflis,) were assembled in little groupes upon the low terraces of their houses, dancing to the sound of tambourin and clapping of hands, to contribute their aid to render this solemn day the least solemn of all the seven

LETTER VIII

TIFLIS

Origin of the Georgians—Geographical divisions of their country—Histori
cal traditions before Alexander and origin of the Orpelians—Subjection to
the Romans and Parthians—Conversion to Christianity—Pakradian kings
of Georgia—Invasion of the Seljookians—Subsequent growth of Georgian
power—Moghúl invasion—Subjected by the Sofies of Persia—Submission
to Russia—Present number of Georgians—Their civil state—Education—
Religion—Complete subjection of the valley of the Koor to the Russians—
View of Colchis—Jews in Colchis and Georgia—Present state of Colchis
—Independence of the inhabitants of the Caucasus—Their religious state
—Missions among them—Papal missions in Georgia and Colchis—Papal
Armenian convent at Venice

DEAR SIR

I HAVE thus far intentionally neglected to speak of the
Georgians in order to make in one place a connected re
port of what we learned respecting that nation   Permit
me now to introduce them to your notice by a few remarks
upon their history

The Greeks knew the Georgians under the name of
Iberes and their geographers divided between them the
Colchi, and *Albani*, the whole of the tract that lies between Armenia and mount Caucasus, extending from the
Caspian to the Black sea , in other words, the valleys of
the Cyrus and the Phasis   The name *Virk*, given to them
by the Armenian writers, seems to be of the same origin
with that used by the Greeks   By the Turks and Persians
they are universally called *Gurjy*, and their country Gurjis-
tan ,* and probably our own name for them is derived

* Perhaps from the river Kür or Koor

20 *

from this origin, rather than from the Greek *georgos*, as some have supposed   The Georgians call themselves *Karth* which name they derive from Kartlos, the second son of Togarmah, as the Armenians do theirs from Haig, his first son   Such a tradition seems at once to be contradicted by the fact that there is no resemblance between the Armenian and Georgian languages, but it evades the objection by replying, that the two nations separated from the original stock before the confusion of tongues *

The original patrimony of Kartlos was bounded on the north by the lower ranges of the Caucasus, on the west by the mountains which separate Georgia from Colchis, on the south by the mountains of Kookark, and on the east by the same Armenian province to the junction of the Khram with the Koor, and then, to the north of the latter river, by the country of Hereti which occupied the valley of the Alazán from its mouth to the north of Telav   The northeastern part of this territory received from *Kakhos*, one of the sons of Kartlos the name of *Kakheti* which was finally extended over Hereti, and is now applied to the whole tract between the Koor and the Alazan   The remainder was called after its original possessor, *Karth*, which is the proper native name of Georgia, and is still

* According to the Georgian and Armenian traditions, Togarmah had eight sons *Haig* the father of the *Haik* or Armenians *Kartlos* from whom descended the *Karth* or Georgians *Bardos* who peopled the valley south of the Koor between the mouths of the Khram and the Aras which was called by the Arabian geographers Aran where he built the city of *Berdaah* *Movakán* whose inheritance was the modern provinces of Sheky Shirwán and *Mooghán* *Heros* who possessed *Hereti* now absorbed in the province of Kakheti of which it formed the eastern part *Lekos* the progenitor of the *Lesgies* who received the eastern part of mount Caucasus from the Terek to the Caspian *Kavkás* to whom fell the western end of the. *Caucasus* from the Terek to the Black sea and *Egros* whose patrimony was Colchis called by the Armenians *Yeker* (Egeria) and sometimes by the Georgians *Egrisi* and *Egoorsi* St Mart vol 2 p 182. Chamcheán P 1 c 1

given to one of the modern provinces, but generally written by foreigners *Kartalini   Somkheti* the third province of Georgia was originally a subdivision of Kartli named from its vicinity to Armenia *Kartel-Somkheti*, or Armenian Georgia * The original capital of Georgia was Mtskheta, a town which still exists at the junction of the Aragvi with the Koor and contains about 200 families It looks up to Kartlos himself as its founder and was the residence of the rulers of Georgia till A. D. 469

Georgian tradition acknowledges that Haig was the most valiant of the sons of Togarmah, and that the descendants of his brethren for a long time professed allegiance to the kings of Armenia But even in those days the fertile north poured forth its inundations, and a flood of Khazars from the plains of Kipchak burst over the Caucasus, and reduced to servitude or subjection its inhabitants and their brethren on the south They were relieved from their oppressors only by a similar invasion from Persia 750 A. C. headed by a general of the famous Feridoon Soon after, the Greeks (perhaps from the colonies in Colchis whose origin dates back to the times of the golden fleece,) came in for a share of the distracted country but were forced to remain satisfied with the country of Egrisi While groaning under the dominion of Kai Khosrov of Persia, 538 A. C. the Georgians saw with astonishment a company of Chinese headed by one of the royal family of that distant empire burst through the gate of Dariél, and come to their aid They were received with joy, their arms were victorious, and the prince was presented with the fortress of Orpet, (called also Samshvilde and Orbisi,) on the Khram, which gave name to his family His descendants the Orpelians afterward distinguished themselves both in Georgian and Armenian history, and now, at Tiflis and elsewhere, they hold their rank among the Georgian nobility,

* The Georgians call the Armenians *Somekhi*

and boast of higher heraldric honors than any of the crowned heads of Europe *

Georgia, like Armenia, submitted to the arms of Alex ander   But, in the next generation, the lieutenant of his successors was expelled by Parnovaz, a native prince, who acquired a power so much greater than any one that had preceded him as to be called the first king of Georgia. To him the Georgians ascribe the honor of inventing their alphabet, while the Armenians contend that it was given them at the beginning of the fifth century by Mesrob the inventor of their own †   As there are two perfectly distinct Georgian alphabets, one used for ecclesiastical and the other for civil purposes, the question might be settled by an equal division, and certainly the resemblance of the former to the letters of the Armenians, seems to show that they are entitled at least to that ‡   During the long and obstinate struggle between the Roman and Parthian pow ers after the removal of Mithridates (to whom Armenian tradition attributes a Georgian origin,) had brought their territories in contact   Georgia, like Armenia, obeyed the will of the strongest, and once we find a prince royal of the former placed by Roman aid upon the throne of the latter §

Ecclesastical history relates that the Georgians were con-verted to Christianity, during the reign of Constantine the Great, by the sanctity and miracles of a captive female slave. The queen, having been healed by her of a grievous disease,

---

* For the preceding traditions see St Martin s notes to the 1st chap of the Hist. of the Orpelians, in his Mém sur l Arm vol ii —and his Introduc-tion to the same vol

† St Mart as above

‡ We obtained at Kars a manuscript of the four Gospels upon parchment, in this character, supposed to have been written in the 12th century   It is now deposited in the library of the Board at the Missionary rooms

§ Chamchean P 3 c 9

adopted her religion, persuaded the nation to erect churches
to the true God and sent to the emperor for Christian teachers * In the consequent persecutions of the Sassanidæ,
they were fellow sufferers with the Armenians, and for a
part of the time aided them in their determined resistance.†
The Georgian church was represented by its Catholicos
and a number of bishops, in the Armenian synod of Vagh-
arshabád which rejected the council of Chalcedon, A D
491, and thus embraced the monophysite heresy ‡ But
within a century after (A D 580) in spite of the remonstrances of the head of the Armenian church, the rejected
decrees were adopted, and the Georgians have ever since
formed a part of the orthodox Greek church §

The Saracen invasion produced nearly the same effects
in Georgia as in Armenia and while the Mohammedans and
Greeks were alternately enforcing their claims by overrun-
ning the country a minor branch of the Pakradians got
effective possession of it, even before their relatives ascended
the throne of Armenia. Their crown or coronet, (for it
hardly deserved the former name) was but a tributary
one, however, sometimes acknowledging the kalif, sometimes the emperor and often more immediately the king
of Armenia, as liege lord.|| Under one title or another,
this family continued to be clothed with the highest native authority in the country, until it finally resigned it
into the hands of Alexander of Russia Even now a Pakradian prince is pensioned by the Persian government as a
pretender to the throne of Georgia. We visited him in
another part of our journey

The invasion of the Seljookians happened at a period,
when the power of these princes of Georgia had been recent-

---

* Theodoret, Eccl. Hist Lib 1 c 24. Compare Mos Choren Lib. 2
c 88

† Chamcheán P 4 c 1 2   ‡ Ibid P 4 c 12

§ Ibid P 4 c 15 || St Mart vol 1 Précis de l'Hist d'Armenie

ly, weakened by a destructive inroad of the Grecian army,
as a chastisement for their revolt against the emperor Basilius whose acceptance of the crown of Armenia so unhappily prepared that country, also for the same disastrous event
Their imbecility was completed by the murder of a brave
Orpelian, A D 1057, whose gallant conduct as generalissimo of the Georgian armies provoked the jealousies of the
other chiefs, and not many years after, hordes of Turks fol
lowed the Seljookian standard over nearly the whole of
Georgia   But in the old age of that short lived dynasty
the Georgian kings issued from their mountain fastnesses,
drove the invaders from their country carried their arms to
the Black sea on the one side, and on the other, after im
posing a Georgian instead of a Seljookian governor upon
the Armenians in their capital of Ani, forced the king of
Khelát to flee before them, and even contended on equal
terms with the Atabegs of Aderbaijan   Tiflis, which, after
having been founded and made the capital of Georgia in
A D 469, had been since A D 853 in the possession first
of the Arabs and then of the Turks, now, in A D 1121,
passed back again into the hands of its proper masters * The
victorious days of the Georgian kings ended soon after the
death of queen Tamar, A D 1206, the most fortunate and
powerful of the whole   for during the reign of her success-
or, A D 1220 occurred the first irruption of the Moghúls †   These singular barbarians in their second invasion
A D 1238 met with little resistance in the conquest of
Georgia and seem to have exhibited there the best specimen of their tolerance ‡   Particularly did the Orpelians,
who, after having been driven from Georgia by the predeces-

---

* St Mart vol 1 p 369 vol 2 p 231 232

† St Mart vol 2 p 247 —Even at this early period Georgia began to
have connection with Russia   The first husband of Tamar and the father of
her successor was a Russian

‡ St Mart vol 1 p 384

sor of Tamar, had during her reign been put in possession
of large estates in the province of Sunik by the Atabeg of
Aderbaijan receive almost fraternal kindness from these
neighbors of their ancestors, and cordially attach themselves
to their fortunes *

Ismael the Sofy, of Persia A D 1519, found Georgia
divided between different branches of the Pakradians, into
the two kingdoms of Karth and Kaketi which had existed
for about a century and easily imposed a tribute upon the
kings of both Under his immediate successors, and in con
sequence of their intrigues and instructions both of them pro
fessed the Mohammedan faith In subsequent dissensions
and rebellions the Osmanlies of Turkey ever ready to do
an injury to the heretical Sofies, found repeated opportu
nities to interfere in the affairs of Georgia and in A D
1576 they built the citadel of Tiflis But that hard heart-
ed despot, Abbas the Great, after prosecuting a pretended
courtship of the sister of one of the kings, until he had betrayed and murdered her brother and carried into captivity
80,000† families of her countrymen as if he would destroy
a nation in a jest , imposed upon Georgia A D 1618, the
following terms of permanent subjection to Persia viz that
the country should not be charged with taxes , that the religion should not be changed , that no churches should be
destroyed or mosks built, that the viceroy should always be
a Georgian of the royal race, but a Mohammedan of
whose sons the one who would likewise renounce Christian
ity should be governor of Isfahán until called to succeed his
father The country was then united under one tributary
viceroy, with the title of *waly,* and the king of Kaketi was
driven from his throne ‡ The influence of a government,

* St Mart vol 2 p. 123

† Chardin must mean that the number was taken from the whole valley of
the Koor though he does not say so

‡ Chardin vol 2 p 47

the head of which was bound by law to be an apostate, must have been bad beyond description. The viceroy himself, attending mosk to please the king and retain his office, and secretly frequenting the church to quiet his conscience, (if in such circumstances he could have any,) and to gratify his Christian relations, learned to carry double-dealing and injustice into all the measures of his government.[*] Most of his nobles, in order to secure employment or a pension themselves, or a place in the harem of the Shah for their daughters, followed his example of hypocrisy.[†] Even the church felt its corrupting influence, for the episcopal sees were filled by the nomination of the prince, and the Catholicos, or head of the church, was of his family.[‡] In one instance A D 1720, the waly having been slain at Kandahar, and the next heir refusing to apostatize from his faith, the Catholicos himself, happening to be the third brother, offered to renounce his religion and ecclesiastical vows, for Mohammedanism and the office of waly The father of the three, though a moslem, was so provoked, that he ordered him to be bastinadoed and kept to his duty.[§]

As early as the subjugation of Georgia by Abbas the Great the grand duke of Muscovy, having already, by the conquest of the kingdoms of Kazán and Astrakhan, become a neighbor to the regions of the Caspian, showed a disposition to meddle in trans-Caucasian matters, by sending an envoy to plead at the court of Persia the cause of the unfortunate king, whose sister was the object of the Shah's pretended affection.[||] In 1674, an attempt was also made by negotiation to reclaim the rights of the grandson of the exiled king of Kakheti, who had found an asylum at the court of Russia.[¶] And Peter the Great, by

---

[*] Tourneforte vol 2 p 310   [†] Chardin vol 2 p. 67

[‡] Chardin vol 2 p. 45   [§] Jonas Hanway's Persia, vol 2 p. 139

[||] Chardin, vol 2 p 60.   [¶] Chardin vol 9 p 146.

passing the gate of Derbénd and destroying Shámakhy gave a more decisive evidence of the same disposition The Georgians doubtless saw with pleasure these their brethren of the same church thus inclined to look after them the imbecility of the last Sofies the invasion of the Afgháns, and the weak successors of Nadir Shah, embold ened them to follow their own inclination in contempt of their masters and finally the waly Heraclius throwing off entirely his allegiance to Persia, put himself by a for mal treaty dated July 24th 1783 under the protection of the empress Catharine This protection however, did not defend him from the wrath of Aga Mohammed who in 1795 sacked Tiflis with every brutal excess of cruelty and led 25 000 captives to Persia * But George, the successor of Heraclius having A D 1801 or 1802, made the em peror Alexander his heir Georgia passed completely under the strong arm of Russia and the Pakradian family ceased to rule One of the lineal heirs received the title of prince and a pension at St Petersburg, and another met with a similar reception in Persia

The present number of the whole Georgian nation, in cluding the Imiretians, Mingrelians and the inhabitants of Gooriel who are of the same race, was stated to us as high as 600 000 souls, but the estimate seems much too large For according to data hereafter to be adduced the whole population of Colchis is only about 150 000, while the highest estimate given us of the inhabitants of Georgia proper including the Armenians already enumerated, was only 360 000 souls, and the lowest made only 20,000 and another 30,000 families of proper Georgians * The

* Mod Trav Persia vol 1 p 220 Malcolm's Hist of Pers vol 2 p 190

† The first estimate was given us by Mr Sirbéd the Armenian professor whom Nérses brought from Paris, and who we were informed was when we saw him employed by marshal Paskevich in investigations relating to th

three provinces of Georgia have been already named. Their principal towns are Tiflis in *Somkheti*, in *Kartalini*, Mtskheta already mentioned, Gori with 600 houses and 8 churches, Sooram and Ananoor, and in *Kakheti*, which has the most fertile soil and brave inhabitants of the three, Signag the provincial capital with 400 houses, and Telav

The Georgians are divided into three classes, viz *free commoners*, *nobles*, and *vassals* The first are few and reside chiefly in towns The last form the mass of the people Formerly their lives their persons, and their property were at the absolute disposal of the nobility who made them labor for months without giving them pay or provisions, and sold their sons and daughters into slavery, or took the latter for concubines, at their will. This slave-trade, as is well known was extensive But it was not by it and by captivity alone, that the harems of Persia were stocked with Georgian beauty The daughters of the nobles themselves often shared the same fate either to gratify the unnatural ambition of a father who considered the situation honorable to his family or to meet the imperious demands of the Shah Early marriage was the only security against it, and so extensively was it resorted to, that ten became a common age for girls to enter the matrimonial state * The condition of the peasants has been somewhat improved by the Russians That they should receive entire liberty from rulers who have serfs themselves at home, could not be expected The vassals of one of the richest of the nobility however, have come so near to it, that they are required to labor for him but one day in the week and are allowed the other five to cultivate for themselves lands, which he gives them upon condition of receiving one sev

Georgians the second is from Le Gamba's book the third was given us by bishop Simeon and the fourth by Serope

* Chardin, vol 2. p. 43, 67 Tournefort vol 2. p. 803, 312.

enthof its produce The power of capital punishment is taken from the nobles, and the slave-trade has of course ceased. The evil of early marriages hardly comes within the scope of the civil law, but archbishop Nérses, in his ecclesiastical capacity, ordered that none of his nation should be married under twelve The influence that has been exerted upon the morals of the Georgians, I have already alluded to

We did not learn that the Georgians have any means of education in Tiflis except the government school already mentioned nor any in the country except a very few small schools in which hardly any thing is taught None of the serfs are taught to read, but all the nobility are more or less acquainted with letters and the females of this class though they have no schools, teach each other, and have generally a better education than the males The nation is possessed, perhaps to an unusual degree, of every faculty needed to facilitate the advance of education but alas! whence shall come the stimulus to provoke to the use of them? The people are too ignorant themselves to feel the need of knowledge their rulers look on with indifference, and their priests contribute not their favor

I have already mentioned that the Georgians are of the orthodox Greek faith, and that they formerly had a head of their church who bore the title of Catholicos. The only difference between the Georgian and Russian religions being found to consist merely in the addition of a few saints to the calendar, and in some acknowledged irregularities, they were easily reconciled, and the rule of the Catholicoses was made to cease with that of the walies, and the nation passed at the same time into the hands of the emperor Alexander, and of the synod of St. Petersburg The treasures of the Catholicos, amounting to 800 000 silver roubles, were transferred to St Petersburg, with his authority and a Russian archbishop was sent from thence to occupy the see of Georgia, and attend to the spiritual concerns of all the professors of the Greek faith south of the Caucasus. The seat of the see, which had hitherto remained at Mtskheta, the ancient capital, was now removed to Tiflis It has two suffragan bishops in Kakheti and one in Imireti Archbishop Jonas, the present incumbent, is a good sort of man, who often preaches, and his sermons are said not to be bad He favors the distribution of the Scriptures and endeavors to promote the education of his clergy We observed the next door to his cathedral some copies of the New Testament exposed for sale, in the Russian, Georgian * Armenian and Turkish languages but, like scriptural truths among the ceremonies and superstitions of the Greek church, they were few and almost hidden by a great quantity of church candles and gilded pictures to the sale of which the shop seemed principally devoted He has a school for the education of candidates for holy orders, at which they are almost obliged to study in order to pass the requisite examination before being ordained The course of study requires several years and embraces the Russian language, and some philosophy and theology, but neither Latin nor Greek receives any attention

The number of Georgian churches at Tiflis was stated to us to be eight or ten † We went into the cathedral one Sabbath during service Its style of architecture resembles that of the Armenian cathedral already described except that its steeple, which is loaded with bells kept almost constantly ringing stands alone on the opposite side of the street. Its interior is of the general character of all Greek churches,

---

* During the existence of the Russian Bible Society two editions of the Georgian Testament were printed at Moscow one in the ecclesiastical and the other in the common character Henderson's Bib Researches in Russia p 522

† The list given by Lauglès in his edition of Chardin contains the names of 15 but some of them may be desert churches of which the Georgians have many or perhaps only the ruins of churches

except that its ornaments and pictures are in better taste, than those of any I had before seen The service too, which was I believe in Russian, was read with solemnity, and without the nasal twang universal in the churches of Greece Nearly the whole audience, which was considerably numerous consisted of officers of the army , and it seemed quite like a government chapel The Georgian churches unlike the Armenian are rich in lands and vassals About one fourth of the soil of Georgia is said to belong to the church But it was suggested to us by one whose opinion is entitled to weight that the funds of the church will probably in time follow those of the Catholicos The priests were formerly numerous, but measures adopted by government have considerably diminished their number They are still ignorant, preaching is extremely rare for few are at all capable of it, some can hardly read the liturgy, and are unable to write There are some convents for men, and a still greater number of nunneries The inmates of the latter are all mendicants

If our account of the Georgians should seem to you meagre as it really is you must accept as an excuse the fact that the thorough amalgamation of their church with that of Russia, by excluding the hope of their becoming a field for missionary effort, destroyed our interest, and discouraged us from prosecuting our inquiries respecting them

The Russian emperor, in taking possession of Georgia, became also liege lord of the several hereditary *khans* (princes) whose territories occupied the valley of the Koor in the direction of the Caspian, and the western shore of that sea preserving to them the rights they enjoyed under a similar control from the Persian Shah The khan of Ganjeh, by nature a tyrant and a bad subject, refused allegiance from the beginning , his power was consequently annihilated by force, and his possessions united to the

crown   The khan of Kara bagh was detected about ten
years ago in a conspiracy against government, and fled into
Persia   His son received a title and a pension from the
emperor, but his province shared the fate of Gánjeh   About
two years after the same course was adopted with the province of Sheky on the occasion of the death of its khan
Shirwán lost its khan in the same way and about the same
time as Kara-bagh, and also shared its fate   Bakoo likewise, had once its khan, but has none now, the khan of
Kooba rebelled and fled into the mountains   and Derbénd
has been subject to Russia since A D 1795   So that
now there is not a province through the whole valley of
the Koor nor along the coast of the Caspian near its mouth,
that is not under the immediate government of the crown
of Russia —We shall take a more minute survey of these
regions from the nearer point of Shoosha   From our present position let us glance at Colchis and the mountains

Colchis is a name borrowed from antiquity, and here
applied for the sake of convenience to the whole basin of
the river Rion, the ancient Phasis   It is bounded on the
north by the Caucasus on the east by the mountains of
Kartalını on the south by those of Akhaltsıkhe, and on
the west by the sea   Its mean length from east to west is
about 45 leagues and its mean breadth is 35 or 40 leagues
from north to south   Its soil is extremely fertile but little
cultivated and covered throughout with dense forests.
Owing in part to this last circumstance, as is supposed, its
climate is so humid that it rains from 120 to 150 days in
the year   Its inhabitants are of the Georgian race, and
speak different dialects of the Georgian tongue   After
having been for a long time united under the king of
Imireti whose family was a branch of the Pakradian stock,
it was separated in the fifteenth century, into the three divisions of Imireti Mingreli, and Gooriel   In the wars which
produced and followed this separation, the neighboring

Turkish pashás were called in to aid the different parties, until the whole country became tributary to Turkey The power of Russia, when once extended across the Caucasus, was felt no less in the valley of the Rion, than in that of the Koor, and supplanted the power of Turkey in the one, as it did that of Persia in the other The king of Imireti rebelled against his new sovereign, was expelled, and his territories were united to the crown The princes of Mingreli and Gooriel still hold their places acknowledging allegiance to Russia , but their countries are filled with Cossack police stations , and the princess of Gooriel having recently fled into Turkey, a doubt was expressed to us whether her heirs, or the emperor, would take possession of her territory

Gooriel contains about **30 000** and Mingreli about **40 000** inhabitants Imireti is about 32 leagues in length by 25 in breadth is divided into the four cantons of Kotais, Vacca Shorapana and Radsha and contained, in 1821, 406 towns and villages, 12 994 houses and 80 793 inhabitants of whom 44,738 were males and 36 055 were females Among its inhabitants as well as those of the two other principalities are many Armenians The capital of Imireti, and in fact of the whole of Colchis, is Kotais, called also Kotatis It contains about 1600 inhabitants, nearly one half of whom are Jews, who have a synagogue Its situation is unhealthy though many parts of Imireti are not liable to that inconvenience In general, however, the whole of Colchis is very subject to bilious affections.

The Jews in Kotais with some others scattered through Imireti, about fifty families near Gori and a few in Sooram, are the only people of that nation which we heard of in Georgia or Colchis Like their neighbors of Akhaltsikhe, they are natives of the country as their ancestors have also been for several generations At Tiflis there are none. A few years ago some foreign Jewish merchants settled there, but unexpectedly an order arrived from St Petersburg for them to leave in two days and they could with difficulty obtain permission to remain a day or two longer, encamped in the public square in order to collect their debts We could learn no reason for such an arbitrary measure for it seemed to be allowed that they were peaceful and useful citizens The order did not affect the native Jews just referred to

For an account of the former state of the people of Colchis I must refer you to Chardin s very full narrative in his 'Journey from Paris to Isfahan ' I shall barely state a few modifications of that account, growing out of the measures of its new rulers —The insecurity to person and property, caused by a semi barbarous government unregulated even by written laws, which placed not only Chardin s jewels but his life in such danger has given place to perfect quiet from one extremity of the country to the other Hardly more than two or three assassinations have occurred in the whole of Imireti since the Russians took possession Decided measures have been adopted to restrain the unnatural inclination which the people of this region have indulged from the earliest ages to sell their children and vassals into slavery, and with much success Still in 1821, travellers ascending the Rion were urged to purchase beautiful girls for 100 or 120 silver roubles each the princess of Gooriel in her late visit to Trebizond offered some of her attendants for sale , and it is supposed that similar instances are numerous. Poty and Akhaltsikhe however, which were formerly convenient slave-trading posts for the Turks, having now passed from their hands into those of Russia, the latter will be able to give more efficiency to her efforts for the suppression of this inhuman traffic

The condition of the peasantry has been improved. With the exception of a few merchants, the population is still divided into only two classes the nobility and the slaves the former owning all the land and the latter doing all the labor   But, as the noble can no longer deprive his serf of his life or limbs nor sell him to a foreign master slavery assumes a mild form   The lord and his serf live together on almost equal terms   It is no longer lawful for the princes to wander about and quarter themselves and their numerous attendants continually upon their vassals, often consuming in a visit of a week the provisions of a year, and leaving want and distress in their train   Still the respectable stranger in travelling through the country will often be escorted great distances by the nobles and their host of retainers meeting at every stopping place a hospitable feast bountiful enough, not only for the enter tainment of their numerous company but also to feed the whole village which furnishes it I am sorry to add, that the Chev Le Gamba to whom we are indebted for our information respecting Colchis after having travelled in almost every part of it assured us that he had never found a single school   Some of the nobility can read a little Russian but their own language they do not read Drunkenness prevails to an incredible extent and almost no limits are set to unchastity in its most offensive and crimi nal forms   The sacredness and validity of an oath are un known

The Catholicos who was formerly the spiritual head of the whole of Colchis, has given place to a Russian bishop, who resides at Kotais and is subject to the archbishop of Tiflis. So that ere this probably the sacraments have been in creased to the usual number of seven by the addition of confirmation and extreme unction the total absence of which so shocked Chardin s papal informant the priests too very likely can no longer obtain a dispensation to marry as often as their wives die and probably the people are more thoroughly drilled into the habit of confessing

Whether correct scriptural knowledge and good morals have been increased, we did not learn. The ecclesiastical books of Colchis are in the Georgian language

We could add so little to what Malte Brun has collected respecting the mountaineers of the Caucasus, that I have very little inducement to attempt any detailed account of that Babel of unnumbered tribes and tongues. In fact, though Tiflis appears on the map to be near to their country, we found ourselves when there, too distant for close inspection We heard much of a general war which marshal Paskevich began about that time to wage against them, for the purpose of reducing all to acknowledge allegiance to the crown of Russia and putting an end to their depredations. Had he not been so soon called to a very different field of warfare in Poland the consequence would probably have been many reported victories, and perhaps the entire erasure from Russian maps of the boundaries of any independent nations in that region. But to reduce them to real subjection is beyond the power even of Russia, until either their character, or the nature of their country is changed Indeed the Russians have already, on their maps, contracted the limits of the independent tribes beyond the effective operation of their government. Nearly half of the country of the Abkház (Abassians) is marked as subject to Russia but in fact the garrison of Sookoom-kulaah (the ancient Dioscurias) live as in a besieged city, and their authority is acknowledged no farther than their guns can reach Swaneti, too, has the same mark of subjection though it is well known that the Swani confine themselves to the neighborhood of the perpetual snows of Elburz in order not to compromise their liberty * Two passes through the mountains, also, are

---

* They are unquestionably a remnant of the *Soanes* of whom Strabo says that they inhabited the highest part of the Caucasus above Dioscurias, and could

marked as Russian soil, but not even the weekly mail is sent through that of Daniel, without an escort amounting sometimes perhaps generally to a hundred soldiers, two field pieces and several Cossacks and if an occasional traveller wishes to try the pass of Derbénd he is not considered safe without a similar guard To the territory of the Lesgies, Russia has a more plausible claim. For that warlike nation, after destroying Shamakhy making itself the terror of all the surrounding provinces, and so perseveringly and successfully resisting the power of Persia, as to give rise to the proverb, "If any king of Persia is a fool let him march against the Lesgies ' was driven by the arms of Nadir Shah to seek protection, in A D 1742, from Russia and swear allegiance to the emperor * And now they pay to the crown a slight contribution of silk or money, and the influence of Russia is effectively felt in the election of officers in the *jumaah* (congress) of their isolated Asiatic democracy † But they are still, even worse than the Cherkes (Circassians) for their predatory and bloodthirsty disposition the Russians instead of residing and having military posts among them station troops along their frontiers to prevent them from pillaging the adjacent territories, and Legistan abounds with both moslems and Georgians, who, by fleeing thither have escaped the execution of Russian justice It is expected, indeed, that the possession of Anapa, through which the Turks, until the last war supplied the mountaineers with arms, ammunition and merchandize in exchange for slaves, will now enable Russia, by drawing a more perfect cordon, to deprive the

muster an undisciplined army of 200,000 men They speak it is said, a dialect of the Georgian language

* In the articles of the treaty they estimated their troops at 66,200 men. Jonas Hanway vol 2 p 410 411

† They have no nobility and their officers are elected by the people at large in an annual assembly

mountaineers of their motive for kidnaping and their
means of defence   But the cause seems disproportioned
to the effect expected , especially, while they are more cel
ebrated than their neighbors, in the manufacture of at least
certain kinds of armor

With the exception of about 200 families of Armenians
among the Cherkes a considerable body of Jews around
Andreva on the borders of Daghistan, and the Lesgies who
are known as bigoted sunny moslems the religion of the
mountains is a nondescript mixture of Mohammedanism,
Christianity and paganism   In the superstitions of some
of the tribes as the Abkház and Cherkes the features of
the moslem faith are predominant , in others as the Swani, Christianity forms the largest ingredient , and in others
still, as the Oset (Osetians) and Ingoosh we find little but
paganism associated it is said, with a strong predilection
for Christianity over Mohammedanism   History tradition,
and monuments in their country, unite with various parts
of their superstitions to testify that nearly all of them once
professed the faith of Christ.   It has been thought that a
people thus circumstanced might be easily induced to embrace the religion of the Bible and our Instructions called
our attention to the report that a missionary effort had been
commenced among them with prospects of success   Such
efforts have been repeatedly made, and by different sects of
Christians   The Scottish mission at Karáss was established
for this specific object   Its operations are well known *
Not many years ago padre Henry, one of the two Jesuit
missionaries stationed at Mosdok a man of zeal and tal-
ent, attempted to convert the Oset and some other tribes to
the papal faith   He had mastered their languages, and
was beginning to reap an abundant harvest , when he was
forbidden by the government to proceed in his labors, as it
professed to have the intention itself of sending mission

* See Henderson's Bib Res in Russia p 446

aries thither In 1821 and 1822, the Rev Mr. Blythe of the Scottish mission labored about nine months among the Ingoosh   As soon as he could speak their language, they listened to the gospel with great interest, and received it with much simplicity and relish , saying, it was just what they wanted their hearts told them it was true.   He was highly respected, and had flattering prospects of success But the Russian government ordered him away, upon the principle, that where the established church has begun to baptize it allows no other denomination to establish a mission   Its baptisms among the Ingoosh, if we were correctly informed, were as follows   The archbishop of Tiflis, re versing Paul s maxim had sent thither two priests, not to preach the gospel, but to baptize, furnishing them with a supply of money and clothing to give effect to their persua sions.   The number of applicants was of course not small and it even happened that some esteemed the ordinance so highly as to get baptized three or four times !   The Russian mission among the Osét which supplanted padre Hen ry s effort appears, from the conversation of bishop Serope already related, and from other reports, to have been con ducted upon similar principles   It consisted of a bishop and ten or fifteen monks, who had an extensive establish ment.   They reported to their synod a large number of converts , but were actually once driven from the country by the provoked natives   The present state of their mission we did not learn

In returning to take leave of Tiflis, permit me to call your attention a moment to the papal missions in Georgia, which have their seat at this place   Their establishment here dates back to A D 1660.*   They introduced themselves to Shahnavaz khan, who was then waly, as physicians the name which they ever afterward bore. In consid-

* So says Chardin, but Le Gamba places its commencement in 1685.

22

eration of the usefulness of their profession, he received them
readily, gave them a house at Tiflis and also at Gori, (where
they soon after established themselves) and liberty to exercise their religion publicly   This hold upon the protection
of the waly with the handsome presents they made him
and his court upon their arrival and every two years afterward, was the only means that enabled them to gain 'and
hold a footing in the country   For the Georgian and Armenian clergy when their proselyting designs were discovered, made every effort to procure their banishment   Medicine not only protected but in part also, supported them.
For their salaries from the propaganda being only 18 Roman crowns, or 72 livres of France each, they were forced
to seek an income from other sources   Besides the practice of medicine, they had several other privileges from
the pope, such as, permission to say mass in all sorts of
places and in any dress to absolve from all sins to disguise
themselves to have horses and servants, to own slaves to
buy and sell, to borrow and lend on interest, and the like
What procured them protection and support, seems also to
have been their only successful employment.   For, so far
were they from creating any partialities for their sect, that
they were themselves obliged to conform to the strict fasts
of the Georgians, and to adopt the oriental calendar in order
to make the natives believe them to be Christians, and thus,
instead of making others papists, became themselves externally Georgians.   When Chardin was with them, five or six
poor people from among their dependents were all that frequented their church, and the school they had established
was attended by only seven or eight little boys, who, according to their own confession, came less to be instructed
than to be fed   In short, the monks allowed that they remained in the country, not for any considerable good they
effected but for the honor of their sect, which would cease
to be the *catholic* church if it had not ministers in all parts

of the world Their mission consisted, in A D 1673, of nine priests and three lay brethren *

We visited their establishment twice It consists of a comfortable convent, connected with a church respectable in size and appearance They still practice medicine and teach a few lads Their parish consists of about 600 souls, mostly, we understood converts from the Armenian church The prefect was a native of Tuscany He had been here six years, and as that is longer than their usual missionary campaign, he was impatiently waiting for his recall They number four members of their mission here, one at Akhal-tsikhe, and one at Kotais They have also a station at Gori, with one church, and about 200 parishioners That at Kotais was established in A D 1670 † and has at present a considerable parish of Armenian converts

The papal missionaries of whom I have now been speaking are Capuchins When Chardin was in Mingreli, (A D 1672,) the Theatins also had an establishment there, at a place called Sipias They came in A D 1627 ‡ and the prince in consideration of their usefulness as physicians gave them a house and lands with a quantity of serfs They consisted of three priests and one lay brother, and their only spiritual labor was the clandestine baptism of children For not considering the Mingrelian mode of baptism valid, and holding like good papists, that it is regeneration and washes away original sin they thought themselves doing a work of great benevolence in performing it *sub conditione*, upon the children of every house which they entered They did it, Chardin says he often

* Chardin vol 2 p 82.—One of Chardin s numerous good qualities for a traveller was that he was a staunch protestant and felt no scruple in reporting what he learned about papal missions

† Chardin vol 1 p 450 Le Gamba says A D 1625

‡ The Jesuits had attempted a mission there 21 years before but the first two of their number having died the enterprise was abandoned

witnessed, by calling for water to wash their hands, and then, while they were wet, putting them upon the foreheads of the sick as if to ascertain their disease, or shaking them into the faces of the well as if in sport. For they thought, if only a drop of water touched the child while the formula of baptism was said mentally by themselves, it was enough The child who a moment before was an heir of perdition thus became a candidate for heaven ' As to making papists of the Mingrehans, they could not even persuade them that they were themselves Christians, because their fasts were too few and easy, and their reverence for images too slight Not even their own slaves would receive the communion at their hands Indeed, they declared to Chardin that they would long since have relinquished their mission as they had already done others in Tartary (Crim Tartary) Georgia Circassia, and Imireti, but for the honor of their church which gloried in having missions throughout the earth and of their society which now had no mission but this * In 1700, there was but one Theatin in Mingreli † and now their is none

In connection with these missionary labors, I may properly state what we learned in compliance with our Instructions respecting the papal Armenian convent at Venice, which has done so much in the same cause That establishment belongs to the order of St. Anthony, and was founded in the island of St Lazarus at Venice in A D. 1706 by the papal Armenian vartabéd, Mukhitár, who was born at Sivás in A D 1665.‡ He was a literary man himself and impressed his character upon his convent Instead of pursuing the denationalizing system of many of the Romish missions among the oriental churches it has done more than all other Armenians together, to cul

* Chardin vol 1 p 354   † Tournefort vol 2 p 317

‡ Mukhitár's Arm Dictionary Arts Mukhitár and Venice

tivate and enrich the literature of the nation One of its first measures was the establishment of an Armenian type foundery and printing press, and its productions have done equal honor to typography and to literature While the mass of the nation has been slumbering under the incubus of Turkish and Persian ignorance and only now and then producing a work often badly composed and still more badly printed, from some little press at Constantinople or elsewhere, this convent has raised up a succession of learned men, who have sent forth publications that would not disgrace the press of London in learning or mechanical execution

It could not be expected that they would entirely neglect controversy in favor of the papal church Formerly they entered into it so warmly that, in A D 1770 heavy denunciations against their books were issued by the Catholicos Simon of Echmiadzin and about the same time by the Armenian bishop of Astrakhán But in latter years controversy has occupied but little of their attention and literary works have been almost their sole publications Through their efforts the Armenian language has been brought up almost to a level with any European tongue in helps both in grammar and lexicography to the study of it either by a native or a foreigner and in several of the sciences as well as in history, a few respectable works are not wanting They have also lent a hand to the publication of the sacred Scriptures As early as A D 1733 they issued a quarto edition of the Bible, which would compare with the best editions of any country at that time One of the editions of the Armenian New Testament circulated by the British and Foreign Bible Society was printed by them And they have also published a Bible with various readings

As to the influence their society is at present exerting upon the nation the result of our inquiries is that in Armenia itself it is small The heavy denunciations

22 *

against their publications just mentioned are indeed forgotten   Not only is no effort made to impede their circulation, but they are held in high esteem wherever the Armenians are scattered, even in India, are received by all classes apparently without suspicion, and are found in the hands of the highest clergy   But, in Armenia, they are extremely rare and difficult to be obtained   We could not learn that the society has an agent in all that region, any farther than that a papal Armenian deacon at Tiflis had offered to procure from Venice any books that might be ordered   With the Capuchin missions, of which I have spoken, we did not learn that the Venice Society has any connection

LETTER IX

DEAR SIR

WE left Tiflis on the 5th of August for Shoosha, where
we hoped to find a cool and healthy retreat, until the season was sufficiently advanced to allow us to proceed to
Tebriz, without exposure to heat or disease As the valley of
the Koor, through which we were to travel is so entirely
depopulated that we should not pass an inhabited spot for
three days we laid in provisions for that length of time
Our conveyance was a large covered baggage-wagon,
without seats or springs, and drawn by four horses abreast
after the Russian fashion   We had hired it of a German
colonist to carry us to Helenendorf, (which was considered
half the distance) in preference to taking caravan or post
horses, on account of the defence it afforded us from the
great heat of the sun

We started at 2 P M and retracing the road by which
we came from Kars for about ten versts to the point where
it leaves the bank of the Koor, continued thence directly
across a parched and uncultivated plain to a low range of
hills which we reached about sunset   In ascending them

our wagon stuck fast in the mud and was extricated only by our lifting a long time at the wheels and finally unloading all our baggage   To avoid a repetition of the accident, we then walked a great distance fatigued as we were and thus reaching a level spot at half past 9 P M near a deserted moslem village stopped for the night   No water could be found except in an extremely muddy ditch, nor any place preferable to the middle of the road to lie upon We had no tent and our cloaks were our only beds and covering

Aug 6. We were on our way at 2 or 3 A M   In crossing a river about sunrise, the wagon again stuck fast. It was extricated by the same process as the last night, and reaching the Red Bridge at 7 o'clock, we stopped to break fast and to bait our horses   Antonio the Armenian who had accompanied us from Constantinople and who was our only attendant had now a burning fever, brought on by fatigue and exposure, and we had no alternative but to prepare our own coffee, the reviving influence of which our feelings loudly called for   The bridge just named is an old and solid structure built over the river Khram   One of its abutments is formed into a large caravanserai *   A road here leads to the right over the mountains to Erivan

We now re-entered Armenia   Its boundary is marked, not only by the river but by a spur of the mountains on the right which follows it down toward the Koor   Hitherto almost no signs of inhabitants had been observed; but now we passed two deserted under-ground villages, which may be the winter residence of some nomads, and in the course of the day occasional stacks of grain indicated a

---

* Chardin speaks of a bridge with a large caravanserai adjoining it at this place both of which were the handsomest he had seen in Georgia. But his description hardly suits this structure and I am inclined to think the ruins a little below are all that is left of them   The neighboring village of 150 houses, also, is no more   Chardin, vol 2 p. 141

little cultivation The province we were in is called Kasakhi, and in the time of Chardin belonged to a distinct khan, who was tributary to Persia Its name is said to be derived from a Mohammedan people called Khazak, who inhabit it and whom Chardin Tourneforte and some modern travellers, suppose to be a branch of the Cossacks As they came into this region however, with the Seljookian armies and speak a dialect of Turkish, St Martin calls them a Turkish tribe and suggests that they may be a branch of the powerful nation of Kerghiz, who are also sometimes called by the same name Unfortunately we found not a human being of whom to inquire and although we repeatedly mentioned their name in the adjacent provinces no one seemed to recognize it

We stopped again during the day for about an hour The spot was selected for a spring which here dropped from a bank of clay Thirst created by the excessive heat of the sun soon led us to taste it, but it was so impregnated with nitre or some other mineral substance, as to be unpalatable We sought for a shade from the fiery sun but could find none except that of the wagon in the middle of the road and of some weeds by its side Reaching at 6 P M a verdant tract of meadow land watered by a limpid rivulet we stopped for the night and soon lay down to sleep congratulating ourselves upon the contrast it presented to our last night s accommodations The grass on which we lay was clean the water was pure, and the air apparently wholesome

Aug 7 We started again at half past 2 A M and reaching at 7 o'clock a post-house on the farther side of a river we stopped two hours Thus far the ground over which we had travelled, with the exception of the hills mentioned on the 5th and those along the banks of the Khram had been neither hilly nor perfectly level but generally arable and of a good soil We had lost sight of the Koor, on the left, since the tenth verst from Tiflis, and on the right, a hilly and mountainous tract had gradually approached us. But soon after leaving the post house to-day, an almost perfectly level plain opened before us, extending in breadth from the mountains on one hand, to the Koor on the other, and reaching in length toward the southeast, (the direction of the Koor,) to so great a distance as to present a horizon like the sea. It was watered with rivulets and canals, and possessed an excellent soil but, with the exception of an occasional meadow, or a field of grain reaped and stacked, it was thinly sprinkled over with shrubs and perfect desolation reigned throughout Not a house was to be seen, and the solitude was broken only by a few antelopes occasionally bounding through the shrubs One needs only to travel through this *fertile desert*, to be convinced of what history tells us respecting the wars and captivities by which it has been produced Reaching a small tree by a water course at 1 P M we were tempted to stop, and shelter ourselves an hour and a half from the sultry sun

We had heard on the road that a deadly disease was raging at Ganjeh, which carried off in a few hours nearly all whom it attacked Its name we could not learn, but from the description of it given by our informants, we could not doubt that it was either the plague or the cholera, though one was not known to exist at all in these regions, and the other had not been heard of nearer than Tebriz in Persia and Bakoo on the Caspian To exchange wagons at Helenendorf, according to our original intention, was now rendered dangerous and impossible For we must pass through the infected air of Ganjeh on our way, and then be arrested by a sanitary cordon which, we understood had been drawn between the two places No course was left us therefore, but to turn aside to the little German colony of Anenfeld, near the ruins of Shamkor, although we had been warned not to stop there, on account of its unhealthy situation.   For not only could we find a wagon in no other place, but it was the only village we heard of nearer than Gánjeh   On starting again, we could distinctly see the pillar of Shamkor eight or ten miles before us   and we soon turned to the right toward the village   We were interested to find, that one of the most common of the wild shrubs which cover the plain around it is the pomegranate   Its fruit   which was now in a green state is said to be good when ripe   We reached the colony about 5 P M

Both because to-morrow was the Sabbath, and on account of Antonio's fever   which continued unabated, we were obliged to stop until Monday   Anenfeld was settled about twelve years ago by 150 German families   but the number remaining was only forty-six, and of these many had lost a father or a mother or children by disease   We saw but little of them, as they were spending the sickly season in a more healthy situation twenty-five versts distant in the mountains and only a few came down by turns to keep guard, three days at a time that their nomadic neighbors might not take advantage of their absence to rob them of their goods and their crops   Their houses are of one story, neatly built and situated upon parallel streets, between which is an open square with a church in its centre   They have no regular pastor but one of their own number acts as their spiritual head The village is surrounded by luxuriant gardens of culinary vegetables, fruit trees, and vines, indicating great fertility   Its soil is also dry, and water good, and we were at a loss to account for its sickliness.   But on Monday morning a southeast wind brought over us a dense fog from the marshes and rice plantations along the Koor, and by almost exhibiting in a palpable form the disease with which it was charged left us no longer in doubt. The site of the village is near the mountains, two, or three versts southwesterly from the ruins of Shamkor   From it the parched steppes across the Koor could be distinctly seen, and far beyond them appeared the immense chain of the Caucasus, with its snowy ridge rising like an eternal bulwark to the skies.

The causes which led to the establishment of the German colonies in Georgia, and their present state, deserve a moment's attention, in fact we were directed by our Instructions to make them a particular object of inquiry. They owe their origin to extravagant views respecting the millennium. Some years ago, several popular and ardent ministers in the kingdom of Wurtemberg maintained in commentaries on the Apocalypse and in other publications, that that wished-for period would commence in 1836, and would be preceded by a dreadful apostacy and great persecutions. These views, in addition to the fascinating interest always connected with prophetical theories being enforced with much pious feeling acquired so great credit as to be adopted by nearly all the religious people in the kingdom and by many others. At the same time, the advocates of the neological system being the predominant party in the clergy, succeeded in effecting some alterations in the prayers and hymns of the church, in accommodation to their errors. This grieved exceedingly all who were attached to evangelical principles, and was taken to be the commencement of the apostacy they expected. Their prophetical teachers had intimated, that, as in the destruction of Jerusalem the Christians found a place of refuge, so would there be one now, and that somewhere in the vicinity of the Caspian sea. Many, therefore, of the common people determined to seek the wished-for asylum, that they and their children, (for whom the better sort were particularly anxious,) might escape the impending storm, and also be able to from an independent ecclesiastical establishment according to their own notions. To these were joined others desirous of change or in straitened circumstances, who, though not at heart pious, professed for the time to be influenced by the same principles

and motives. In fact the latter finally became the most nu
merous. The company when it left Wurtemberg, consisted of 1500 families But no adequate arrangement having
been made for the journey, and the sinister motives of the
majority contributing to create disorder, they suffered ex
ceedingly on the way, and before they reached Odessa,
two thirds had died There they found a large number
of their countrymen, and received a reinforcement of 100
families.

They reached Georgia in 1817, and settled in seven
colonies One divided into two villages called Marienfeld
and Petersdorf, is on the Iori in Kakheti, two others, New
Tiflis and Alexandersdorf are on the left bank of the Koor
near Tiflis, two more, Elizabeththal and Katherinenfeld, are
in Somkheti not far from the same city, and Anenfeld
and Helenendorf are here in the vicinity of Gánjeh The
emperor, in the same spirit of encouragement toward foreign
settlers, which has actuated many of his predecessors almost
from the foundation of the Russian monarchy, and which has
recently stripped the adjacent Persian and Turkish provin
ces of their Armenian population, granted them a ready re
ception and considerable privileges They were allowed
to have their own municipal officers and internal police,
free from the interference of the Russians, and were never
to be draughted for soldiers They received a quantity of
land, free from taxes for a certain number of years, and the
loan of a sum of money from government, to aid in building their houses and commencing agricultural operations *
Those who should refund this loan after a certain number of

---

* Our principal informants respecting these colonies were the German
missionaries and they did not give exact numbers Le Gamba says of Mari
enfeld and Petersdorf that each family was allowed 35 disseatines, (about 90
acres) of land to be free from taxes for ten years, and then to pay 20 kopecks
(about 15 cts.) the disseatine and that their houses cost the crown only 125 silver roubles (about $94) which was to be repaid in ten years without interest

years, were to remain free foreigners, with the liberty of going
and coming when and where they might choose, those who
should not, were to become subjects of the crown   At first
they did not flourish   some were sickly, and others had internal dissensions   The two near Gánjeh were driven away
by the Persians in the last war and lost almost every thing
Individuals were even carried into captivity, and when we
were at Tebriz, a poor colonist came there in search of his
wife and child who, he had heard, were in the harem of a
Persian noble in that vicinity   He recovered his little boy,
but his wife was dead   At the same time, another scourge
visited them, as dreadful as it was unusual   A number of
hyenas from the neighboring mountains where they abound,
descended upon the colony of Helenendorf   They traversed
the streets for several days, attacking all who were exposed
to them and even flying furiously at the windows where
they heard the cry of a child or caught the glimpse of an
individual within   Many graves, also, were robbed by them
of the bodies of the dead   Several persons were wounded,
but only one, a young man was slain   The colonists are
now prospering more in their worldly interests but it is
doubtful whether many of them will not fail to fulfil the condition upon which their liberty depends   Their whole number is at present about 2000 souls

The arrival of the German missionaries in Georgia in
the spring of 1823 was the commencement of some ecclesiastical order among them   They were found entirely
without pastors and deplorably destitute of religious privileges and those gentlemen, induced by their earnest request as well as by their condition devoted to them the
whole of their first summer   Then finding that too much
of their attention was thus called away from the proper object of their mission, they wrote to their society to send out
a man specially for the colonists, and the Rev Mr Saltet
was accordingly commissioned for this purpose   They re-

ceived him with joy but another pastor arriving soon after
with a commission from the German consistory of St Petersburg they were of course immediately resigned into his
hands   Although the latter was an evangelical man, the
colonists, having fled from Germany to escape a similar ecclesiastical authority, declared that they were under no consistory, and would have nothing to do with him   In support of their pretensions they appealed to a promise to
that effect from the emperor Alexander which he had probably given, at least verbally   An account of the whole matter was sent to the consistory by their delegate , but before
it was settled he died   About this time count Diebitch,
who has since so distinguished himself in the Turkish war,
arrived in Georgia   Being himself a protestant he took a
deep interest in the colonies and entered into the most
full consultations with Mr Saltet respecting their ecclesiastical affairs   At the suggestion of Diebitch, they were
assembled in a council and the plan of a separate re
ligious establishment was drawn up, with the aid of the
missionaries and presented to the emperor   He consequently
granted that agreeably to their request they should be in
dependent of the consistory   that they should be supplied
with pastors from the society of Basle   and that Mr Saltet
should be the spiritual inspector of the whole   He also gave
them 27,000 silver roubles (about $20,250) for the erec-
tion of a church and a parsonage in every colony, and 250
silver roubles (about $187) per annum for the support of
each pastor   Two pastors in addition to Mr Saltet, had
already arrived when we were in Georgia , one of whom
was settled in Elizabeththal, and the other not yet located
We have also, since met two others, one at Constantinople
and one at Malta, on their way   Mr Saltet s lamented
death I have already mentioned   Subsequently the Rev
Mr Dittrich, at the request of the minister at St. Petersburg
addressed first to himself and then to his society, was ap-

pointed to his place   Rejoiced as we were 'that the colonies should obtain a spiritual director, so well qualified by talents and piety and an intimate acquaintance from the beginning with all their spiritual concerns, we could not but sympathize with him, in the trial his feelings endured in view of the consequent interruption of his labors among the Armenians and are on the whole gratified to learn, that the arrangement is likely to be overruled in favor of his remaining at Shoosha

When the missionaries first arrived among the colonists, they were received with open arms, and were delighted to find every mouth full of the most pious conversation   They soon perceived, however, that much of it was a mere show and that a majority were at heart men of the world   Still, wherever they preached some profited and proved themselves to be branches of the true vine   Under the excellent influence of Mr Saltet, their spiritual state has improved, and it is hoped they will ultimately exert a most salutary influence upon the natives of the country

Aug 9   By the blessing of God upon our prescriptions, Antonio s fever left him yesterday and nothing now prevented our starting but the want of a conveyance   With post horses which we had authority to take, as the general at Kars had given us an order without our knowledge that extended even to the Persian frontier we should be obliged to pass directly through Ganjeh   Such quarantines had been established on the road in consequence of diseases that no one would take us to Shoosha in a wagon upon any condition   At last we persuaded a man to carry us to the next post beyond Ganjeh, without going through that place, but were obliged to pay him a considerable sum, on account of the quarantine of fourteen days to which he would thus subject himself on his return   We started at half past 3 P M

The east wind, even after the fog of the morning had

subsided had seemed all day surcharged with noxious vapors, and before reaching the column of Shamkor, I felt symptoms of approaching fever Still we stopped a moment to examine that antiquity   It is built of brick, has winding stairs within to its top, and is said to be 180 feet in height. On a stone near the bottom is an inscription in the Arabic character, and another reaches nearly around it at the top where it is also surrounded by a gallery with a door opening upon it from within   Its origin is not known, but it was evidently built for the same purposes as the minaret of a mosk   The other ruins of the place are the foundations of a large caravanserai, and several small moslem tombs   Shamkor was a powerful and important city in the ninth and tenth centuries,* but now, not a human being inhabits its ruins   The small river which passes them is divided and scattered over a large surface in canals, but very little use seems to be made of it for cultivation, as we saw only two or three small cotton fields   Mr Dwight was now seized with the same febrile symptoms as myself and the pains in our heads and limbs were so increased by the jolting of the wagon, that we became almost insensible to every object on the road   At half past 8 P M we stopped by a little rivulet for the night, and were surprised to find that, notwithstanding our bargain with the wagoner, we were almost within a stone s cast of Ganjeh   We had not then been able to learn, what we afterwards ascertained, that the disease which existed there was the cholera, and the uncertainty perhaps made us more fearful of the infected atmosphere, than if we had known the real extent of the evil   There was no remedy, however, and racked with the pains of a burning fever, we lay down under our cloaks by the wheels of our wagon, in a much better state to indulge in delirious longings for the comforts of home, than to sleep

* St Mart vol 1 p 90

Aug 10 After a night which I would rather forget than describe, we started again at half past 4 A M with our fever unintermitted We passed Ganjeh by just skirting its suburbs on the east, instead of going directly through it This city lays claim to Kobad who reigned over Persia in the beginning of the sixth century, as its founder [*] It was called Kantság of the Aghovans by the Armenians, to distinguish it from Tebriz, which was also named by them Kantság Its distinctive appellation was derived from the Aghováns, whose Catholicos resided here for some time; and under them about the tenth and eleventh centuries, it attained its greatest importance [†] I have already spoken of its passing from the hands of a Persian khan into those of the Russian emperor In the last war with Persia, it was instigated by a mollah to rise upon and murder the Russian garrison that occupied it, and the greatest battle that occurred between the belligerent parties was fought in its vicinity [‡] It is still the most important place in this part of the Russian provinces has about 12 000 inhabitants, and is the capital of a small province, which contains as many more, and produces considerable silk The plain where it is situated, is fertile and well watered, but contrary to what seems to have been its character once, the site is considered pecliarly unhealthy The Russians have given it the name of Elizabethpol

On reaching the post house at the Koorek-chai, 18 versts from Ganjeh we found ourselves unable to proceed farther, and were obliged to stop for the day It was a day of suffering and anxiety The same pestiferous wind continued, and the scorching rays of the sun, either were in themselves uncommonly oppressive or were made to seem so by the diseased state of our bodies The houses of the post

---

[*] Mod Trav Persia vol 1 p 109   [†] St Mart vol 1 p 150

[‡] Mod Trav Persia vol 1 p 245.

were little cabins sunk completely under ground, and the walls of the one we occupied were almost black with musquetoes which tormented us all day and all night Food or medicine we did not expect to find at such a place, nor did we need them, for we had no appetite for the one, and with the other we were supplied Not the slightest article of convenience, not even a vessel for bathing our feet could be obtained, and a few rough planks for our bed was all that the post afforded Yet even in such circumstances, did God give efficacy to the means we used for recovery and kindly broke our fever

Aug 11 We arose extremely weak and without appetite, but the fever had left us and the wind too had changed and purified the atmosphere Starting at half past 5 A M with post horses we proceeded over the same level plain It afforded nothing to note except a few fields of rice and cotton irrigated by canals of the purest water, till we reached the next post, a distance of 18 versts Finding no shelter from the sun so comfortable as the stable, we threw ourselves upon the ground there and hardly rose till 5 o clock P M Then we mounted again to accomplish another stage of 22 versts The rivers which so abundantly water this plain, are generally composed of perfectly pure and limpid water We crossed this afternoon the only exception of a muddy one Like all the others it was divided into a great number of artificial canals, as if for purposes of irrigation though, as usual, there was hardly any thing but uncultivated fields to be irrigated At length after crossing the main channel of the river Terter and all its numerous canals, we reached our post house at 9 P M I had now been more than two days without eating any thing but a small bit of bread We had indeed laid in at Anenfeld a stock of provisions similar to what we had provided at Tiflis and for a similar reason, as on our road between Ganjeh and

Shoosha we were to pass only naked Cossack stations, but I had no appetite for any thing. Happening now, however, to think of some arrowroot which we had brought from Malta, I succeeded in swallowing a little. Another similar dish was the only nutriment I took till we reached Shoosha. Mr. Dwight was in almost as diseased a state as myself. The Cossacks at this post could furnish us with no place to lie upon but the open ground. They themselves slept upon a scaffold elevated several feet to avoid the musquetoes, which were here more numerous than can easily be credited. The bushes around the inclosure of the post were the next morning black with them. After trying various expedients in vain. I succeeded at last by wrapping myself closely in a cloak, keeping on my boots, defending my hands with leather gloves, and tying a double handkerchief tight over my face, in getting a little sleep in an empty wagon.

On the same river, farther toward the Koor, there is a small village called Berdaah, and also the ruins of the city which once bore that name. It was the capital of the Armenian province of Oodi, and in the eighth century was the residence of the kings of the Aghovans. It was often mentioned by the Arabian geogaphers, as the chief city of this region, called by them Aran, and at one time there was no place nearer than Rey and Isfahan, that would compare with it * The Oodians too an Armenian tribe, that once inhabited this province, and toward the beginning of the tenth century becoming almost independent, carried their arms to the Caucasus on the one side, and into Armenia on the other † seem not to be entirely extinct. The German missionaries have found, in their travels in the province of Sheky, at a village called Vertashin, two or three hundred families of a peculiar denomination of Christians called Oodi. Others of that name were also heard of

* St Mart vol 1 p 87   † Ibid vol 1 p 226

in different parts of the same province But their principal place of residence was found to be in the district of
Char * among the Lesgies, by whom they have been se-
verely oppressed, and not allowed to have priests. As that
district has now however come under Russian control,
their condition is much improved The Armenians say
they once belonged to their church, while others affirm that
they were of the Georgian faith At any rate, they are
now united to the Georgian church, and have Georgian and
Russian priests They are believed to speak a language
peculiar to themselves —At a little distance above the
post, on the same river Terter, is a village of some
300 families of Nestorians, who emigrated from the prov
ince of Oormiah with the Armenians, when the Russian
army retired from Persia But, as our informant had made
them but one short visit he could tell us little respecting
them It was reported that their priest had died, and that
they had applied for one of the Russian church

Aug 12 At half past 5 A M we commenced another
stage of 30 versts The rays of the sun, beating upon our
diseased bodies from above, and reflected from a dry and
dusty soil beneath, created as the morning advanced, a degree of thirst that was almost intolerable, and which the
infrequency of rivers here prevented us from quenching,
as on other days, till we neared the post-house Then, a
stream fresh from the mountains which we had now approached, crossed our path, and offered us an abundance of
the purest water A cup doled it out in potions too small
for my craving appetite, and I lay down by its side and
drank in no measured quantities I could not bear to
leave it and came back once to its farther side to repeat
my draught. I was now too weak to support myself on
horseback without much difficulty, but, by alternately
changing that position, for the top of our baggage wagon,

* Probably the Dzanar of the Armenians See St Mart vol I p 233.

succeeded in getting through this long stage   We reached
the post-house, an old castle called Shah boolak, at half past
11 A M and remained until 6 P M   Not far beyond,
our road entered the mountains and the chillness of the
night air that blew from them added to our enfeebled
state, made the next stage of 17 versts seem almost interminable   Before it was completed our wagon broke down,
and poured baggage and Antonio, who was riding upon it,
into the road   Leaving him to guard it until fresh horses
could be procured we pushed on to the post house which
we reached at half past 11 at night.   Our lodging place
was the musqueto scaffold, raised ten or twelve feet from
the ground and undefended by the slightest covering   The
mountain breeze that swept over us seemed to chill us to
the heart , the Cossacks who lay by our side talked and
snored, and shook our frail platform by their motion   the
trouble of bringing up our baggage caused loud talking and
scolding among the surijies till almost morning and all together produced such an effect upon my weak nerves that
to sleep was impossible, and I lay and wept like a child

Aug 13   The morning sun showed us Shoosha elevated high before us at the end of a long mountain ravine   Though so far below it, we had already sensibly
changed climates.   The fresh herbage of beautiful meadows and pastures in the valleys, and the verdure of the
trees that clothed the sides of the mountains afforded
a delightful contrast to the parched plains we had left.
After a stage of 17 versts, the latter part of which was a long
and steep ascent of a mountain, we reached the quarantine
ground of Shoosha   Through the mediation of the missionaries, and the politeness of the commandant, our baggage was only subjected unopened to the *form* of smoking,
and after three or four hours, we found a home with our
Christian brethren and sisters in the mission house   We
immediately forgot the fatigues and exposures of the journey,

in the kindness and comforts which surrounded us, while they, instead of being surprised at our illness wondered that we had accomplished so unwholesome a ride with no more injury, and all of us united in admiring the goodness of God, through which we had been led to escape even thus, from the destructive epidemic, which it now appeared was hurrying off its victims in every direction

It was at Shoosha that we found a refuge from the cholera, while it passed by us through the isthmus between the Caspian and Black seas on its way to Europe, where it has since committed such fearful ravages After having been several years advancing from India, it made its appearance at Reshd on the southern shore of the Caspian before the last cold season was gone Thence in the summer, it spread over Aderbaiján on the one side, where together with the plague which followed it it carried off about 36,000 souls among which was a tenth of the population of Tebriz, while on the other it broke out at Bakoo From Aderbaijan it spread into Nakhchevan and Eriván where about 700 died of it From Bakoo it continued along the shore of the Caspian and branched off into the valley of the Koor In the latter direction Shamakhy Ganjeh and Tiflis felt its ravages At Ganjeh two hundred had already died of it when we passed along In the neighboring colony of Helenendorf ninety four were attacked but under the medical treatment of Mr Hohenacker the physician of this mission who happened to be there, only twenty nine died His chief prescription was calomel and opium, and in every case where salivation was produced it proved effectual At Tiflis where it broke out while we were on the road to Shoosha, the number of deaths was variously estimated from three to ten thousand The inhabitants deserted the town and it ceased On the shore of the Caspian, it passed through Kooba and Derbénd to Kizlar, and then spread along the line of the Terek In the whole Govern ment of the Caucasus, it is supposed to have destroyed as many as in Aderbaijan So that while we were at Shoosha, more than 70,000 died of it in the regions around us

We hoped for some time, that the elevated situation of that town would defend us from it, though the inhabitants feared it excessively, and Armenians and moslems endeavored, each according to their respective superstitions, to appeal to the clemency of the Deity We shall long remember to what a pitch our compassion was excited for the latter, as they passed repeatedly by our window in formal procession, bare-headed, with banners flying, and calling loudly upon God, on their way to their cemetery, where they hoped their prayers would be more effectual We could distinguish nothing but *ya Allah ! ya Allah !* (oh God ! oh God !) uttered in different tones as fast as the sounds could be repeated At length it made its appearance among us, but in so mild a form that few died of it In the mission house however, we had a severe case in the person of the Rev Mr Zaremba, a valuable member of the mission He had been at Tiflis during the worst of it there, and Mr Saltet had died in his arms Soon after he arrived in Shoosha, he was seized himself, and speedily the symptoms of approaching death cut off all hopes of his recovery But God heard the prayers of his anxious brethren and raised him up from the grave We left him convalescent but his enfeebled constitution has since obliged him, much to the sorrow of all his associates as well as his own, to relinquish the mission, and return to his native Poland No one, so far as we heard, thought of the cholera s being contagious like the plague, until the doctrine of quarantines was brought down from Russia, after it had almost ceased in the trans-Caucasian provinces.

Not only the prevalence of the Cholera around rendered a long delay at Shoosha expedient, but our own ill health, and especially mine, made it absolutely necessary We all arrived there invalids. I was extremely weak, my blood seemed to circulate without force, and I felt as if I had been poisoned. I was not surprised, therefore, at being seized, a week after our arrival, with the ague and fever; but grateful that Providence caused the disease to assume so mild a form Antonio was next attacked by the same disease, and Mr Dwight soon after with a more severe remittent Every case, however, easily yielded to medicine, and in a few days we were all convalescent. My hopes of speedy recovery were soon disappointed by a relapse, which was followed by another and another, which not only prevented me from leaving, but almost confined me to the house, till the first of November Nor did the evil end then , the seeds of disease implanted in the valley of the Koor, produced constant returns of the ague and fever in both Mr Dwight and myself for more than a year, and were only eradicated, in my case by calomel, after our return to Malta There must have been something extremely deleterious in the atmosphere at that time affecting the general health even of those in whom it did not produce the cholera Although only one of the six persons who composed the mission family had the cholera, not one remained in good health Some of the time almost every one was confined to his room, and the house was like a hospital We were able to meet for divine worship only the first Sabbath after our arrival And Mr Dittrich was obliged to be carried away for a change of air sometime before we left.

We were pained in the extreme, to add by our presence and sickness, to the cares of families thus worn down themselves by disease But the hospitality and kindness we experienced from them, were not, in consequence of their afflicted circumstances, the less cheerfully given, and they have, I trust, impressed upon our hearts an indelible sense of gratitude to those beloved Christian brethren It is not only for comforts contributing to the restoration of our health, and perhaps even to the prolongation of our lives,

24

however, that we are indebted to the missionaries at Shoosha.
To them, especially to Mr Dittrich, whose cultivated mind
was stored with well digested information respecting the
Armenians, are you to credit most that is valuable in
the results of our tour   Whenever his and our own health
would permit we sat down with him, pen in hand, and
brought under review the several topics of inquiry suggested in our Instructions   And though in the form in which
our journals are finally embodied the information thus elicited is so scattered through every part, that we are unable
to give credit for the individual facts and opinions, we
cheerfully confess, that, however small may be the value of
our communications they would not have possessed the
half of that especially in a missionary point of view, had
we never visited Shoosha *

* Finding Mr Dittrich possessed of so much valuable information respect
ing the Armenian church we urged him to present it to the Christian public
in a publication of his own and have been gratified to learn from him since,
that such a work has been prepared and printed   We have not yet had access to it

LETTER X

Description of the town—Province of Kara bagh—The Aghováns—Adjacent
provinces—Tenure of lands—Nomads—Language of the moslems—Their
domestic state—Moral character—Religious opinions—Priesthood—Intel
lectual state of the Armenians—Family education—Desire for education—
Education of females—Number of schools—School books—Sources of in
telligence—Modern Armenian language

DEAR SIR

SHOOSHA is the capital of the province of Kara bagh
which embraces the ancient Paidagarán, with parts of Oodi
Artsákh and Sunik, and occupies the space between the Koor
and the Aras at their junction, being washed by them on two
sides for some distance   In the reign of Nadir Shah, somewhat more than eighty years ago, the Armenian chiefs, who
had then gained a sort of independence in its mountainous in
terior, were forced by their own dissensions and the power of
that conqueror, to receive a moslem khan for their governor
He built the town of Shoosha, and called it *Penah-abád* or
city of Penáh, which was his own name   That name is now
almost lost in the more common one of *Shoosha-kulaasy*, or
fortress of Shoosha, (written in Armenian, Shooshi,) which
it has borrowed from a neighboring village   His memory,
however, is effectually preserved in a coin that was struck by
him and the *penabád* in this and the adjacent provinces, takes
the place of the *abbas*, by which the name of the great Persian Shah is perpetuated in a coin at Tiflis   It was his son
that lost the province by fleeing into Persia, and his grandson
that now lives upon a Russian pension, as already related

Nature has done much to render Shoosha impregnable. It is a mountain formed into a natural castle. The ravine by which we approached it, separates at its base into two, which, each with its stream of the purest water, continue up on either side. From the same point, an almost precipitous path winds, sometimes along the face of a ledge of rocks, a tedious distance to the gate at the top. On every other side a perpendicular precipice of a giddy height prevents the necessity of artificial defence, except at the Erivan gate. There, a tremendous chasm opening toward the mountains, with the precipice rising up in two immense towers on each side as if formed by nature to guard this weak spot in her fortification, is defended by a short wall. The top presents an uneven surface gently sloping to the northeast, of which the town occupies only a small space in the lowest part, and the remainder is covered with a green sward. So surrounded is it by rugged and weather-beaten mountains still higher than itself, that one is not aware of its elevation, till, from the edge of its precipice he looks into the frightful ravines around it, so deep that the mountain torrents at their bottom seem only noiseless rills, or through the opening formed by the ravine to the north, sees the valley of the Koor at a great distance below, or just discerns in the same direction, as far as the eye can reach, the giant Caucasus towering above all the adjacent peaks for nearly a quarter of the horizon.

The houses of the town are built of stone, frequently two stories high, and open to the streets like those of Georgia and Turkey. Unlike, so far as I recollect, every other place I had seen since leaving America, their roofs were covered with shingles, in the wooden pegs however, by which, instead of nails, they were fastened, we did not recognize a custom of our country. They had in general a ruinous appearance, and one extremity of the continuous

arcade of shops, which line the two sides of a street
almost the whole length of the town, and form its bazár, had
been broken down by an earthquake Its climate was as
cool as we had expected, but in regard to its salubrity our
anticipations were not realized It is by no means free
from intermittent fevers and billious affections In my
own case, I fancied that its water was particularly injuri
ous None but well water is to be found within the walls
and all of that is so impregnated with saline matter as to be
very unpalatable We at last procured what we had oc
casion to use, from a pure spring, just without the Erivan
gate, and my health rapidly recovered

The town itself contains about 2000 houses, of which
700 are Armenian, and the rest Mohammedan The Armenians have two large and two small churches which
are served by fourteen priests There is also a nunnery
with one inmate The moslems have two mosks The
province of Kara bagh derives its name, which signifies
black garden, from the extreme fertility of the alluvial
plain of the Koor which it embraces Its interior is
mountainous, and in general well wooded with a variety of
forest trees Armenians and moslems, in nearly equal
numbers, compose its population, and amount in all to
about 50 000 souls The former are under the jurisdic
tion of two bishops One of them resides in the convent
of Datev, and will be spoken of hereafter The other
spends his winters in Shoosha, and the remainder of his
time in the convent of Kántsasar about a day s ride farther
to the west, where he has a chorepiscopus, one vartabed,
and two deacons He has sometimes been called a fourth
Catholicos of the Armenians, in addition to those at Echmiádzin, at Sis, and at Aghtamár, which have been already
mentioned But his more proper title was Catholicos of
the *Aghovans*, and the mention of him reminds me to say

a word respecting that nation, which occupies so prominent
a place in the history of these regions

The Aghovans were called *Albani* * by the Greeks and
Latins, who describe them as the possessors of the whole
valley of the Koor from Georgia to the Caspian sea. Their
original country seems to have been between the Koor and
the Caspian, and to have corresponded nearly with the
modern Shirwán. According to Armenian tradition, it
was called *Aghovank* after a prince of the race of Haig,
who conquered it and gave that name to its inhabitants.†
They seem to have continued very intimately connected
with the Armenians though the latter allow that they
spoke a different dialect, and the Romans and Greeks regarded them as a distinct people Strabo affirms that they
were more numerous than the Georgians, and could muster
60,000 armed men From the first of the Armenian Arsacidæ they received a governor by the name of Aran;‡
but in the third century of the Christian era, they threw off
the yoke of Armenian rule and probably never again submitted to it. In the subsequent wars of the Armenians
with Persia, they took a hostile part, and though, when
the Sassanian persecutions came upon both, they were
allies for a time, yet, after the fall of the Arsacidæ of Armenia, the Aghováns made large encroachments upon several of the northeastern provinces of that country, and
even transferred the capital of their kingdom to the south
of the Koor § Here they afforded an asylum to the Armenians, even after Armenia had fallen before the Sar-

---

* The names are the same, for the Armenians always write the letter *l* in
foreign names by *gh* and the Greek *beta* has the sound of *v*

† Chamchean P 1 c 2.

‡ St. Mart vol 1 p 218.—Perhaps the name by which the Saracens
knew this region was derived from him

§ Chamchean P 3 c 16, 22 P 4 c 1 St Mart vol. 1 p 220

acens, and the Seljookian Malik-shah got possession of their country only by marrying their queen *

The gospel was preached to the Aghovans by a grand son of Gregory Loosavorich, and he is supposed to have founded the see of their Catholicos, which, at different times had Gánjeh, Berdaah, and Kantsasar for its seat They shared in the monophysite heresy with the Armenians from the beginning, and there seems to have been uniformly a good understanding between the primates of the two nations.† We hear little or nothing of the Aghovans in this region, since the invasion of Timoor, of whom tradition asserts, that he transported numbers to Kandahár, where their descendants are now called Afghans.‡ The nomadic tribes of Kara-bagh are said to have even now, a corresponding tradition, that the Afgháns and they have exchanged countries. Difficult as it may be, to believe in the transportation of an entire nation, we encounter almost as great a difficulty in whatever way we attempt to account for its total disappearance § Once they had a written language of their own, having received letters from the inventor of the Armenian alphabet ,|| but now there is no relic of their di-

* Chamchean P 5 c 16   † Ibid P 3. c 15. P 4 c 12

‡ Chamcheán P 7 c 1   Lett Ed et Cur vol 4 p 25.

§ The difference of the two names has been urged as an objection to this tradition But the mission library at Malta contains a history of the exploits of Nadir Shah written in Armeno-Turkish by an Armenian who accompanied him to Delhi, in which the Afgháns are always called Aghováns It is certain, however that a people of that name existed at Kandahár some centuries before the time of Timoor (See Langlès' notes to Chardin.) An enterprising countryman of ours is now travelling in Afghanistán. After having already spent several years there and ascended as far as Cabul he came to Tebriz to make himself better acquainted with the history of the country and returned again just before we reached that place. The acting English embassador kindly lent us his journals. He found no Christians at Kandahár nor in any part of the country except a few Armenians at Cabul

|| Chamcheán, P 3 c 28. Moses Choren. Lib 3. c 54

alect in books, and none also in the tongues spoken among the natives of the country unless something should hereaf. ter be discovered in a *patois* which is said to be used by the peasants near Bakoo. Their name was preserved until recently, in connection with the see of Kantsasar. But the Russians have now reduced its occupant to complete dependence upon Echmiádzin, and changed his title of Catholicos of the Aghovans, into that of a simple Armenian archbishop.

Shoosha is the usual residence of the governor of that division of the trans-Caucasian territories of Russia, which bears the name of Mussulman Provinces. It will be proper, therefore, from this point, to glance at Sheky and Shirwan, of which, together with Kara bagh it consists and also to say a word upon Daghistán.—The capital of *Sheky* is Nookha. The province contains some villages of Armenians, and in the town a large number of that nation is assembled. Most of them, however are strangers, drawn together by commercial enterprise, as an extensive trade with the Lesgies centres at that place.—Old Shamakhy long remained a deserted monument of the wrath of Nadir Shah, who, for the trouble it gave him in holding out a temptation for Lesgian and Russian invasions razed it to the ground, A. D. 1734, and transferred its inhabitants and its name to another spot.* But it has now resumed its honors as capital of *Shirwán*, and is fast becoming a place of consequence. Whether it will ever regain the great commercial importance it formerly had, is uncertain, but its salubrity and other advantages of situation bid fair to make it soon eclipse New Shámakhy, the deadly air of which has already caused it to sink into insignificance. The almost unequalled productiveness of that part of the province of Shirwán along the Koor, of which, under the name of the plain of Albania, Strabo asserts, ' that its verdure is perpetual, that

---

* Jonas Hanway vol 2 p 388

every fruit and plant comes to perfection uncultivated, that a field once sowed produces two or three crops, and that irrigation here is more perfect than in Babylonia or Egypt,' is still proverbial I need only add, that in later times, it is not less distinguished by extreme insalubrity, the thorn so usually implanted by Providence in the rose of fertility In the town there are 200 families of Armenians, and in the province 50 villages of the same nation *—The province of which Bakoo is the capital, contains 19,700 inhabitants, of which 5150 are in the city itself and the rest scattered in 39 villages Only 80 families of them are Armenians, and they are all in the city Silk and saffron are among the principal productions of Bakoo, and the former is said to amount to 80,000 pounds a year Naphtha is also among its exports, and the burning fountain in the vicinity of the city is still an object of worship to a few of the followers of Zoroaster, who resort thither from Persia and from India.†—The territory of Kooba is said to contain 60,000 souls, of which 5 000 are in the town ‡ A few of the villages are inhabited by Armenians who are tenants of a Mohammedan lord In the town their number is very small —Derbénd contains 600 or 700 Armenians, among its 7000 or 8000 inhabitants but in the villages belonging to it there are none

Before separating the moslems from the Armenians for distinct subjects of remark, permit me to say a word respecting the tenure by which the peasantry of both relig-

---

* These numbers were given us by Mr Zaremba as the result of his own personal inquiries They accord exactly with the statements of the Jesuits before the destruction of the place See Lett Ed et Cur vol 4 p 14, 34

† The only relic of the fire worshipers now existing in Persia is found in the city of Yezd They are called Guebres and amount to nearly 4,000 families Though extremely oppressed they are distinguished by their enterprising commercial spirit, their wealth and their general uprightness

‡ This statement is from Le Gamba, it seems incredibly large.

ions, in this vicinity, hold the lands they cultivate We could not learn, that such a thing as a freehold estate in the hands of a cultivator of the soil, is known in Kara-bagh In Gánjeh the last khan owned not only the soil but the persons of those who tilled it the peasants of Shirwán were also serfs of their prince, and the same was true of nearly all in Bakoo Of course as the emperor succeeded to the rights of the former rulers, the peasants of those provinces are now serfs of the crown   In general it may be said, that the soil is owned either by the crown, by Christian *mehks* (princes) and Mohammedan *begs* (lords, or gentlemen,) or by convents and that its cultivators bear to its owners the relation, if not of slaves, at least of very degraded vassals Government always claims of the peasant a poll tax, which, though generally fixed at a ducat, (about $2 25) sometimes varies and amounts to two thirds more Whoever may be his landlord makes another still heavier exaction of services or produce, rather than money It varies according to the will of different proprietors, so that it would be difficult to estimate its amount, but the universal poverty impressed upon houses, furniture, clothing, and all the necessaries of life and meeting the traveller at every step, affords abundant proof, that it is so heavy as to leave but the very scantiest means of subsistence So far as we learned, too that very important check upon oppression, which arises from the ability of the peasant to forsake at will an overbearing for a more tolerant master, is destroyed, by his being attached to the soil

The moslems of these provinces, with the exception of a few Kurds in the mountains of Kara bagh, who will be spoken of hereafter, are generally called by the Russians and other Europeans *Tartars* That name, however, is believed to be unknown among the natives of the country, for the Armenians call them *Toork*, and they name themselves *musulman* and, as their language plainly shows their origin to be purely Turkish, I see no occasion for using it. A part of them are wandering nomads, and the rest stationary inhabitants of villages The condition of the latter as cultivators of the soil has just been explained The former, compose somewhat more than half of the moslem population of Kara bagh and Talish, but in the provinces north of the Koor their number is comparatively small In the winter they collect along the warm banks of the Koor, and live in caves being, in fact as historical conjecture would make us believe all the inhabitants of the earth once were, *troglodytes* As the warm season comes on they issue from their confinement, and spread out their tents upon the plain the drought soon cuts short their pasturage there, and forces them gradually to ascend the mountains, upon their highest summits, with their flocks and herds, they enjoy a cool climate and unwithering verdure during the hottest months, and then the approaching snows force them to descend again gradually toward their winter-quarters They live almost entirely upon the produce of their flocks and only cultivate grain enough in the plain to furnish bread for the winter months Inconvenient as their mode of life is, the charm of freedom exalts it in their estimation far above the slavish condition of a tenant Government designs, it is said, to induce them, by a grant of peculiar privileges, to locate themselves as cultivators of the soil, but hitherto, suspicions on their part of sinister designs, and the want of a properly organized plan on the part of government, have prevented any considerable result In Shirwan, however, some have forsaken the nomadic life Their origin and habits are probably the same with those of the pastoral Turkish tribes of Persia. Still, there will be no error in classing them, for the following remarks, with the fixed Mohammedan population of these provinces, if we merely bear in mind, that in their character they are a little more honest, more free, and more inclined to robbery Respecting the civil rights of both, I would just remark, that Mohammedanism is fully tolerated by the laws of Russia; its professors being burdened with no extra taxes and generally admissible to office like Christians We did not learn that they are ever draughted for soldiers, though in the Turkish war many voluntarily enlisted

A few words respecting their language, will serve to illustrate the state of education among them   It is a dialect of Turkish, differing from that of the Osmanlies of Turkey, of the Crim Tartars, and of the Tartars of Kazán. The population which uses it is not small, embracing nearly all the moslem inhabitants of the trans-Caucasian provinces of Russia, and of the northwestern parts of Persia It has none of the dignity and sweetness of the Constantinopolitan tongue; and differs so much from it in pronunciation, grammatical inflection, and meaning and arrangement of words, that persons speaking the two dialects can with difficulty comprehend each other, and the books of the Turkish capital are not intelligible here. It does not even hold the rank of a written language We could not learn that any work has ever been printed in it at all, nor any composed except by the missionaries at Shoosha.

The moslems not only possess very good natural talents, but are decidedly in advance of the Armenians in their desires and efforts for the education of their children They have schools occasionally in the villages, and in the towns always. Shoosha has six schools Even a number of their females, especially the daughters of mollahs, are taught to read, and in Nookha there is the phenomenon of a public school for moslem girls, which is not small. With the exception of the Koran, which is read in Arabic but not understood, all their school books are in Persian, which language they study by means of grammars and dictionaries, not only for objects of business, but that they may read the distinguished poems which it contains The latter attainment is the highest point at which their education aims Still, comparatively few of them, and of the nomads very few, are able to read , and no improvement has been attempted or desired in their school books not even that of having them in the vulgar dialect Public or private libraries can hardly be said to exist , though many of the rich begs (or beys) have a number of books in Persian , which they are not remiss in reading

Their domestic state, under the influence of a religion that views the conjugal relation in the light in which the Korán presents it, cannot but be miserable Polygamy however though sanctioned by that authority is not gen eral To have two wives may not be very uncommon , but a greater number is found only in the harems of khans and begs It is prevented by the inability of the common people to support a multitude of women Divorces also though placed by the law within the power of every husband, are rather uncommon in practice They are pre vented like polygamy, not by any considerations of domestic quiet or affection, but of economy, as the divorced wife is entitled to the restitution of her dowry But, in the regard which the stronger sex has for the weaker, the abominable influence of the religion of Mecca is fully felt Women are generally looked upon as an inferior race made for the service and pleasure of the men, rather than as equal companions for the increase of their social enjoyments. With the exception of a few instances among the peasantry and the nomads, where something like pure con jugal affection sometimes appears such a thing as esteem for females is apparently unknown According to the spirit of the Mohammedan religion, the thought of them is always unchaste As a natural consequence, they are confined, by being cautiously kept from the view of visitors and rarely permitted to go abroad , and degraded to a rank that allows

25

their voice almost no weight in the family, unless it in some instances derives a little from the fact that they have borne children Some exceptions are found among the lowest peasants and nomads. Ladies of noble birth, too occasionally enjoy much liberty and assume no little authority Indeed, it is not uncommon for a nobleman to be completely under the control of some favorite or troublesome wife In such a domestic state, it is needless to remark, that real family government, producing uniform obedience and respect of children toward their parents does not exist

Respecting the moral character of the moslems you will expect me, though the task be unpleasant, to speak as plainly as I have done of their domestic state They have the reputation of being inclined to robbery , but fear of the Russian government is so great, and so universal, that any actual attempt of the kind almost never occurs In their habits of labor though they find much leisure, and, instead of the active stirring industry of Europeans, seem to work with little energy, they ought not to be called an indolent people The sacredness of truth they know not, but are so universally given to lying that their word can never be trusted Profaneness, too the most shocking is heard from every body, and nothing is thought of it The extreme jealousy of husbands renders infidelity of married females, it is believed, a rare crime But many who are unmarried, especially in towns abandon themselves to a life of sin. Unnatural vice, too, is not uncommon In a word, the whole heart of the people is polluted The most filthy conversation is in the mouths of all it obtrudes itself upon the missionary in his most serious conversations; he hears it from the youngest children as he passes through the streets. It has even affected the very state of the language

In religious opinions, a part of the moslems of these provinces rank themselves with the *sunnes* (orthodox) of Turkey, and a part with the *sheeies* (sectarians) of Persia. Nearly all in Kara bagh are sheeies, and the same is true of those who inhabit the towns of Bakoo and Derbend. But in the country around, and in the provinces of Shirwan and Sheky, the sunnies are most numerous, and as you approach the mountains, whose moslem inhabitants are all of that sect, they form the mass of the population. Notwithstanding the bitter animosity and bloody wars that have separated the two sects for ages, they here live together without manifesting any hostility in the ordinary concerns of life. They would doubtless soon amalgamate, were they not reminded of their difference of sect and taught to consider each other as enemies, by the feast of Moharim, which celebrates the martyrdom of Hossein the son of Aly the head of the sheey sect. In fact, they manifest little sincere regard for their religion at all. Few regularly perform the five stated daily prayers, and they are often neglectful of attending at the mosks, though in this respect there is great irregularity and sometimes their meetings are crowded. In sentiment they are so lax that in argument, they will readily give up the mission of Mohammed if their opponent will say nothing of the divinity of Christ, and they are many of them in reality complete infidels. Yet they contend violently against the exalted character of Christ, and deem opposition to his religion, even when carried into persecution, a merit.

Their clergy of every rank bear the common name of *mollah* with the exception of a very superior class who are called *mujtahids*. The former are about as numerous as the Armenian priests, the latter are extremely few, and are, I believe, peculiar to the sheeies. Shoosha has one, and there is one at Tiflis with the title of chief mujtahid of all the sheey moslems of these provinces. The latter was the person, who carried the keys of Tebriz to the Russians, as they approached that city in the last war, and invited them to enter His present office is his reward The authority of the mujtahids always extends over the mollahs of their own town and those of a certain district around

The education of the moslem clergy is various Some children designed for that profession only learn to read of a common village mollah, others seek the instructions of one more learned in the nearest town, others still go to a distinguished teacher at a greater distance and those who wish to perfect their education, resort to the celebrated shrine of Hossein at Kérbela near Bagdád Among them all however, the number of those that can understand the Koran, (which they have only in Arabic,) is exceedingly small With the exception of a few in towns, and now and then an individual in the villages, who are learned they actually know little more than to read and write In Persia the appointment of the mollahs depends upon the mujtahids and we did not learn that it is otherwise in these provinces North of the Caucasus government acknowledges but one mollah in a village as entitled to the privileges of the order These are, an exemption from taxes, a legal claim to his fees from the people, and in some instances, perhaps in all, pecuniary aid from government If in any case a village has two mollahs the second has no such rights It is not known that these laws have been formally promulgated south of the Caucasus but they are believed to be acted upon as circumstances are supposed to render it expedient

The support of the moslem clergy arises from a contribution given by the people each individual's proportion of which is regularly understood from gifts at certain festivals, and from fees for particular services To those who are engaged in teaching that is also a source of profit, and others seek additional income by engaging, like com-

mon people, in husbandry and trade   Their duties, besides
teaching, which is considered as almost exclusively belonging
to them, are to lead the devotions of the mosk, to read the
Koran on particular occasions, and to perform the other
ceremonies of their religion   Preaching rarely occurs, and
then is performed by persons specially appointed   Particularly during the thirty days preceding the feast of Moha
rim, are pains taken thus to provide that all the sad tales
connected with the event which it celebrates, shall be duly
narrated   Their influence is sufficiently great to procure
from the people at least the show of obedience   It springs
however, rather from a reverence for the clerical office,
than for any respect for the persons of the mollahs, for
the former is sincere, but the latter is little more than ex
ternal   In real principle they are no farther from infidelity
than the people, though they sometimes make a show of
great zeal   Nor is their moral character at all more exem
plary   They are generally however, in favor of education,
and in this respect decidedly surpass the Armenian clergy
In fact, it is believed, that education is entirely in their
hands

Most of the information which we obtained from our
missionary brethren at Shoosha respecting the *Armenians*
is introduced in other places, as occasion presents the dif
ferent topics to which it relates   I shall give here only
so much as will serve to illustrate their intellectual condition, mingling with it the results of our own observations
and inquiries, in order to give my remarks a general appli
cation to the whole of Armenia which we visited —At
home very young children here, as in every part of the world
are left almost entirely to the management of their mothers.   But unfortunately an Armenian mother has too little
education, and holds too low a rank in the family herself,
to instruct their minds or govern their passions to any good
effect.   The father is indeed sufficiently absolute in power,

but, instead of being led to a steady and firm exercise of it by a wisely directed desire for the good of his child, undisciplined parental affection makes him forget it in injurious indulgence, until it is called forth with altogether disproportioned severity by some sudden fit of anger The result is, that that invaluable instinct, of which nature has given an Armenian parent his full share, most unhappily directly fosters a rapid growth of evil passions in the child, causes him to become disobedient and vicious, and finally eradicates from his heart all corresponding filial affection.

As to the instruction in books which is usually obtained in schools, the common people have so little desire to procure it for their offspring that they are not only not willing to make any sacrifices for it by contributing to bear the necessary expences, but will hardly bring themselves to exercise sufficient parental authority to induce their children to a punctual attendance at school   Still there is no prejudice against the education of boys, and were schools established gratuitously they would like a sick man when medicine is brought to him, take them   After a while, a taste for education would be acquired, and then they would help themselves   The small effects that have resulted from the mere toleration of education by the Russian government, already alluded to most clearly illustrate and prove, that the Armenians need something more than being negatively left to themselves   Some positive stimulus must rouse them from their lethargy of ignorance

The education of girls is not only not desired, but decidedly disliked, and in some places the prejudice against it is strong   Its novelty gives alarm, an ability to read is considered a qualification hardly becoming any but nuns, an immoral tendency is apprehended and the shocking custom of writing letters to gentlemen is specially dreaded! As might be expected, therefore, the number of females that can read is extremely small   An estimate, founded indeed upon very scanty data, would not make the proportion so great as one in two hundred   We heard of no female school in actual existence throughout the whole of Armenia, and the only one of whose history we learned, was kept about twenty years ago in a nunnery at Akoolis, on the northern bank of the Aras to the east of Nakhcheván It contained about sixty pupils   The nunnery has been destroyed and the scattered nuns no longer teach. Its happy effects, however, are still manifested, by the existence in that vicinity of a decided wish for the education of girls, and of a more than usually strong desire for that of boys also   Two or three girls are allowed to read in a boy's school at Ganjeh and at Shamakhy, at Shoosha also the same is tolerated in a school of ten or twelve boys taught by a nun   But farther than this it is not known that girls are found in any school either in Russian Persian, or Turkish Armenia, and there is a decided prejudice against allowing the two sexes to attend together

The proportion of males who are able to read is estimated by the missionaries, in the region that has come under their observation at two in ten for the towns, and two, or at the most three, in a hundred for the country The result also of inquiries made by ourselves personally in the villages we visited at different points of our journey, and of estimates obtained from individuals respecting many others, presents for the country an average of little more than *two per cent !* This small number consists generally of the priests, and their assistants in the church services. Even of them many are unable to write and some even to read writing This estimate is believed to be a very near approximation to the truth, still perfect accuracy cannot be expected where the premises are so few and the conclusion so extensive

It is much easier to count the number of schools, and estimate the means of education which they afford   In

Kara-bagh, not including the schools of the mission, which will be mentioned hereafter, there are, in Shoosha itself, one of thirty scholars taught by a vartabed, and another of ten or twelve taught by a nun, in the country, a vartabed who occupies alone the convent of St Hagop, has long made himself useful by teaching from 10 to 20 boys, and some 20 lads from the neighboring villages are also taught at the convent of Datev Ganjeh has a school of 30 scholars, and Shámakhy another of 80   There is one likewise in Sheky Bakoo has none   Nakhchevan is also destitute. But at Erivan there are two, one lately commenced in the town, and another in Ashterag, a neighboring village It was reported also, that not far from Gumry the people were anxious for a school, and had commenced gathering one If we add to these the schools already mentioned in Erzroom Kars, Bayezeed, and Tiflis the first three of which have in fact been destroyed and consider that in Persian Armenia, as will hereafter be seen, there are none, we have at the most, only 14 native Armenian schools of any kind, in the whole of the region over which our inquiries extended

The schools of this and the adjoining provinces are all taught by men who hold some clerical rank, which in part unites their interests with those of the clergy, being either vartabeds, priests deacons, or clerks   They are generally men of slight education and their pupils are taught little else than to read mechanically without understanding, to write, and to perform some simple sums in arithmetic. In Gánjeh, however grammar is taught, and through the influence of the mission, it is coming into use elsewere The study of it is very important, as affording a key to the ancient language in which their only books of any kind, including the Bible are written

Their school books are the following, and in the following order For spelling and reading, a spelling book, the

first of the nine divisions of the Psalms divided into syllables, a small prayer-book, the remainder of the Psalms, the
four Gospels, and the church hymn book, are used, and all
of them, being in the ancient dialect, are not understood
In arithmetic, a large and able work has been printed at
Venice but, on account of the difficulty of obtaining, and
also of understanding it, as it is in the ancient tongue, no
book is used, and the science is taught orally In grammar, a similar difficulty was formerly experienced, as only
a few copies of the large one by Chamcheán could be obtained but recently two others one by Michael Salamteán
of Moscow and another by the missionaries, have been
partially introduced Should any Armenian student wish
to advance farther, (which, however, never happens except
with some learned vartabéd in a convent) he would find in
geography, nothing but a great work in twelve volumes 'printed at Venice and exceedingly rare, rhetoric he could learn
only from a thick octavo from the same press, filled with the
technical terms of the old school of Quinctilian, and which
he would hardly be so fortunate as to find and logic,
metaphysics, and moral philososophy, he would have access
to, only in a very scarce work of three volumes, also from
Venice, and wholly conformed to the Aristotelian school
As to improvements in the system of education, I need only
say that none have been made

The sources of intelligence accessible to the people are
even more easily summed up than their means of education Not a newspaper is printed any where in the Armenian language, and a mere glance at the location of
the different printing presses already mentioned, will show
how few publications of any kind can find their way hither
We have only to add a press at Echmiadzin, which has
not been in operation for about twenty years, to the establishments at Venice, Constantinople Moscow Astrakhán
and Tiflis, and our list of presses of native origin that can

possibly have any bearing upon Armenia is complete. The efficiency even of these most unfortunately diminishes rapidly, in proportion to their nearness to that country, so that the sum of their united influence which actually reaches it, becomes almost imperceptible A new book in circulation is an extremely rare phenomenon, and to hear one inquired for with interest is still rarer Little more is accomplished than to supply the churches with the necessary books for public worship. In fact, the prayer book, the hymn book, and the book of martyrology, are almost the only sources of intelligence to be found, and even these, with the exception of the latter, which unfortunately is in a style sufficiently modern to allow its fabulous legends to be understood, are sealed up in a dead language I wish the sacred Scriptures could be added to the list, not only of accessible but of intelligible books, but besides the copies that have been distributed by the missionaries, they are very rarely to be met with out of the churches even there only the prescribed lessons, can sometimes be found and in no case are they in the vulgar tongue None therefore can understand them nor any other books, except those who have studied the ancient dialect, how many such there are you can judge from what has been already said of the means of education Preaching in other countries such an extremely valuable source of religious information accessible alike to the learned and the unlearned we can here hardly take into the account A few family libraries exist if a collection of sixty or seventy books can be so named, but they are carefully stowed away, and the more valuable works perhaps folded in a covering of two or three handkerchiefs, so that the owners themselves rarely read them, and access to them by others is extremely difficult.

Permit me to add a few remarks upon the modern language of the Armenians, to this view of their intellectual condition. Its variations are almost as numerous, as are the countries where the scattered members of the nation reside and all so corrupt that the uneducated can it is believed no where understand even the general meaning of books in the ancient tongue. These numerous variations, however may be considered as embraced in *two* dialects, differing so that while all who speak any of the branches of one of them are mutually understood, they are unable to comprehend a book written for those who speak the other. As one has Constantinople for its centre, it may be named the dialect of Constantinople, while the other, from its being spoken in Armenia, may be called after the celebrated mountain in the centre of that country, the dialect of Ararat. The former it is believed, extends from the capital of Turkey through Asia Minor and the pashalik of Erzroom, and has borrowed not only many terms but also forms of construction from the Turkish. The latter is spoken throughout the rest of Armenia and both in the words used, and in their arrangement is nearer the original language. The missionaries here from whom we received this theory know that books printed for Constantinople are not understood in these parts while their own in the dialect of Ararat have been found perfectly intelligible throughout the Georgian provinces the pashaliks of Kars and Bayezeed, the province of Aderbaiján and even at Bagdad.

In the dialect of Constantinople, several works have been printed especially at the press in Venice, and a translation of the New Testament has been published at Paris by the British and Foreign Bible Society. But in the dialect of Ararat the books printed by the missionaries here are the only ones so far as we learned, that exist. It is a curious fact that we found not an Armenian in our whole journey, that did not speak at least two languages. One of them was always Armenian, and the second generally a dialect of Turkish. Of these, Armenian in Armenia itself is much the best understood, and, for that reason, as well as because those who speak it are partial to it, on account of its being their native and also a Christian tongue, is undoubtedly to be preferred to Turkish for missionary publications for that region.

LETTER XI

DEAR SIR,

THE original design of the missionary society of Basle in Switzerland respecting their mission in these provinces was, that it should be located somewhere within the Russian boundaries on the Persian frontier, between the Caspian and Black seas, for the purpose of propagating Christianity among *Mohammedans*, especially in Persia The first step was taken in 1821, by sending the Rev Messrs Dittrich and Zaremba to St. Petersburg, to obtain the approbation of the emperor, and a charter for a colony

The necessity for the appendage of a colony arose from the nature of the ecclesiastical principles of the Russian government. The established church is understood to claim the right to baptize and hold in its communion all converts within the limits of the empire, who are not made by any of the tolerated Christian sects Foreign missionaries, therefore, as such, labor under serious embarrassments. The expedient of a colony, consisting of a large proportion of lay members, engaged in agriculture and the mechanic

26

arts, and possessing chartered rights as citizens of the empire, divests them of their foreign character Connected with it, they come to stand in the light of ministers of a tolerated sect of the empire, and are thus entitled to the right of making converts from nations not Christian A charter for such a colony was given by Alexander to the Scottish missionaries at Karass in 1802, which has been renewed by the present emperor, for the express purpose of allowing the missionaries to preach the gospel to the mountaineers of the Caucasus

The German missionaries found the disposition of the emperor Alexander not less favorable to them, than it had been to their Scottish brethren In a private interview of some length, he laid aside the attitude of an emperor for that of a Christian brother, entering with interest into their plans, and developing freely his own Christian experience Alluding to the temptations which surrounded him, and his need of divine grace to direct his influence aright, he earnestly besought an interest in their prayers Wishing them success in their enterprise, he promised that if they needed any thing in addition to the provisions of their charter, their requests directed to him personally would be readily attended to And they left him with a favorable impression of his piety, which they retain to the present day The provisions of their charter were liberal They were to travel in the trans-Caucasian provinces, for the purpose of selecting a site for a colony, which, when it should be formed, was to have the privileges of Karass, including the liberty of baptizing converts And they were to be allowed to have a printing press, to establish elementary schools, subject only to the immediate inspection of the minister of education; and to organize a seminary for teaching the higher branches of science

At St. Petersburg the two brethren were joined by three others, one of whom, however, died at that place. The

four survivors proceeded in 1822 to Astrakhán, for the purpose of studying languages, and there were hindered by
sickness and other causes, so that they did not reach Tiflis
till the spring of 1823 The attention of Messrs. Dittrich,
Zaremba and a third brother, who were the only ones that
then arrived in Georgia, was first arrested by the German
colonies The part they took as advisers in organizing
their ecclesiastical matters, has been already explained.
You will observe however, that no connection has ever existed between the colonies and the mission Their time
was thus occupied until the autumn

When the documents relative to their mission were laid
before general Yermoloff, who was then governor of these
provinces, he informed them, to their surprise, that govern
ment possessed no land on the Persian frontier that could
be spared for a colony, and of course such an establishment could not be formed He declared, however, that
they should be welcome to a building and garden spot for
themselves simply as missionaries, in any town or village
they might select that they were at liberty to commence
their labors immediately, and that, if they should be blessed with converts, he would use his influence that they might
have the privilege of receiving them to their own commun
ion by baptism The colony they had ever considered a
serious evil, and were glad to be relieved from it, but to
lose this important privilege they deeply regretted. Neither
the promise of the governor, nor the friendly disposition of
the emperor and of his minister Galitzin ever availed to secure it to them.—They left Tiflis for Shoosha early in September At Helenendorf near where we were ourselves
attacked by sickness, one of their number died The surviving two, Messrs Dittrich and Zaremba, fixed upon
Shoosha for the seat of their mission, at their first visit, but
continued their journey as far as Shámakhy and Bakoo.

They had hitherto had in view only Mohammedans,

as the object of their labors. But on becoming acquainted with the people among whom they were thrown, they found a large Armenian population, who were without schools, and so ignorant, that the Armenian Scriptures which the brethren had with them could be read by few, and understood by still fewer. So unchristian, too, was their character that all arguments intended to convince moslems of the excellence of Christianity, were parried by a reference to them, (the only representatives of Christianity at hand,) as triumphant proof that its practical influence was no better than that of Mohammedanism. The Armenians themselves said, 'Why do you pass by us and go to the moslems? come to our aid, establish schools for us!' Touched by their wants, and feeling in fact, that efforts for the undermining of Mohammedanism would be of little avail, so long as they should be paralyzed by such sad examples of Christianity the missionaries determined to do something if possible for the Armenians. Letters were addressed to the archbishop Nérses at Tiflis, and to the Catholicos at Echmiádzin, explaining the condition in which their people had been found, and expressing the hope that their Christian brethren of the west of Europe, would aid by their charities in the establishment of schools provided that in those schools the New Testament and Psalter might be used as school books. To these letters no answer was ever received. It is interesting and encouraging to missionaries in Turkey, where the laws of the country oppose obstacles to their directly attempting the conversion of moslems, and oblige them to confine their instructions almost exclusively to the native Christians, to find these brethren, where the accessibleness of the two sects is nearly reversed, led by evident expediency to a similar course. In fact the reformation of Christians seems an almost indispensable preliminary to the conversion of moslems.

Mr Dittrich now returned for a season to Germany, and

Mr Hohenacker, who had until then remained at Karass, proceeded to Shoosha, that Mr Zaremba might not be alone Here Messrs. Pfander and Woehr subsequently joined them, but the latter was soon removed by death. Mr. Zaremba at this period opened a school for teaching Russian It was attended by Armenians, and a few moslems The sacred Scriptures were his only school books, and he had the satisfaction of perceiving that not all of his pupils remained unaffected by what they read The society in the mean time, on learning the condition of the Armenians, consented that two of their missionaries should devote their labors to them, and sent Messrs Dittrich and Haas to Moscow for a year, to study their language Thence Mr Dittrich was called to St Petersburg to attend to the expediency of uniting the Shoosha and Karass missions as branches of the same colony Such a union was found unadvisable, and the project was abandoned Mr Haas made an attempt to join his brethren at Shoosha but the Persian war prevented, and he stopped on the other side of the Caucasus

That war put the mission in great peril It was commenced without the formality of a declaration, and the whole Persian army marched directly upon Shoosha, before Gen R who was then its governor, had time to make any preparation of troops, ammunition, or stores The town was besieged for six weeks by about 50,000 Persians commanded by Abbas Mirza in person, while the Russian garrison within hardly amounted to more than 600. Its batteries were mounted by only two guns, one of which was almost useless, of powder and provisions only very small quantities were on hand, and the moslem population secretly favored the enemy Had it surrendered, the missionaries have reason to believe that they might have fallen a prey to the enmity, which their previous operations had excited in some of its more bigoted Mohammedan inhabit-

26 *

ants. But the Lord defended them, and the seige was raised.

It was in 1827 that the missionaries were first assembled at Shoosha in circumstances to give form to their plans of operation. They were five in number: viz Dittrich, Zaremba, Haas, Hohenacker, and Pfander. A part of their arrangement was, that Messrs. Zaremba and Pfander, who together with Mr Hohenacker were to labor for the moslems, should spend most of the year in travelling, and the remainder in visiting the people in the bazárs of Shoosha, or in preparing such books and tracts in the vulgar Turkish dialect, as might be usefully circulated. In prosecution of this plan, Sheky, Shirwán, Bakoo, Daghistan as far as Derbend, Nakhchevan and Erivan have been traversed. Recently, also, as has been already related, an extensive tour has been made into Turkey. Persia, which was the primary object of their mission, it was thought superfluous to visit, while so much needed to be done directly around them. Then came the war to prevent any such movement, and after its close the two newly acquired provinces claimed prior attention. Recently Mr Pfander, in order to make himself familiar with Arabic and Persian, has accompanied Mr Groves to Bagdad, with the intention of spending some time in Persia. No other visit has been made by them to that country.

In the preparation of books, they could for a long time find almost no native help. The Armenians were unable to write Turkish, and the moslems were so reluctant to contribute their aid to the circulation of the opinions of the missionaries, as to consent only with great reluctance even to copy the smallest articles. At length Providence furnished them with a very competent helper. He was born of Armenian parents, in an obscure village on the Aras in this province, and was named by them Harútún. During a war between Persia and Russia in 1810, a moslem khan of Kara-dagh, at the head of a horde of robbers, crossed the Aras, plundered his village, and carried him, then a mere boy, into captivity. Mohammedanism of course now became his religion, and with it he received the name of Mirza Ferookh. He was soon sent as a present to one of his master's wives who resided at Tehran, and she, having recently lost a son of about the same age adopted him as her own child. No pains were spared in his education, the best masters were employed to teach him, and he was instructed in all the literature of Persia. Eight years passed away thus in the enjoyment of uninterrupted maternal partiality and fondness from his new mother, when the khan, heedless of her remonstrances, took him away to be afterward about his person. For nine years he was the companion of his master, almost constantly travelling in different provinces of the kingdom. But he still remembered his parents and his native village. The last Russian war afforded him an opportunity he had long wished and escaping at the hazard of his life, he returned to the home of his childhood. He yet retained his Mohammedanism for a time, but at length embraced again the religion of his fathers. Wishing to add a knowledge of Russian to his other attainments, he came to put himself under the instructions of Mr Zaremba at Shoosha, and was thus introduced to the missionaries. As a translator his qualifications have given them entire satisfaction. He has accompanied Mr Zaremba in two missionary tours, and proved himself a valuable assistant. Being little attached to the errors of his church he is a candid receiver of religious instruction. And if not already truly a Christian, the missionaries hope that he is not far from the kingdom of God. Thus by leading him in a way that he knew not, has Providence prepared him admirably to assist in one of the most important and difficult branches of missionary labor.

With his aid the missionaries have made copious extracts

of such parts of the Scriptures as they wished to read to the moslems in their travels, have translated a small tract; and have composed another on the truth of Christianity and falsity of Mohammedanism. He has likewise translated the whole of the New Testament, and only a revision is needed to prepare it for the press Mr Hohenacker has made some progress in composing a grammar of the Turkish of these provinces No other books, so far as is known, have ever been composed in that dialect; and even none of these have yet been printed Hitherto the missionaries have been destitute of Arabic types, nor, on account of the poverty of their society, have they any expectation of being supplied, except through the aid of the British and Foreign Bible Society, which has promised to transfer hither a font in its possession at Astrakhan Unfortunately, they are so different from the Persian form of letters that books printed with them would hardly be read A font of the new types with which the latest edition of the Persian Testament has been printed at London, would be a real acquisition. No attempt has hitherto been made to collect a regular congregation, to establish schools, or to prepare school books, from a conviction that neither would succeed Lately, however, some hopes have been entertained that a school might be commenced at Shoosha

The chief aim of the missionaries in their intercourse with the moslems, has been to urge as directly and simply as possible, "repentance toward God and faith toward our Lord Jesus Christ." Instead of endeavoring to gain respect by paying liberally for their entertainment, they have aimed to go among them, as far as possible, in the spirit of those who were commanded to ' provide neither gold, nor silver, nor brass in their purses. On entering a village, they have inquired who was willing to entertain them, and thrown themselves upon his hospitality The consequence has been, and it is no unimportant one, that report has never accused them of endeavoring to make proselytes by money, and though an individual has occasionally presented himself as an inquirer, evidently with the hope of some worldly advantage from them or from the Russians, the number has been small The moslems even accuse them of want of wisdom in this respect   Once after a long con versation in the bazar of Bakoo, their hearers proposed to meet them again at a certain hour upon the sea-shore The hour arrived, but none except the missionaries came At last a venerable old moslem approached them and said ; ' Friends, your arguments are all very good but allow me to tell you that you do not take the right course   arguments alone will accomplish nothing , you should use money too , with that you can make as many Christians as you choose '

From the fact that many of the moslems do not really believe their own religion nor practice it any farther than its precepts agree with their carnal inclinations we might expect little difficulty in obtaining a candid hearing for the doctrines of Christianity   But if they care little about their own faith, they care less about any other , and the levity which allows them to laugh at Mohammedan doctrines and forms of worship, assumes the form of absolute contempt for those of the gospel   In a word, their skepticism, in- stead of producing a disposition to inquire has created absolute indifference, or rather a state of mind positively opposed to inquiry   For they are still deeply imbued with that part of Mohammedanism which consists in a bigoted enmity to Christianity, and consider opposition to it, or even the murder of any moslem who may embrace it, a meritorious deed   This spirit the missionaries have found most prevalent in towns   Not having access to the people at their houses, they have talked with them in the bazárs and caravanserais.   Conversations with individuals have often been long and interesting, but have generally been terminated by a reference to the mollahs   When they have been called, and their arguments been refuted, the greatest levity and indifference, or violent rage, has often been the only result. More promiscuous and larger assemblies have mingled extreme heedlessness, with an inclination for the most vehement dispute. Once at Nookha, they were violently thrust out of the town, and their lives so much endangered that they were generally reported to have been murdered. The protection of government, however, and the impression still prevalent, though often studiously contradicted that they are employed by the emperor, generally prevents forcible opposition, and procures them respect.

In the country, the missionaries have frequently found the common people simple, and not unwilling to hear the truth, and their mollahs though esteeming themselves learned, yet feeling that their knowledge is imperfect. Among them, especially among the mollahs there are some in an inquiring state, and upon frequent intercourse with such, they found their hopes of success. A mollah at Shoosha and another at Bakoo, are convinced of the truth of Christianity, and have in consequence suffered some persecution. The former having become sensible of the great evil of profaneness once exhorted his brethren in the mosk against it, and proposed that they should make a resolution to reform. Some pledged themselves to abstain from the practice, under a penalty of forfeiting a certain sum of money at every offence. A temporary reformation was the consequence, but it is to be lamented that they have long since forgotten their good resolutions. The one at Bakoo is considered in even a more hopeful state. But neither has yet had the boldness to make an open profession of Christianity, nor, if they desired it, would the brethren feel authorised to baptize them, as they do not give sufficient evidence of a change of heart.

Messrs. Dittrich and Haas, to whom was assigned the

Armenian department, had a most delicate course to pursue. It was wholly without consultation with government, that this branch of labor was added to the operations of the mission. The laws of the empire were understood to forbid one denomination to make proselytes from another, and even to clothe the clergy of any tolerated Christian sect, with power to prevent their flock from forsaking them, except to join the established Greek church. Education, however, is not considered by government as under the direction of the clergy, and any attempt on their part to control it, is even regarded with jealousy. Yet wherever *religious* instruction is given, they have a right to interfere. Here a small door was open therefore, and yet so guarded was it by hindrances and difficulties, as to be exceedingly strait. The use of the press, too, is not entirely prohibited, but through the censorship, the control of all religious publications is thrown entirely into the hands of the clergy. Their course was, by all means, to steer clear of any collision with these government restrictions, and still make progress in usefulness.

In such circumstances they determined as vitally important to direct all their labors, in enlightening and reforming the Armenians, to the simple point of bringing them to be coadjutors in the great work of converting the Mohammedans and thus to place this department in the light of only a subordinate branch of the original and primary object of the mission. They aimed to enlighten the Armenian church without drawing away its members, and for this end, intended to lay the fundamental doctrines of redemption by Jesus Christ, justification by faith alone and sanctification by the Holy Ghost, simply and clearly before individuals, as often as opportunity should present, but to forego all attempts at preaching or expounding in meetings, public or private, and to avoid controversy even in conversation. No intention was formed, however, to conceal fundamental truth, nor to refuse an answer to direct inquiries on controversial points. In regard to such topics, their usual course has been, to refer to the declarations of the Bible, and let them form the answer and the argument. *Schools* and the *press* were expected to occupy their time, and to constitute the principal means of effecting the reformation at which they aimed. In them they hoped to find a field of usefulness sufficiently extensive and fruitful, without drawing upon themselves the opposition of the clergy, or the condemnation of the law. And if the ultimate result of the light they might thus communicate, should be a determination of some no longer to adhere to the rites of the Armenian church, they trusted that Providence, by giving more liberality to the laws or to the clergy, would prevent any fatal consequences to the mission.

Before noticing these two branches of their operations, permit me to say, that the brethren who have travelled among the moslems, have not failed to do good as they have had opportunity to the Armenians also. It is a lamentable fact, that they have found but one native who gave them the least evidence of being pious and him they saw but a short time. He was an old monk, who seemed to participate in their Christian feelings, and manifested for them the attachment of a brother. Downright infidelity, however, is not an enemy with which they have had to contend. It hardly exists among the Armenians in these parts. The great evil is a superstitious reliance upon the external observances of religion, to the neglect of its vitality. The common people have almost no idea of spiritual religion, nor in fact of any doctrines, but such as tell them when and how to make the cross, to fast, feast, confess, commune, and the like; and the only practical effect of their religion of course, is to cause the performance of such ceremonies. In this state their minds rest perfectly indifferent and spiritually dead. No spirit of inquiry has

been found any where Efforts to excite such a spirit,
however, have not been in vain The missionaries are in
deed looked upon as chargeable with great heresies and
none the less so for being the followers of Luther and Calvin
who, probably through the influence of papal missionaries,
are generally regarded as heresiarchs But the Armenian
church does not imitate the exclusiveness of Rome, in con
demning as heirs of perdition, all who are without its pale
and its members are taught to regard other Christians, as hold
ing indeed to doctrines and rites inferior to theirs but as mem
bers of the catholic church of Christ Instead therefore, of
being turned away at once, the missionaries have found no
difficulty in obtaining a hearing They have been gratified also to find that though the Armenian church receives
as decidedly as any other, the canons and traditions of the
Fathers in addition to the word of God as its standard of
faith and practice still, the common sense of the communi
ty, when the question of paramount authority is started, al
ways decides in favor of the Scriptures They are consid
ered and felt to be of binding authority, and an appeal to
them in argument is generally final and satisfactory Thus
a firm support is found for appeals to the conscience and
the common people have often been seen to feel the force
of the plain preaching of the gospel, and to listen to it
with interest In some places especially in Bakoo and
Shámakhy the most pleasing fruits have attended the dispensation of divine truth In the former place a few, and
in the latter twenty five or thirty meet together privately
for the reading of the Scriptures and attending to other
means of grace, and have virtually separated from their
church With them the brethren correspond by letter,
and also send them religious treatises in manuscript, which,
not being subject to the censorship, can be more explicit
in doctrine than if they were printed Encouraging hopes
are entertained that they will persevere unto the end, and

27

information as late as August 4th, 1831, says 'that many awakened souls in Shámakhy and Bakoo go on with firmness in the midst of the opposition they have to encounter.'

When the missionaries first came to Shoosha, not a school existed in town, nor any but that of the old monk of St Hagop, in the province All attempts to establish a *female* school have, till the present time, been unsuccessful. No native female could be found capable in the least degree of acting as teacher, except an old nun Proposals were made to her, but her usual employment of begging, being not only more congenial to her indolent habits, but in fact more lucrative than teaching, she absolutely refused They then sought to teach a few girls in their own house, but such an indelible opprobrium would public opinion cast upon a girl who should thus frequent the house of a foreigner, that none would come This prejudice is so strong that to this day they are unable to obtain any native female servants for their families, and are obliged to procure help from the German colonies The English families at Tebriz experience a similar difficulty, and the ladies there bring their maids from England

The want of a *male* teacher was supplied by bringing one from the gymnasium at Moscow, and a school for boys was opened in the spring of 1827 So decidedly was he disqualified however for teaching, that it did not prosper until a vartabed named Boghos, who had in the mean time opened a private school in the place, was called in as principal. He was not only a popular but a good teacher, and the number of scholars soon increased to 130 They were taught reading writing, arithmetic and grammar, and, at the request of Boghos, a few also studied rhetoric. The Psalter and other parts of the Scriptures were the reading lessons. But Boghos, after quarrelling away several assistants for insubordination, at length found himself, also, in the predicament of disobedience to his superiors, and was likewise obliged to leave His original contract bound him to teach a religious catechism, and also every morning to read the Scriptures and explain them in the vulgar dialect Of this part of his duty he was from the first extremely neglectful and an intimation from the missionaries at last, of the necessity of attending to it, only called forth from him a more positive refusal Desirous as they were to retain so able a teacher, they felt that without at least this small amount of religious instruction, they would no longer be authorized to support the school, and plainly told him their connection must be dissolved

A school was then opened in their own house, which shortly increased to as many as their room would accommodate A school house was then erected for it within their premises, and that was also soon filled Religion was now made more prominent, for the teacher was one of their converts, and the school was daily opened with prayer and reading the Scriptures either by him, or by one of the missionaries. It continued to flourish until near the time of our arrival when its scholars amounted to sixty We found also another school of about thirty scholars under their patronage Only about two thirds of the teacher's salary was contributed by them, the remainder being supplied by tuition fees Besides the effects of these schools in giving knowledge to the young tending to produce enlightened views of religion and of the prevailing superstitions, the missionaries have noticed with pleasure an increased desire of parents for the education of their offspring, and a distinct impression beginning to be made in favor of school books in the common dialect The use of such books is one of the two improvements which they have been aiming to introduce The other is the rejection of the old church books, which have hitherto been universally used The Lancasterian system they have not attempted

The great want of teachers, which forced itself so distinctly upon their observation in their own experience, led them early to contemplate some method for supplying it With this view, half of their new school house has been fitted up for the accommodation of a seminary for the education of teachers It is a favorite object and one to which they intend their principal efforts in this department of education shall be directed Mr Haas to whose lot in their division of labor the business of education has fallen, was expected on his return from Moscow where he was at the time of our visit, to open it in form In the mean time, as an incipient step, some half a dozen young men had been already admitted to a private course of study, which some in fact had pursued so far as to be almost prepared to commence their profession How they will be received, coming out as they do under missionary patronage, and being the first proper lay school masters in the country, remains to be seen But let their usefulness to others be what it may they have themselves at least been benefited by the instructions of the missionaries Two or three have been received into their families where indeed no direct attempt has been made to lead them to fall out with their church but they have attended family devotions and heard much religious conversation , and though no satisfactory evidence of their being truly pious has been observed, they yet are in a promising state of mind their views are generally scriptural and their conduct has given the greatest satisfaction

The most gratifying effects of the labors of the missionaries upon individual character have been observed in two deacons, of whom I must be allowed to give some account. They originally belonged to a convent on an island in the lake of Sevan But in search of theological knowledge, they left that convent , and even had so strong a desire for the object of their pursuit, as to form the secret purpose of

going to Venice, could they not obtain it nearer Not
finding it at Echmiádzin, where they spent some time, nor
being admitted to the school at Tiflis, whither they subsequently went one of them came to Shoosha, and engaged
himself as assistant to Boghos, while he was principal of
the mission school for the sole compensation of receiving
his instructions Being dismissed by him for some friv-
olous reason it came to the knowledge of the missionaries
that he was desirous of studying Latin and Greek, and they
took him into their family He subsequently assisted them
in their school, and was the pious teacher already alluded to.
His name was Moses He was not long in mentioning his
friend to them, and at their request, he also soon joined
them The two deacons already understood their ancient
tongue, and were in the estimation of their countrymen,
learned But their thirst for additional knowledge was so
great that notwithstanding the serious difficulties to be encountered from the total want of the requisite elementary
works their progress in Latin and Greek was good, and
one of them learned considerable English The Scriptures,
too, were embraced in the circle of their studies and though
the errors of their Church were never pointed out they were
not slow to detect them The practice of praying for the
dead was early brought forward by Moses, in an inquiry
respecting its lawfulness Mr Dittrich chose to reply by
merely pointing out some passages in the Bible opposed to
it The deacon needed no more, he was already prepared to reject it He soon, indeed, began to give pleasing
evidence of a change of heart His companion had not
advanced so far, and for some time opposed, not forbearing
to apply to him the epithet of heretic He, too at length
became convinced, but the signs of his conversion, though
such as to give encouraging hope were never, owing perhaps to his natural temperament's being of a more intellectual make, so distinctly marked Not having been convert-

27 *

ed in the school of controversy, both were more inclined, in conversing with their countrymen, to urge the great *duties* of repentance and faith, than to wrangle about points of speculative *doctrine*, however important Thus their usefulness was great, and their enemies few In fact, so mild and inoffensive was their deportment, that whatever they said was listened to, and such efficient coadjutors did they bid fair to become, that the missionaries contemplated sending them to some European seminary, for a more complete education, than could be obtained at Shoosha They never forsook the Armenian church, nor did they ever commune with the church of the mission

The press was an original part of the missionary establishment, contemplated by the charter of Alexander It has hitherto been furnished with only Armenian types The superintendence of it, with the preparation of books, is Mr Dittrich s particular department The laws of the Russian censorship are understood to direct that all religious works before being printed shall be inspected by the synod of St Petersburg or persons appointed by it, if in the Russian language ; if in German by the Lutheran consistory of the same city , if for the papists, by the papal archbishop also resident there, and if in Armenian, by the Armenian archbishop of the province Of course archbishop Nerses, as wekeel of the Catholicos and president of the synod of Echmiadzin, had the inspection of the publications of this press So long as he continued at Tiflis the necessary *imprimatur* could be easily obtained With his approbation the following works were printed chiefly for schools viz the Sermon on the Mount, as a first trial of the press , the first portion of the Psalms in syllables, intended as a sequel to the spelling book , a short history of the Bible , a small grammar of the ancient Armenian, historical extracts from the Old Testament , and a large collection of Scripture passages, in both ancient and modern

Armenian   Since his banishment, only a small dictionary of the ancient tongue for schools has passed through the censorship, and that so soon afterward that the approbation was given in his name   The censorship is now exercised by the synod of Echmiádzin   but three works, viz Vivian's three dialogues on the way of salvation the Negro Servant, and an original treatise on Christianity and Mohammedanism, all in the vulgar tongue, have been sent to the press at Moscow, where the rector of the gymnasium both superintends the printing, and performs the office of censor   An edition of the first arrived at Shoosha while we were there and the last has since been finished   Agents have recently been sent abroad with them, and they are now extensively scattered throughout the trans-Caucasian provinces   None of their publications have met with any opposition   nor could they be opposed, bearing as they do the approbation of the censor upon their title page

The most important work which Mr Dittrich has attempted, and the one from which the most good is anticipated, is a translation of the New Testament into the vulgar dialect of the Armenians   The copies of the Scriptures possessed by the people when the missionaries first came to these provinces, were extremely few   They have increased their number by distributing about 700 of the ancient Armenian New Testament between the Koor and the Aras But the small proportion of the people that can understand it in that dialect necessarily sets very narrow limits to its circulation   In the vulgar dialect the firmest belief is indulged that it would be eagerly received by the common people   With the intention of making them so valuable a present, Mr Dittrich undertook with the aid of the deacon already mentioned who was not engaged in teaching, to translate it   The first copy of the whole was completed, and the four gospels were revised for the press, when we were at Shoosha , and since then the revision of the re-

mainder has been completed   The British and Foreign
Bible Society had authorized an edition to be printed at its
expense   But a *veto* from the censor arrested it. The
Gospel of Matthew, on being prepared, was duly laid before the synod of Echmiadzin, for its approbation   For
several months nothing was heard from it, and Mr Zarem
ba, on his return from Turkey, made a visit to the convent
to obtain a final answer   After considerable delay, the vartabéds reluctantly consented to call a meeting of the syn
od, at which he was present. Various objections were
urged to its being printed   The work was declared to be
so important that a long time would be necessary to ex
amine it and form their opinions   This difficulty he overruled   They promised to make a translation themselves
He replied that they would not complete it in fifteen years,
and ' were they willing to be responsible for the souls, which
during that time would be lost through ignorance of the
word of God ?'   Then, with much violence of temper, they
unanimously declared their unwillingness that the Scriptures should be printed in the vulgar tongue   Still, promises of acceding to his request, mingled with intrigue and
tergiversation, were given and recalled, till despairing of
success he left them in disgust. The Gospel of Matthew
has finally been printed   But no hope is entertained of
getting the *imprimatur* of the synod for the rest, and without this, it cannot, according to the decision of government,
be printed in the empire. The operations of the press in
every department, are in fact now entirely stopped by the
inimical opposition of the censors   Thus is the Armenian
hierarchy by the aid of Russian laws exercising, with the
spirit and rigor of papacy, a power of which it would otherwise hardly have dreamed   For the anathemas already
mentioned as having been uttered against the publications
of Venice only to be forgotten, are the only instances
known of a formal attempt on the part of the Armenian

clergy, to control the reading of their countrymen, or even the right of private opinion, until these laws at the same time suggested to them the idea, and clothed them with the necessary power

Permit me now to give you an account of the storm of persecution which burst upon the mission not long before our arrival, and to which it was exposed during our visit. Nearly all the opposition which protestant missions in the Mediteranean have encountered, may be traced directly or indirectly to the adherents of the church of Rome. Unfortunately a missionary can hardly set his foot upon any spot in that field, without encountering some sentinel of the "Mother of Harlots,' ready to challenge him, and shout the alarm. Papists are the first Christians he meets, and before he has worked his way through them, to the Greeks, the Armenians, or the Copts, for whose benefit specially he intends to labor the chance is that they become so alarmed and prejudiced by papal misrepresentation, as to give him but a reluctant welcome. The missionaries at Shoosha had no obstacle of this kind to encounter. We know not that within the whole field of their labors, there is a papist nearer than Tiflis * Unexpectedly however the see of Echmiadzin was found ready enough, without instigation or advice, to act the part of the see of Rome.

The subject that first opened the eyes of the deacons to the errors of their church, was the first that brought them

---

* The Jesuits once had a mission at Shámakhy. It was a branch of their mission at Isfahán and was chartered by the Shah at the solicitation of a Polish envoy the protection of whose government it continued for some time to enjoy. The station was selected with particular reference to the European merchants who visited the place many of whom were papists. The first missionary was assassinated in 1687. But the field was considered too important to be abandoned and two others were appointed to his place. (Lett Edif et Cur vol 4 p 44—53) We neglected to inquire for any remains of this mission but from the fact that we heard nothing of it I infer that there are none

into collision with their countrymen   At a feast of sacrifice for the dead, made by a man, who, as a pilgrim to Jerusalem and a punctual observer of the laws of his church, was reputed very religious, they expressed a caution against relying upon masses for the dead, and some similar errors. Provoked that his good deeds should be called in question, he reported abroad that they had renounced praying for the dead, and the worship of saints and images and a general opposition to them broke out.   One morning the principal Armenian of the place rose upon them in church, abused them with the most violent language raised his cane over them, spat in their faces, and forbade them ever to appear there again.   Things remained in this state when the bishop came as usual to take up his winter residence in town.   He immediately began to condemn them, and even wrote a letter of complaint to the missionaries. Their answer, and the winning meekness and simple piety of Moses, exhibited in a personal interview, calmed and overcame him   He became friendly   even put under the daily instruction of Moses two of his own deacons, and the storm was allayed.

The calm however was but a prelude to a more violent tempest   A few weeks before our arrival, an Armenian who through the instructions of the missionaries had embraced the truth came from Bakoo and was immediately carried by his zeal into the bazár to converse with his countrymen   Much attention was excited, and though his manner was winning and his theme was the great doctrines of salvation nearly all opposed   The storm, however, burst not upon him, as he was a stranger, but upon the deacons   On a subsequent Sabbath morning, a letter from the bishop was read in one of the churches declaring 'that he was ordered by the Catholicos to send the two deacons to Echmiádzin, and commanding them to be immediately bound and delivered to him   An appeal to the local authorities prevented the execution of this command at the time, but, it being repeated after a few days, the governor concluded to refer the whole case to the governor-general and accordingly sent the deacons to Tiflis We met them on their way in company with two Cossacks, at Shah-boolak. Mr Zaremba preceded them, in order to make the necessary explanation of their case After reading a written statement of the proceedings of the missionaries, and listening to Mr Zaremba s verbal explanations, the governor-general asked with surprise, 'How is it that you being Germans, are interfering with the Armenians? Remain Germans yourselves, and let them remain Armenians He declined at first to take cognizance of the case, saying 'The deacons are ecclesiastical men they have committed an ecclesiastical offence, and must be judged by an ecclesiastical tribunal ' But at length he concluded to lay it before the emperor, and to send them in the mean time to Echmiádzin, under the civil protection of the governor of Erivan A petition to the emperor was accordingly written by them, and, together with the statement of the missionaries, was immediately forwarded I ought to add, that though, as a plain man and an executor of Russian laws, the governor expressed himself abruptly, he was in reality very friendly to Mr Zaremba. A similar testimony is given by the missionaries of the local authorities of these provinces generally They have uniformly countenanced them, and manifested a disposition to facilitate their operations.

In the mean time a wekeel of the Catholicos arrived at Shoosha early in September, to withdraw the Armenians from the influence of the missionaries. Let us return thither and view his proceedings Belonging to a distinguished family, holding the rank of high vartabed, and clothed on the present occasion with the delegated authority of the Catholicos, he assumed a haughty carriage, and

menaced the missionaries with threatenings of grievous
import   His first blow at the mission was to drive an
apprentice from the printing office, by accusing his broth-
er-in law and guardian, how was a priest, of *German-
ism* and threatening to send him in chains to Echmiad
zin   The school he attacked by publishing the names
of all whose children had attended, and forbidding them,
under penalty of excommunication, to send them again
The consequence was that when the school which had
hitherto been closed on account of the cholera was open
ed a few days afterward, only eight or nine, out of the
former number of sixty attended   The young men too,
who were preparing to be teachers he forced, by threaten
ing their fathers with excommunication and by menaces
directed to them personally, to cease their attendance at
the mission house

Shall we look a moment at the instructions he was himself
giving to his countrymen, while thus engaged in driving
them from those of the missionaries?   In a sermon preached the Sabbath after his arrival in praise of the Virgin
who as chief of the saints was considered to be treated
with special indignity by the protestant doctrines, he argued,
that, ' as Adam could not live without the woman neither
can Christ be mediator without Mary , she is the queen
mentioned in the 45th Psalm the most beautiful of women
whose charms are celebrated in the Song of Solomon and
as Christ did all that she required at the marriage in Cana,
so will he now always regard her intercessions   ' Who,'
said he in conclusion, (bowing before her image as if to
restore her lost honors) ' who are these Germans, that
have dared to speak against her?   Cursed be they, and
all who have to do with them !   May the disease which
now rages destroy them !'   On another occasion, he was
reported to assert not only that Christ could not be mediator without Mary, but even to say that he would take up-

on himself to affirm, that she was equal to either of the persons in the Trinity!

The decision of the imperial government was waited for by the missionaries with anxiety. When it came, both of the deacons were already taken from their earthly trials, one having been carried off at Tiflís while the cholera was raging, and the other having died in the convent of Sevân. In reference to them, however, after declaring that no evidence appeared of the missionaries' having attempted to proselyte, the decision laid down the important principle, that should a person be fully determined to leave the Armenian church, the clergy have no right to retain him by force, but shall leave him immediately to do what he pleases—a principle of religious liberty never before, it is believed, acknowledged in Russia, and entirely subversive of that prohibition of dissent, which denies the right of every man to worship God according to the dictates of his own conscience. Of the schools, government distinctly declared its approbation, though it neither could nor would interfere, to prevent the clergy from opposing schools established by men of another denomination. The missionaries, therefore, have no longer reason to apprehend the interference of government to the injury of their schools, and have only to contend, as best they can with the help of God, against the inimical moral power of the clergy. "Surely the king's heart is in the hand of the Lord, as the rivers of water he turneth it whithersoever he will."—In August of 1831 the mission had five schools, which were going on in tolerable quiet, and the opposition at Shoosha had grown weaker. But unfortunately the strength of the mission had seriously diminished. The departure of Mr. Zaremba, one of its oldest and most valued members, on account of sickness, has been previously mentioned. Mr. Hohenacker's feeble health has obliged him likewise to leave, and he has settled at Helenendorf. The mission now consists of Messrs.

Dittrich, Haas, and Pfander, already named, of Mr Yudt a printer, and Mr Spromberg a brother recently arrived.

The experiment which these brethren have made is exceedingly important Let us gather some of the fruits of their experience They have been led to doubt whether their original design of enlightening the Armenian nation without drawing away any from the Armenian communion, can be carried into complete execution. As the people become enlightened, they will of course wish for spiritual food, and for a rational and evangelical mode of worship, both of which must be sought elsewhere than in their own church Some, also, will be the victims of persecution and excommunication A mission church cannot refuse to open its arms to such as are thus excluded, by conscience or by opposition, from their own Still, so many barriers are set up by prejudice against foreign influence, that neither foreign missionaries alone, nor converts who have united with them and thus come to be viewed as foreigners and apostates, can hardly expect to effect the entire reformation of the Armenian church The work must be done by enlightened persons rising up from the midst of the church itself, and the greater the amount of light that is diffused through the nation before it is attempted, the more sure and complete will be the result.

The missionary, therefore, instead of aiming to make proselytes to his own communion, although he may receive individuals who wish or are forced to come, should shape his measures so as to draw as few as possible. To this end, he should avoid unnecessary controversy. By it ceremonial and unessential points are magnified into essentials in the estimation of the convert, and his conscience made so sensitive as to force him speedily from the communion of his church, while the clergy at the same time are irritated, and urged to search out and persecute or excommunicate all who are inclined to heresy On general princi-

ples, too, it is inexpedient   For, instead of conveying
important truth to the mind, it awakens prejudice to shut
the door by immediate opposition, while by a contrary
course, the seed might be widely scattered and become
deeply rooted, before the occurrence of such an event.
The brethren confess, too that stated and formal preaching to a regular congregation, although, did the laws of
the country allow, their feelings would strongly urge them
to attempt it as the most effectual mode of religious instruction, tends more than almost any thing to bring opposition
upon inquirers for the truth, and to draw a line of separation between them and their church

You will expect us to suggest, in some part of our journey, what American Christians can do toward diffusing
evangelical light in Russian Armenia   Our suggestions
can be given nowhere more advantageously than here, in
the light of the experiment of the Shoosha mission   In
order to accomplish so desirable an object, no attempt, of
course should be made to transgress the laws of the land
Principles of expediency, of our society, and of religion,
equally forbid it   And yet it must be confessed, the door
of entrance if we would infringe upon none of them, is exceedingly strait.   That an additional *printing press* could
not be advantageously established, you hardly need that we
should intimate after what has been said of the press at
Shoosha.   So many difficulties would there be, also, in the
way of sending *missionaries*, that we would not take upon
ourselves at present to recommend it.   Still, we are far
from being ready to abandon, as inaccessible, so large a portion of the Armenian nation, (embracing now the emigrant
population of Persian Armenia, and of the northern part
of Turkish Armenia,) as is assembled in the trans-Caucasian provinces of Russia   The door of entrance, though
strait, is not entirely closed   Government has still left,
and in a measure guarantied to the German missionaries,

a very important sphere of usefulness, in allowing them such scope in the establishment and direction of *schools*. And we attribute to it the more importance, from a firm persuasion that the emperor looks upon their operations with pleasure, and that his inclinations would lead him to increase, rather than diminish their privileges. Still, through want of funds, they are unable to cultivate the field that is thus open to them. Before our visit, their society, on account of the smallness of its income, had directed them by no means to enlarge their system of gratuitous instruction, which is the very thing that is needed in the present intellectual condition of the people. And the letter which communicated to us the decision of the emperor, said, "We fear our society is not able to carry into effect what is most needed—schools and printing." We would therefore strongly recommend to you to consider, if it be not expedient to extend to them a helping hand by furnishing them with the means, in money and books, of putting into operation the extensive system of schools that is called for. You cannot need a word to convince you of the extreme desirableness, that so important a field so providentially opened, should be immediately occupied. Of the gentlemen whom you would thus make your agents, we happen, owing to changes that have occurred since we were there, to be acquainted with only one who is ordained. Respecting him, it gives us pleasure to testify, that we have no expectation of your being able to send out from our own country a man of higher qualifications for judgment, learning and piety.

www.ingramcontent.com/pod-product-compliance
Lightning Source LLC
Chambersburg PA
CBHW062034090426

42740CB00016B/2908